Retirement: Ready or N

How to Get Financially Prepared —In a Hurry

By
Lee Rosenberg, CFP

Retirement: Ready or Not

How to Get Financially Prepared —In a Hurry

By
Lee Rosenberg, CFP

CAREER PRESS
180 Fifth Avenue
P.O. Box 34
Hawthorne, NJ 07507
1-800-CAREER-1
- 201-427-0229 (outside U.S.)
FAX: 201-427-2037

RETIREMENT: READY OR NOT
HOW TO GET FINANCIALLY PREPARED—IN A HURRY
ISBN 1-56414-052-0, $14.95
Cover design by A Good Thing, Inc.
Printed in the U.S.A. by Book-mart Press

To order this title by mail, please include price as noted above, $2.50 handling per order, and $1.00 for each book ordered. Send to: Career Press, Inc., 180 Fifth Ave., P.O. Box 34, Hawthorne, NJ 07507

Or call toll-free 1-800-CAREER-1 (Canada: 201-427-0229) to order using VISA or MasterCard, or for further information on books from Career Press.

To the best of the author's knowledge, the following information provided in this book was the most current and accurate available at the time of printing. However, the material is for reference purposes only and is subject to change pending new tax and other laws that may be passed. Readers should consult with their own financial advisors for the latest information and to confirm the use of the strategies based on their personal circumstances.

Library of Congress Cataloging-in-Publication Data

Rosenberg, Lee, 1952-
    Retirement, ready or not : how to get financially prepared—in a hurry / by
Lee Rosenberg.
        p. cm.
    Includes index.
    ISBN 1-56414-052-0 : $14.95
    1. Retirees--United States--Finance, Personal--Miscellanea. 2. Retirement income--United
States--Planning--Miscellanea. 3. Retirement--United States--Planning--Miscellanea. I. Title.
    HG179.R676   1993
    332.024'01--dc20   93-13789
                                                                                            CIP

Dedication

To Zachary, Alexandra and Taryn

Prepare well for your future.
It is where you shall spend the rest of your lives.

To Saralee

Talent and hard work got us to the foot of the mountain.
Faith will get us to the top.

Acknowledgments

Behind every "by" line is a chorus of voices—people who willingly lend their knowledge and expertise to further the understanding of important issues and topics. *Retirement Ready or Not* is no exception, and could not have been written without the help of many individuals who provided the latest available data and trends regarding financial products and services. A special thanks goes to representatives of Kemper Financial Services, Oppenheimer Funds, Phoenix Funds, Ibbotson Associates and HSH Associates for sharing the "goods." I am also grateful to Phil Gambino and John Clark at the Social Security Administration for their painstaking efforts to review several drafts and be ready with the facts.

I'm always thankful to have the personal support and expert advice of my attorney, Bob Lehman. His integrity, sincerity and "right-on-the-money" answers continue to inspire me.

I am deeply indebted to my business partner and friend of 18 years, Anthony Spatafore. The tremendous success of our financial planning practice, ARS Financial Services, is very much a tribute to his diligence and ongoing efforts to develop state-of-the-art retirement planning strategies. None of this is possible without the continued support of our family of clients. They are the real catalysts for this book. Because of their trust and confidence, we have been able to develop the best possible plans for retiring with financial security. And if experience is my teacher, then I have learned from the best. Art Grant, Mac Cadaret, Norlyn Feldman and BJ Johnson and other dedicated colleagues at Cadaret, Grant & Company, Inc., have worked tirelessly to help me achieve my personal and professional goals.

My parents, Dan and Rita Rosenberg, were the first to teach me the value of a buck and the benefits of saving for a rainy day. I am proud (and relieved) that they practiced what they preached. My children, Zachary, Alexandra and Taryn, are my guiding lights. In their eyes I see hope and fulfillment.

As with any chorus, I relied deeply on a "soloist." My wife, friend and partner, Saralee, is truly the star of this book, as well as of our other collaborations. Her unwavering support is always music to my ears.

Contents

Contents

Introduction

Every day, it seems, another study comes out revealing something new and incredible about Americans—that we're eating more vegetables and suffering less heart attacks, we're spending more time with our children, and, my favorite—the recent magazine poll that divulged what people *most* like to do in bed. The poll indicated that 76 percent said their activity of choice was eating ice cream! It's not how I would have responded, but I still respected the survey in the morning.

Of all the statistics I've seen, the one that intrigues me the most has to do with older Americans. I recently read that by the time 50 percent of this country's workers retire, they have become millionaires.

It sounds preposterous, until you consider that, for example, the typical 65-year-old man has spent more than 40 years bringing home a paycheck. If he averaged a salary of $25,000 a year or more, he legitimately earned in excess of $1 million over the course of his lifetime. At the same time, he came of age during the post-World War II boom, when the country witnessed a tremendous number of favorable economic conditions occurred:

- The stock market prospered (common stock dividends have grown by 400 percent since 1970 alone).

- Investors had a virtual heyday when T-bills were paying 8 percent to 10 percent, CDs were paying 15.7 percent and the prime lending rate hit close to 20 percent.

- Corporate America introduced lucrative employee pensions and stock option plans to encourage job loyalty, while the government started offering its own incentives to get Americans to save for their retirement. IRAs, KEOGHs and 401ks provided a desirable outlet for deferring taxes on income.

- Social Security benefits have increased to 20 times their initial payout.

- Home appreciation has literally gone through the roof (the average housing price in 1968 was $22,300; in 1992, the average housing price was $130,900).

- Finally, the two-income family became as accepted as a blue business suit, allowing for two paychecks, two pensions, two sets of benefits, etc.

As a result of these simultaneous events, this decade's crop of retirees is the wealthiest in our country's history. To make money, they didn't have to be financially savvy. They didn't have to read bank advertisements with a magnifying glass to find the true mortgage rate (points and all) and they certainly never spent their weekends poring over investment prospectuses, trying to figure out which would deliver the highest rate of return. In fact, with so many factors giving them the edge, they just rode the wave and made money quite by accident!

Yet in spite of their good fortunes and good timing, this very wealthy generation approaches retirement age stone broke! According to the latest U.S. Census figures, today only one of every 10 Americans is financially prepared to retire when they reach age 65. The others range in readiness from, "We need to work a few more years" to "Who knows if we'll ever be able to retire!"

How is this possible? Because it never mattered what people made at work or in the market, it only mattered what they kept. And there's the catch. In spite of living through one of the most prosperous periods in our time, older Americans have also had to contend with the black sheep of the economic family—taxes and inflation. Since 1970, the dollar lost 70 percent of its purchasing power and many workers started paying in federal income taxes what their parents could

only have dreamed of earning! (In 1975, a joint return listing two dependents paid $14,260 in federal income tax on an adjusted gross income of $50,000.)

At the same time, the Depression mentality so many people were raised with ("Save it for a rainy day") went the way of hoop skirts and hit parades. By the 1970s, the number-one song was "Don't spend over the limit dear, with anyone else but me." Everyone was so enjoying their disposable income, they didn't realize how much of it they were disposing. As of 1992, consumer debt topped $800 billion dollars, due mostly to the proliferation of the credit card (bet it was invented by the same guy who gave us the boomerang).

Never did access to so much financing do so little for our personal wealth. In fact, we have never earned so much and had so little to show for it. Although median incomes have more than tripled since 1970, the disposable income that Americans save today has actually declined to 5 percent. In other words, we spend the other 95 percent.

We could somehow muddle by with these spending/saving habits if not for a new "wrinkle." We are living longer—much longer. Whereas previous generations died in their 50s and 60s, today's retirees aren't considered old until they are in their 80s! The average man or woman who turns 65 this year can expect to live another 15 to 18 years respectively, and 50 percent will live into their 90s. This is a miracle until you consider the other side of the sword. Who can afford to live that long?

Now you understand why you can't pick up a newspaper or hear a report about retirement that doesn't come standard-equipped with emergency warning lights. The red lights are blinking because at the rate that most Americans are saving for retirement, they will most definitely outlive their money! And how quickly the glow of the golden years loses its tarnish when the quest to remain financially independent is in constant jeopardy.

That's where this book will help. Unlike the volumes of material that have been published on the subject, *Retirement Ready or Not* won't bore you with lectures about being fiscally irresponsible and/or downright stupid.

As a Certified Financial Planner in practice for over 18 years, my approach has always been to help clients put their problems into perspective without making judgment calls. On a personal level, I have a growing family and know first-hand the hundreds of decisions and circumstances, financial and otherwise, that alter our good intentions every year. The point is, we all do the best we can.

I wrote this book, not to scold or lay blame, but to give you the benefit of my expertise. Here are not only my most proven strategies and winning ideas for saving for retirement, but words of inspiration so you can finally take charge of your personal finances...even if you are in the ninth inning and losing badly.

Retirement Ready or Not tackles the tough questions on Medicare and Medicare supplements, long-term care, beating inflation, Social Security, the best investments, real estate options, company pensions and virtually dozens of other issues that have a direct impact on a secure retirement. Together, we'll also try to project the size of your retirement nest egg based on your current savings, as well as predict how much you'll need based on your age and number of years left to save. We'll even get into ways to prepare for an early retirement, so you can try to take advantage and get a jump-start on the good life.

To maximize your "return" (of time and money), each chapter is divided into three sections. The first section provides an in-depth overview of the latest available facts on the subject (never forget, knowledge is power). Next comes "Good Question"—an insightful question-and-answer segment that proposes solutions to real-life dilemmas. Finally, the last section, "What I Tell My Clients" is where I share the insights I've gained in my close to 20 years as a professional financial advisor. Here you'll find the "behind-the-scenes" or "insider's" look at what the experts know, but don't always tell.

Your retirement will be a once-in-a-lifetime experience. But as a Certified Financial Planner, I've made the journey over 800 times. That is why I have dedicated this book to all of you who have dreamt of a fulfilling retirement, but who have been so overwhelmed with the task of getting ready, you haven't been able to get past wondering and wishing.

Here is your chance to "take the course" and pass with flying colors. It has probably never mattered more.

Lee Rosenberg, CFP
October 1993

1

It's never too late to get financially prepared for retirement

It has been said that retirement is the fine art of spending all your time without spending all your money. Nice concept if you can get it. But what about the millions of Americans who reach their 50s and 60s and are still wrestling with the question, "When can I afford to retire at all?"

For many people, the best they can do is make predictions based on the "depend" system. Retirement "depends" on whether they can sell the house for the right price so they can live off the equity. Or maybe it "depends" on whether they can hold onto their job for a few more years so they can finally start to save. Or perhaps it simply "depends" on being able to pay off enough old debts so they can live comfortably on a fixed income.

But regardless of a person's circumstances and the age he or she hopes to check out of the work force, the reality is the same: The only feasible way to *ever* retire is to build up a sizable nest egg.

How much is enough? Again we turn to the "depend" system. It depends on the kind of lifestyle you'd like to have and, equally important, how long you plan to live! Of course, since none of us come into this world with a firm departure date, the only logical thing to do is to consider the latest statistics.

According to IRS mortality tables, the average retiree today can expect to live to at least 75. And that's just on average. Men and women who are currently 65 are expected to live for another 15.6 years and 19.3 years respectively. Further, there is a 50-percent chance that you or your spouse will live to 90.

If you are still years from retirement, the chart on the following page provides the pension industry's life expectancy projections as of 1993:

What the pension experts say about life expectancies

Your age today	Men could live another____ years	Women could live another____ years
50	25.5	29.6
51	24.7	28.7
52	24.0	27.9
53	23.2	27.1
54	22.4	26.3
55	21.7	25.5
56	21.0	24.7
57	20.3	24.0
58	19.6	23.2
59	18.9	22.4
60	18.2	21.7
61	17.5	21.0
62	16.9	20.3
63	16.2	19.6
64	15.6	18.9
65	15.0	18.2
66	14.4	17.5
67	13.8	16.9
68	13.2	16.2
69	12.6	15.6
70	12.1	15.0

Source: Ordinary Life Annuity Table, Pension Coordinator, 1993

What these figures show is that the typical retirement is expected to last 20 to 30 years, or more than a third of a person's life! But not only are we living longer, we are living better. Today's older Americans travel, go to college, begin new careers, start businesses and literally run with the best of them. The beloved George Burns sums it up best with his apt remark, "I can't die. I'm booked."

All it takes is good health and *money*! And therein lies the problem.

With this country's continued economic uncertainties, spiraling health care costs, an alarmingly high number of companies forcing workers to retire early, and a recession that has beaten many of our investments to a pulp, it is entirely likely that this and future generations of retirees will outlive their money. A recent Gallup poll found that

40 percent of all Americans were convinced they'd be in this boat.

As a Certified Financial Planner in private practice for over 18 years, I've known without benefit of a fancy survey that people's biggest fear about retirement is running out of money. Sure, they are deeply concerned about illness, death, loneliness, separation and other emotionally charged issues, too. But this is nothing compared to the anxiety of one day being dependent on family, friends or the government for financial survival.

And yet in spite of this, better than 90 percent of Americans fail to save enough money prior to retirement to allay this fear. Instead, they convince themselves that somehow they'll be spared any serious misfortunes. They rationalize that with lower living costs, a decreased tax burden and the need to support only themselves, their financial needs will be greatly reduced. They also assume that the profits on the sale of their home and/or a business, their Social Security benefits, and savings and investments will provide an adequate nest egg.

I'm always hopeful that they're right, but it's my experience that most often they are not. Every week I meet with new clients who are a few years into retirement and who are in a panic because their nest egg is starting to crack under the stress. They tell me they never expected to have so many financial burdens, such as having to help out their grown children with down payments—or their parents with the cost of home health care. They are discouraged because doing battle with inflation when you're working is one thing. When you're trying to live comfortably on a fixed income and your CDs are no help at all, it is entirely different. Adding to this, they worry that their good health won't last forever and that the cost of being cured will wipe out their savings completely.

I know this sounds disheartening at a time when there are so many positive aspects of retirement lifestyles to consider. But that's the reason you picked up this book. You don't want to reach retirement age and face the music. You want retirement to be your pay-back time for your years of hard labor, as well you should!

That is the reason it has never been more important to insure *in advance* that you have adequate income and assets to eventually retire with financial security. In other words, you deserve for your money to work as hard for *you* as you did for it!

But before you can get started on that road to financial security, we'll discuss the reasons people have traditionally failed to save enough for retirement. For one thing, it is always helpful to discover you are not alone, and just as important, that you are not lazy, crazy or out of control (in spite of what your mother-in-law claims).

In this chapter, we'll also take a look at the most common and costly financial mistakes people make in preparing for retirement so that you don't fall into the same traps. Next, we'll try to project the size of your retirement nest egg, looking at your current, age, assets and income as predictors. We'll also look realistically at how much you'll need to retire (and stay retired). But of greatest importance will be the no-fail strategies you can use to build a retirement nest egg, even if you are convinced that it is impossible to put money away.

Why aren't we able to save any money?

Most of us consider ourselves to be responsible, mature people who work hard, pay taxes and raise our children to the best of our abilities. When it comes to money, our intentions are good. We want to do what's right, but no matter how often we say we're going to start saving for our retirement, somehow life keeps getting in the way. Between braces, sleep-away camps, out-of-state colleges, nose jobs, therapy, family vacations, new cars, outdoor patio furniture, big weddings and the 1,001 "must-haves" we dole out for, it's a wonder we can put anything away at all.

And yet, our materialistic, "throw-it-on-Visa" lifestyles are not *totally* to blame for our lack of preparedness for retirement. Although we are the most affluent generation in history, over the past 10 to 20 years, we have been up against a tidal wave of economic changes that have made it more difficult than ever to save money. Consider this:

- Just about every year for the last 30, inflation has eaten up another 5 percent of our purchasing power. Since 1970 alone, the purchasing power of the dollar has declined 70 percent.
- Thanks to the won't-say-die recession, the term, "job security" sounds as prehistoric as ice box or princess phone. To translate, not since the Depression have the odds been greater that you will be unemployed at least once (if not more) during your working years.
- If job security is outdated, so is job loyalty. It seems that the only way

to move up is to move out. But because of job switching, millions of workers don't stay at a company long enough to get vested in a pension plan. (The Pension Rights Center in Washington, D.C., recently reported that 60 percent of American workers don't have pensions).

- Even if an employee does stay with a company for many years, there is no longer any guarantee that the company will contribute to a pension plan at the same rate they used to. In fact, you can expect that, during this decade, pensions, stock options, employer-subsidized health care coverage and other traditional benefits will be a mere shadow of what they once were. The bottom line is that health care and retirement planning will ultimately be the responsibility of the employee.

- What about finding ways to pay for your childrens' college education while still being able to take in an occasional movie and dinner? Between 1986 and 1992, tuition increased 7 percent to 10 percent *annually*, making it increasingly difficult to pay for schooling while paying the rest of your overhead. Today, one year of schooling runs $5,434 for a public university and $15,936 for a private university.

- Finally, the other change that has drastically affected this generation's ability to save is that it took us so much longer to get the ball rolling. Unlike our parents and grandparents who were married with children in their 20s, today the typical 50- to 55-year-old is still supporting a family. The timing is rotten because it meets head-on with the point in life when our retirement savings efforts are supposed to be in high gear. Furthermore, since the children of the 50-plus people are presumably of the age where they have grown up but not out, their financial requirements are endless. As one friend complained, "Who can save for retirement when my kids are demanding the 3 C's: college, cars and cash?"

In the end, we could finger-point all day long or, worse, beat ourselves up for not putting away 10 percent of our income since we were 30. But that will not change one simple fact. *You still can not retire until you can afford it!*

That is why I want to show you the steps you need to take to get financially prepared for retirement, no matter if you are in your 40s, 50s, 60s, or even in your 70s. It's going to be a challenge and require some serious belt-tightening (translated—you'll have to "retire" your debts first). But if you consider not only the benefits of being financially independent to the end, as well as leaving a legacy to your children, I know you'll agree the preparation will be worth it!

Myths, misconceptions and mistakes about retirement

One of the things I've found beneficial when a new client is ready to get serious about planning for retirement is to discuss some of the more common and costly mistakes others have made. To help you from falling prey to what are mostly false assumptions and old myths,

we are going to nip those notions in the bud right now.

1. If only there were glasses for short-sightedness. In this society where instant gratification is thought to be a constitutional right, many of us get more satisfaction from spending our money on things we can show off than we do from investing money for our future. Where is the glory in getting a 14-percent return on a mutual fund when you could possibly have a Q45 in the driveway? Couple that with our "mañana" attitudes ("We'll do a better job of saving next year"), and it is plain to see why 90 percent of all Americans reach retirement age with barely enough money to last a few years. *The moral of the story? We don't plan to fail, we simply fail to plan!*

2. "It's just going to be the two of us." Back in the '70s, everyone talked about coping with the "empty nest" syndrome. Today, many retirees would call that a dream-come-true! Since 1975, the number of adult children ages 25-29 living with their parents has almost doubled. Taking in and supporting elderly parents who can't live alone is another growing trend. Almost 60 percent of dependent seniors live with their adult children. And what about the cases where a child's marriage is failing or a divorced parent dies? Suddenly Grandma and Grandpa are back supporting dependents. In fact, according to a national support group, there are an estimated 5.2 million children in this country now being raised by grandparents. But even if nobody actually moves in with you, that's not to say they won't require financial support. *In* *essence, it is unrealistic to think that retirement means cutting financial ties with your family.*

3. Putting one egg in the basket. Too often people count on a single source of income as their key to financial security in retirement. They assume that the equity in their home, a buy-out of their business or professional practice, an inheritance, a pension plan, etc., is going to be so large, they don't have to be concerned about putting more money aside. Adding to the problem, they presume that this "fail-safe" investment won't fluctuate in value. Then when nearing retirement, they discover the actual worth of their assets is considerably less than expected. *The solution is to never count on one source of retirement income. The more diversified your retirement portfolio, the better.*

4. "Hello retirement, good-bye big tax bill." It used to be that when you retired, high taxes became someone else's problem. But that was then. Today, state and city taxes, property taxes, luxury taxes, sin taxes, occupancy taxes, sales tax, etc., will *not* retire when you do. If anything, retirees actually see a greater percentage of their income go toward taxes than when they were working. And what about the granddaddy of 'em all—federal income tax? High income earners—retired or not—just got pushed into higher brackets. Effective with your 1994 tax bill (for tax year 1993), those with taxable income over $140,000 (joint filers and surviving spouses), $127,500 (heads of households), $115,000 (singles) or $70,000 (marrieds filing separately) will be subject to the new 36-percent tax bracket. A

39.6-percent tax bracket will apply to those with taxable income exceeding $250,000 ($125,000 for married filing separately). But even if you end up in a lower tax bracket at retirement, with the recent tax law changes, the effective tax rate is pretty much the same because retirees may lose certain deductions and exemptions. *That is why it is so important that your retirement portfolio is invested in growth and income vehicles that can withstand the one-two punches from taxes and inflation.*

5. "OK, so our living costs will be less." To some extent this is true. The cost of commuting and dressing for success will be gone. And perhaps you'll trade in your larger home for a smaller one or move to a part of the country where it is less expensive to live. Hopefully, at some point, you will only be supporting yourselves. But unless you are extremely frugal, you are likely to find that there are many unexpected costs that pick up the slack. Paying for leisure activities, travel and hobbies, small business ventures and other interests add up quickly. In addition, health care costs have been rising at a rate of 9 percent to 10 percent annually. This is double the rate of inflation! What's worse, these inflated costs are occurring at a time when you are most likely to need medical attention. *For these reasons, the rule of thumb is that you'll need at least 80 percent of your pre-retirement income to live on if you hope to maintain the status quo.*

6. The price of procrastination. Every time you tell yourself you'll worry about saving for your retirement next year, you push yourself further behind.

Let's say your goal was to save $250,000. The chart below shows how much you would need to put away every month, depending on how many years you had until retirement:

Years to Retirement	Amount Invested Monthly to Save $250,000	Total Investment *
30	$168	$60,480
20	$424	$101,760
10	$1,367	$164,040
6	$3,402	$204,120

* Based on annual return of 8%, compounded yearly.

Another example: If you invested $5,000 a year between the ages of 35 and 45 (a total of $50,000), and not a dime after that, you'd have a nest egg of about $725,000 at age 65. Compare that to waiting until you reached 45 to start saving. If you put away $7,500 a year for the next 20 years (a total of $157,500), you'd never reach the size of the first nest egg. In fact, you'd have only accumulated $561,000. That means that for every year you wait, you have to put away a higher amount for ultimately a smaller return. That's why the price of procrastinating is too high.

It is never too late to get ready for retirement

Once you have a feel for why retirement planning is so essential, you *should* be anxious to improve the prospects of your own future. The first step is to take inventory of your current personal and financial affairs. I call it the "Personal Starting Line" and it is a good way for you to focus on the current circumstances that have a direct bearing on your ability to earn, save, and spend.

Are you in your late 50s with a fair-sized pension and a growing portfolio, or are you in your 60s with only a few thousand in the bank and a job your boss thinks some 30-year-old can do? How much do you own compared to how much you *owe*? Are you still supporting a family (or two), or are you free as a bird? Do you have considerable equity in a home or are you planning to cash in some long-standing investments to raise money?

These are just some of the situations we need to assess before we can shoot the starting gun for what could well be the race of your life!

To get started, answer the following questions as best you can, recognizing that some of your responses will be mere predictions or wishful thinking. The purpose of this exercise? It's not to give you a test and a final score (this is usually so discouraging). Rather, it is simply to help you become conscious of the many factors that determine when—and with how much money—you can eventually retire.

Your Personal Starting Line in the Race of Your Life
**(If both you and your spouse are working, you may want to
fill this out separately)**

AGE

How old are you?_____

Ideally, what age would you like to retire?_____

How many years does that give you to save?_____

Using the chart on page 16, what is your life expectancy?_____

Based on your life expectancy and the year you plan to retire, how many years of retirement do you need to plan for?_____

FAMILY

Are you currently supporting dependents and/or a former spouse?_____

How many more years do you expect to be financially responsible for your children and/or former spouse?_____

Do you anticipate having to support parents, adult children, grandchildren and/or other family members when you retire?_____

If married, have you considered the effect on your income if your spouse dies before you? (For example, Social Security will reduce your benefits by dropping the lower of your two monthly checks)?_____

EMPLOYMENT

Is your career still in high gear or are you approaching the end of the line?_____

If working full-time, are you taking advantage of employer-sponsored retirement savings programs?_____

If you have an employee-sponsored savings plan or 401k, are you putting away the maximum amount every year?_____

If you are a business owner, have you set up a retirement program for yourself?_____

If you are a business owner, have you recently assessed the worth of your business should you plan to sell when you retire?_____

When you do retire, do you anticipate doing some consulting or part-time work? Is there any possibility you will open a business or franchise?_____

Your Personal Starting Line in the Race of Your Life
(pg. 2)

REAL ESTATE

Do you currently have a balance on a mortgage (and/or home equity loan or second mortgage)? If so, what do you owe (in total)?_____

Approximately, how much equity do you have in your home?_____

When you retire, do you plan to live in this home?_____

If you plan to live in the house, do you plan to pay off the mortgage before you retire?_____

If you sell the home, do you plan to rent or buy another?_____

If you buy another, do you hope to trade up or trade down (price-wise)?_____

When you retire, do you plan to stay in your community or relocate?_____

When you retire, do you plan to maintain more than one residence (i.e. be a snowbird)?_____

If you do plan to buy a new home when you retire, would you expect to pay cash or take out a mortgage?_____

SAVINGS AND INVESTMENTS

Do you put money aside for your retirement on a regular basis?_____

Are you and/or your spouse going to have a pension plan when you retire? If so, how much do you estimate it will pay you each month?_____

If you will not have a pension, what other investments will you have (such as IRAs and 401ks) that can replace your income when you retire?_____

Are you altering your investment strategy so that the closer you get to retirement, the more you are focusing on growth and income, tax-deferred and tax-frees, etc.?_____

Are you aware if your investments are designed to keep up with or exceed the rate of inflation so that you maintain your standard of living after you retire?_____

Can you anticipate your tax bracket when you retire, based on your sources of income?_____

LIABILITIES AND DEBTS

Are you aware of your current monthly expenses?_____

Do you know the extent of your outstanding debts (loans, credit cards, etc.)?_____

Do you know the interest rates you are paying on your outstanding debts?_____

The typical reaction to answering this questionnaire is, "Boy, I never thought about half these things, but they do make sense." Which is the point exactly. Once you can start to focus on all the "what-if's" and "should-we's," you'll have a much clearer sense of what it is going to take to prepare for a comfortable, secure retirement. In other words, now you'll really know where your personal starting line is.

Next comes the hard part—putting a pencil and paper to where your *financial* starting line is. For most people, this is about as much fun as stepping on the scale in January. But much as you may deny it, you really do want to know where you're at or you wouldn't be reading this.

The process of assessing your financial starting line is also called establishing your net worth, and it is a way for you to get a ready-or-not snapshot of your personal wealth. You have to know where you are starting from in order to know where you're going!

So first, we'll look at the value of your combined assets. This would include your home, investments, pension(s), savings, etc. Then we'll size up your liabilities, such as mortgages, installment loans, etc. When you subtract what you owe from what you own, this is your net worth.

Establish your net worth

Cash reserve assets. Add up your cash or near-cash resources such as checking accounts, savings accounts and money market funds. These are your "liquid" assets because they can be liquidated quickly without penalties.

It's also possible to include the cash value of a life insurance policy as well as a bank Certificate of Deposit (CD). These vehicles are liquid to the extent that it's possible to tap into them in an emergency. However, doing so may result in penalties for early withdrawal or, in the case of borrowing from the cash value of a life insurance policy, trigger interest charges on the value of the loan.

In my opinion, between 15 percent and 20 percent of your total assets should be liquid and there should be enough ready cash to cover your living expenses for a minimum of three months, preferably six.

Equity/retirement assets. Generally, the most valuable asset in your portfolio is the equity in your home. But, hopefully, you will also have a combination of other investment assets including stocks and options, mutual funds, taxable and tax-free bonds, T-Bills, annuities, investment property (not your residence) and/or equity in a business. Retirement assets include IRAs/KEOGH Plans, 401ks, vested pension plans, employee savings and stock option programs. In tandem, these should represent 50 percent to 60 percent of your total assets.

Keep in mind that if you do sell off investment assets, it will more than likely trigger tax liabilities and possibly penalties for early withdrawal.

To establish the values of these assets, ask your insurance agent, stockbroker, realtor and Certified Financial Planner for assistance. You can also refer to recent price quotes in the newspaper. Although establishing values for real estate limited partnerships and vacation timeshares is complicated, it is acceptable to place the value at 50 percent of the price you paid (for the purpose of this exercise, you are trying to

Assets

Cash Reserve Assets
Checking accounts/cash $ _____
Savings accounts   _____
Money market funds   _____
Certificates of Deposit   _____
Life insurance (cash value)   _____

Equity/Retirement Assets
Time deposits (T-bills)   _____
Stocks and options   _____
Retirement savings (IRAs/KEOGHs)   _____
Annuities (surrender value)   _____
Pensions (vested interest)   _____
Profit-sharing plans   _____
Collectibles   _____
House (market value)   _____
Other real estate/limited partnerships   _____
Business interests   _____
Personal property (auto, jewels, etc.)   _____
Loans owed you   _____
Other assets   _____

Total Assets $ _____

Liabilities

Mortgage or rent (balance due) $ _____
Auto loan (balance due)   _____
Credit cards   _____
Installment loans   _____
Annual tax bill   _____
Business debts   _____
Student loans   _____
Brokerage margin loans   _____
Home equity loans/2nd or 3rd mortgages   _____

Total Liabilities $ _____

Total Net Worth $ _____

establish the most realistic price in the event of a quick sale). Finally, to determine the value of your 401k or other company benefit programs, ask your benefits department to help calculate.

As for personal property—clothing, furs and jewelry, cars, furniture—appraise their value by estimating how much money they would generate if they were sold today.

Liabilities. This represents the outstanding balances on your mortgage(s), cars, installment loans, credit cards, etc. It also includes your projected state and federal tax bill. Ideally, your liabilities should represent no more than 30 percent to 50 percent of your total assets.

If you don't have a current net worth statement, fill out the form on the previous page. If you need help, consult your financial planner or accountant.

As you review your net worth statement, you should be asking, "Do we or don't we have enough to retire on?" That's why the next steps are to try to predict, as best we can, the size of our nest egg, depending on our current net worth and other potential income sources.

The following section has been designed to help you "guess-timate" the amount you can expect to receive from your pension, Social Security, savings and investments and other outlets.

How much will you have to retire on?

This first chart will help you estimate your Social Security benefits based on your present age and annual earnings (Chapter 2 outlines the formulas for Social Security in greater detail). Circle the number that best reflects your benefit amount. If necessary, round up to the next highest age and income ranges.

Projected Social Security benefits
Worker with spouse (line 1)   Single worker (line 2)

Present age

Annual Income	35	40	45	50	55	60
$30,000	$20,964 $13,980	$20,094 $13,398	$19,224 $12,816	$18,186 $12,126	$17,148 $11,436	$16,140 $10,764
$40,000	$23,808 $15,876	$22,692 $15,132	$21,576 $14,388	$20,058 $13,374	$18,540 $12,360	$17,226 $11,484
$50,000+	$25,248 $16,836	$23,934 $15,960	$22,620 $15,084	$20,874 $13,920	$19,128 $12,756	$17,652 $11,772

Figures based on maximum contributions made up until retirement at age 65.

If you're currently contributing to a company pension plan and plan to continue to do so, the next step is to try to predict what your annual payout will be at retirement. Using the chart on the next page, match up your current annual earnings with your age to determine the estimated amount. Circle the figure that best reflects your benefits. If necessary, round up to the next highest age and income ranges to calculate.

Projected annual pension benefits

Present age

Annual income	35	40	45	50	55	60
$30,000	$45,230	$33,798	$25,526	$18,873	$14,103	$10,538
$40,000	$60,307	$45,065	$33,675	$25,164	$18,804	$14,051
$50,000	$75,383	$56,631	$42,094	$31,455	$23,505	$17,564
$60,000	$90,460	$67,597	$50,512	$37,746	$28,206	$26,077
$70,000	$105,537	$78,863	$58,931	$44,037	$32,907	$24,590
$80,000	$120,613	$90,129	$67,350	$50,328	$37,608	$28,103
$100,000	$150,767	$112,662	$84,183	$62,910	$47,010	$35,128
$125,000	$188,458	$140,827	$105,234	$78,637	$58,762	$43,911
$150,000	$226,150	$168,992	$126,281	$94,364	$70,515	$52,693

Source: Kemper Financial Services, Inc. Figures based on an estimated 35-percent payout at retirement and 6-percent annual raises until retirement at age 65.

Potential annual income at retirement from personal savings and investments, based on their current value

Present age

Current value of personal investments and savings	35	40	45	50	55	60
$25,000	$26,972	$17,660	$11,563	$7,511	$4,959	$3,245
$40,000	$43,454	$28,255	$18,500	$12,113	$7,931	$5,193
$50,000	$53,943	$35,319	$23,125	$15,141	$9,914	$6,419
$75,000	$80,915	$52,979	$34,688	$22,712	$14,871	$9,737
$100,000	$107,866	$70,638	$46,251	$30,283	$19,827	$12,982
$125,000	$134,858	$88,298	$57,813	$37,853	$24,784	$16,228
$150,000	$161,829	$108,958	$69,376	$45,424	$29,741	$19,473
$175,000	$188,801	$123,617	$80,938	$52,994	$34,698	$23,719
$200,000	$215,772	$141,277	$92,501	$60,565	$39,655	$25,964
$250,000	$269,716	$176,596	$115,626	$75,706	$49,569	$32,455

Source: Kemper Financial Services, Inc. Figures based on a 8.5-percent fixed rate of return, compounded monthly, with no additional investments made or any declining principal. Payout at age 65 is from interest income only.

Then, try to establish the current value of your savings and investments so you can predict how much annual income they will provide when you retire. This includes stocks and bonds, IRAs, CDs, etc. *It doesn't include the value of your primary residence or personal prop-erty*. Circle the figure that best reflects your potential annual income. If necessary, round up to the next highest age and income ranges to calculate.

Next, to determine your projected annual income at retirement, simply add the three numbers:

Source	Potential Annual Income
Social Security	$_____
Company pension	$_____
Personal savings and investments	$_____

In addition to these income sources, you may be able to count on the sale of a primary residence, a vacation home, a business or private practice, an inheritance, an insurance or legal settlement, a severance package, royalties, commissions, etc. Ideally, it would be helpful to work with a Certified Financial Planner and/or your accountant so that you are able to better establish the potential annual income you could expect from these sources.

Source	Potential Payout	Potential Annual Income
1.		
2.		
3.		
4.		
5.		
6.		
Projected Annual Income	Total $_____	

How much will you need?

Projecting how much money you will have accumulated by the time you retire is clearly a top priority. But just as important, you also must try to determine how much you'll need to live on when you retire. Unfortunately, this is not a science. As we've established, the typical retiree needs at least 80 percent of his or her pre-retirement income to live comfortably. So, one possible strategy for establishing future financial needs is to base them on *current* earnings. As you'll see from the next chart, you can try to project how much money you will need to live on based on your current age and annual earnings. For example, if you are 45 and currently earning $60,000 a year, if you retired in 20 years (age 65), you would need an annual income of $144,321 to maintain your current standard of living.

On the chart, circle the figure that best reflects your income needs. If necessary, round up to the next highest age and income ranges to calculate.

How much annual income will you need at retirement to maintain your current lifestyle?

Present age

Current income	35	40	45	50	55	60
$30,000	$129,229	$ 96,567	$ 72,161	$ 53,923	$ 40,924	$ 30,110
$40,000	$172,305	$128,756	$ 96,214	$ 71,897	$ 53,725	$ 40,147
$50,000	$215,381	$160,945	$120,268	$ 89,871	$ 67,157	$ 50,183
$60,000	$258,457	$193,134	$144,321	$107,845	$ 80,588	$ 60,220
$70,000	$301,533	$225,323	$168,375	$125,819	$ 94,019	$ 70,257
$80,000	$344,609	$257,512	$192,428	$143,793	$107,451	$ 80,294
$100,000	$430,762	$321,890	$240,535	$179,742	$134,314	$100,367
$125,000	$538,452	$402,363	$300,669	$224,677	$167,892	$125,459
$150,000	$646,143	$482,835	$360,803	$269,613	$201,470	$150,550

Source: Kemper Financial Services, Inc. Figures based on needing 75 percent of current income starting at age 65. Annual inflation and 6-percent salary increases are factored in.

You know what comes next. You've got to subtract your income requirements at retirement from your projected annual income at retirement to find out if there's a shortfall. We call this "future shock" because the typical bottom line shows a difference the size of the Delaware Water Gap. Others will show a surplus. Either way, you'll now know where you stand.

The Bottom Line

Estimated annual income at retirement	$_____
Estimated annual income needed at retirement	$_____
Income gap or surplus	$_____

The effects of inflation

One of the biggest shocks people experience when looking ahead to retirement is the realization that inflation is the biggest, baddest enemy of all. A typical reaction is to look at the chart entitled "How much annual income will you need at retirement to maintain your current lifestyle?" and declare that the figures are total hogwash. They do seem pretty remarkable when you think in today's prices. But you aren't retiring today. You'll be retiring in five or even 25 years from now, and that's what you have to consider. If the numbers still don't seem plausible, take a look at this example of what things cost in 1970, 1980 and today. Or, even better, ask yourself if, back in 1970, you would ever have imagined paying $7.50 to see a movie or $35,000 to buy a car. If the inflation rate continues to increase 4 percent to 5 percent a year, living costs will close to triple every 20 years.

Average prices	1970	1980	TODAY
Postage stamp	.06	.15	.29
Loaf of bread	.23	.43	$1.25
Automobile	$3400	$6,910	$18,000
House	$25,600	$64,000	$99,468

Once you accept that living-cost increases will be as predictable as Christmas in December, you'll better understand the impact inflation will have on your overall purchasing power. The chart below is useful in that it compares the value of $1,000 today and 25 years from now.

4% annual inflation rate						
Monthly income: Per $1,000	Today	5 Yrs.	10 Yrs.	15 Yrs.	20 Yr.s	25 Yrs.
How much you'll need to have same purchasing power	$1,000	$1,220	$1,480	$1,800	$2,190	$2,670
What $1,000 will be worth	$1,000	$822	$675	$555	$456	$375

Explanation: If the annual rate of inflation is 4 percent, in 10 years you will need $1,480 to buy what $1,000 bought today. The reason? In 10 years, $1,000 will only be worth $675.

Can your retirement nest egg go the distance?

As I mentioned earlier, the good news is that people are living longer and the bad news is that because of inflation, their money is likely to expire first. As a result, I am often asked if there is any way to predict how much staying power a retirement nest egg will have. Of course, much of this is predicated on where the retirement portfolio is invested and the true rate of return after taxes and inflation. But the number of years your money can last also depends on how much you withdraw every year.

The chart below will give you the life expectancy of a retirement nest egg, based on varying rates of return.

Number of years your retirement dollars will last

Rate of withdrawal annually	5%	6%	7%	8%	9%	10%
6%	37	*	*	*	*	*
7%	25	33	*	*	*	*
8%	20	23	30	*	*	*
9%	16	18	22	29	*	*
10%	14	15	17	20	27	*
11%	12	14	15	17	20	25
12%	11	12	13	14	16	19

* Capital will never be depleted

Explanation: If you withdrew 10 percent of your retirement nest egg every year, and it averaged an annual growth rate of 7 percent, your money would last approximately 17 years.

Another way to get a fix on the strength of your retirement account is by looking at the total amount of funds you're starting with. Refer to this next chart to see how many years the money will last if you take out a certain dollar amount each month for "X" number of years.

How much money can you withdraw?

Size of Nest Egg	If you withdraw this amount each month for the following number of years, you'll have a "0" balance.				If you withdraw this amount each month, you won't be touching the nest egg at all.	
	10 yrs.	15 yrs.	20 yrs.	25 yrs.	30 yrs.	35 yrs.
$15,000	$174/mo.	$134	$118	$106	$99	$59
$25,000	290	224	193	176	166	118
$50,000	580	448	386	352	332	285
$80,000	928	718	620	564	532	467
$100,000	1,160	896	772	704	668	585

Note: These figures are based on 7% net annual growth (after taxes).

In combination, all of the charts and personal surveys we've gone through are like Bloody Marys at a Sunday brunch. They are real eye-openers. But at least you now know what all the clamor has been about. You know why so many books, magazine articles, TV shows, lectures and seminars are constantly shouting at us: "Start saving for retirement today." And of course they are right. The question is, are you going to listen?

If you are prepared to get your financial affairs in order so that you can live comfortably now and in retirement, then follow me. This next section and, for that matter, the rest of this book, will lead you down the path toward financial freedom.

How to save money for your retirement

Whether you were ready or not, you have just taken a crash course in retirement planning. Overall, you've learned about the obstacles that have gotten in the way of saving for retirement. And for the most part, unless you've been a member of Congress, they weren't your doing.

But, now, we must move on to something that may very well have stood in the way of saving for retirement—something you most certainly *do* have control over: your family's personal spending habits.

It comes down to this. Unless you have an incredible week in Vegas, or are adored by rich relatives, the only way you're ever going to be able to save enough money to retire is if you 1) create a monthly budget and live within it, 2) do away with the credit cards that eat away at your paychecks and, most important, 3) consistently earmark a percentage of your earnings for savings and investments.

To help you achieve these financial goals, you must be willing to get what astrologers call your "money house" in order. And the first step in doing so is to examine your current income compared to your outgo—what you earn compared to what you spend. It's called a cash-flow analysis.

Using the charts on pages 34 and 35, first fill in the information regarding your current sources of income. To collect the data on your expenses, go no further than your home office, or wherever it is you stash your checkbook register, monthly bank statements, tax returns and credit-card receipts.

At the same time, it also important to dig a little deeper to try and track some of the more invisible expenditures—cash purchases. These are often the true culprits of cash-flow problems, because the proof of the purchase disappears into thin air, as though it never existed.

To figure out where the money goes, add up your cash withdrawals for a three-month period, multiply by four and then write down the types of things you usually pay for with cash—lunches, dry cleaning, hair and nail care, movies and videos, the drug store, lottery tickets, photo developing, etc. Not only will you discover where your cash disappears to, you'll also realize how innocent and unimportant small purchases seem—until you add them up. Most of us don't deliberate about spending money. We buy now and ask questions later.

But you are going to change that now that you are committed to saving for your retirement. To make this goal a reality, you need to establish a budget you can live with.

I have one client who thinks a balanced budget is when the month and the money run out at the same time, but that's not what I mean. A budget is a contract you make with yourself to spend up to a certain amount per month so that you can live within your means.

Yes, I know that in some households the mere mention of the "B" word brings out these foot-stomping, head-shaking gyrations. And you should see what happens when the *kids* hear about it! Unfortunately, with today's high-priced lifestyles and unending material desires, your toughest but most important job will be rallying the troops to cooperate.

But before you start your campaign, consider this. Budgeting has earned a very bad rap over the years. When you strip the word bare of all the associations, the truth is a budget is a plan for spending your money. It doesn't mean you can't spend money, it means you're going to decide *in advance of spending it,* where it's going to go.

Budget systems

The first step in creating a working budget is deciding what it will look like.

One of my clients set up this elaborate budget tracking system on his personal computer. He had spreadsheets and forecasting tools and year-to-date figures and variance analyses...and, you guessed it. He never entered a single piece of information. "Takes too much time," he told me.

That's an important lesson. So here are some less-complicated ideas for keeping a budget that might work for you.

1. Monthly reviews. Every month, add up what you spend in each category and compare it to what you were budgeted to spend. See where you're overdoing it, or not spending what you anticipated. After three months, look for trends and readjust the budget accordingly. While this system may not keep you from splurging, you'll be able to count on having a good sense of where the money is going—12 times a year. If things start getting out of control, just apply the brakes.

2. Accountant's spreadsheets. This is an extended version of the monthly review. But in this case, the information is confined to ledger sheets, which can be found at any office supply store.

The advantage of using this format is you can put an entire year on one sheet, or "spread it out" on a quarterly basis. The other major difference is that there is room on the spreadsheet to record your banking transactions, paychecks and investment income—giving you a complete bird's-eye view of your finances at a moment's glance. If you are computer-literate, you can set the system up on your PC and let the software do your year-to-date totals and projections. By the way, projections are made by comparing "actual" expenditures in a category thus far, to the amount that is budgeted for the remainder of the year. It will immediately indicate an overspending situation.

3. "The envelope, please." This system is simple yet effective. It involves cashing your paychecks or other income, dividing the cash into envelopes labeled by expense categories, and paying the bills from that cash.

Cash Flow Analysis

Income

Husband's salary/bonus/commissions $ _____

Wife's salary/bonus/commissions   _____

Dividends and interest   _____

Child support/alimony   _____

Annuities/pensions/Social Security   _____

Rent, royalties, fees   _____

Moonlighting/freelance work   _____

Loans being paid back to you   _____

     Total Income $ _____

Taxes

Combined income taxes $ _____

Social Security contributions   _____

Property taxes   _____

     Total Taxes $ _____

Living Expenses

Rent or mortgage payments $ _____

Food   _____

Clothing and uniforms   _____

Utilities   _____

Dining out   _____

Furniture/electronics   _____

Vacations/recreation   _____

Entertainment   _____

Cash Flow Analysis (continued)

Living Expenses (continued)

Gasoline	$ _____
Car payments	_____
Auto repair and maintenance	_____
Financial and legal services	_____
Medical care/medications	_____
School tuition/day care	_____
Life and disability insurance	_____
Car insurance	_____
Health insurance	_____
Property and casualty insurance	_____
Pet care	_____
Birthday and holiday gifts	_____
Babysitting/housekeeping	_____
Commutation (tolls, trains, etc.)	_____
Cable TV	_____
Household maintenance	_____
Telephone bills	_____
Religious institutions	_____
Books, magazines and papers	_____
Clubs, sports, hobbies	_____
Dues—union and others	_____
Alimony/child support	_____
Parental support/nursing home	_____
Personal allowances (kids, lottery, etc.)	_____
Other	_____
Total Annual Living Expenses	$ _____

When the envelope is empty, you stop spending in that category. Of course, you can always rob Peter to pay Paul, but you get the idea. This idea is probably best for those on a fixed income whose financial needs are uncomplicated and predictable.

4. The bank account method. This is a more sophisticated version of the envelope method, but similar. It involves setting up three different bank accounts: a savings account for long-term goals (investments), an interest-bearing checking account or money market fund for short-term goals (tuition payments) and a checking account for bills and cash withdrawals. Budget how much is to go into each account on a monthly basis, and withdraw a certain allotment for bills. If your withdrawals exceed the budget for the month, stop taking the money out.

Truthfully, the final execution is the least relevant. What's important is that the tracking system is simple enough to use *on a continuing basis*.

Budget tips

Once you and your budget are comfortable with each other, here are some suggestions to keep the ball rolling.

As in Monopoly—pick the banker first. If the wrong person is in charge of the funds, your best intentions could be wasted. Decide which family member is the most organized, has the better memory for dates and obligations, likes working with numbers, has the most free time to handle the record-keeping, bill-paying, etc., and is preferably the *saver*, not the spender. If both adults are equally capable or incapable of these functions, split the chores to keep each other in check.

Build in a reward system. There has to be both small and large payoffs for good behavior. Make sure that rewards are given as often as possible. Perhaps a family membership at a health club is a way to say thanks—or a nice vacation, dinner out. You get the idea. Keep 'em happy. Everyone deserves a break now and then.

Charge yourself a "check" fee. Some people find that they can save small amounts of money if they deduct $10 or $20 every time they write a check. They call it a check fee, and after a month of bill-paying, they've accumulated a few hundred dollars that can be thrown into an interest-bearing account.

Leave home without it. That's right. You can leave your American Express card home, along with your other credit cards, and you will survive. You'll also cut back on credit-card spending in a big way. If you use your cards, let them be for planned purchases. Also, if you're not always carrying your cards, you'll be less likely to ever have to report them lost or stolen.

As with anything that is experimental, you can expect the first few months of money-watching to have some ups and downs. You'll discover luxuries you absolutely can't live without, expenses you overlooked, and overall bad ideas, like serving macaroni and cheese every third night. But at least your heart and your pocketbook will be in the right place. And when you *do* work out the glitches, you'll be amazed at the size of the surplus that's ready to work for you.

Public Enemy #1

Creating a budget and sticking with it can be as hard as losing weight and keeping it off. But there is one thing you can do to make your job easier. Stop being a member of the "debt set."

In my view, debts have become Public Enemy #1. At last count, according to the Federal Reserve Board, the national debt topped a record $4.1 trillion dollars, with consumer debt representing almost $800 billion of that (not including mortgages).

Hopefully, the amount you owe your creditors pales by comparison. But regardless of how much you owe, make no mistake, if you don't get your personal spending in line with your income, you will never have enough money to save for your retirement.

Simply put, unless you get out from under the credit-card bills, outstanding loans and other forms of indebtedness that have commandeered your pocketbook for who knows how many years, you will do nothing more than lose precious time. For every year that you dole out hundreds to thousands of dollars trying to pay down your high interest charges, you lose out on the chance to invest in your retirement nest egg.

It is also important to understand how expensive borrowing is today. Not only does credit debt prevent you from maximizing your earning power, the debts aren't even deductible anymore. Gone are the days when you could rationalize away your Visa bill by telling yourself you could deduct the interest from your income tax. Furthermore, the interest on installment debt is still hovering as high as 18 percent to 21 percent on unpaid balances, while our savings accounts are earning a not-very-

exciting 3 percent to 5 percent. Add to that the cost of annual membership fees, the exorbitant penalties for late payments and over-the-limit charges, and in another era, it would have been called highway robbery.

Just how much do you owe?

The first step in getting a handle on your debt is to determine the percentage of your after-tax income you are spending to pay off installment debts.

The conservative school of thought is that you should be spending no more than 15 percent to 20 percent of your take-home pay (this does not include your mortgage payment). If you are currently spending 20 percent to 30 percent, or higher, it's time to apply the emergency brakes.

The best way to get a feel for how much of your income and savings are being eaten away every month by credit debt is to take a piece of paper and write down every creditor. Next to that, put the interest rate being paid, the average monthly payment and the total amount due. If there is a maturity date (when the loan will be retired), list that as well. Add it all up, and that's exactly where you're at.

Whatever the bottom line, don't give up. If you're willing to fight this battle, there are any number of ways you can win. I have a client who swears that the only way to acquire a second home, a second car, and a second vacation is to get a third income. I told him that's the hard way. Here are some practical suggestions to get you started on the road to fiscal fitness and to stay in good standing with the creditors you don't ultimately cancel out on.

Lee Rosenberg's best tips for chopping debts

- **Cut, cut, cut.** Find the biggest, sharpest scissors in the house and start cutting up credit cards. All but the ones you need for emergencies—gas cards, one bank card (Mastercard or Visa), and one dining card (American Express, Diners Club, etc.) Anything else will get you into deeper trouble.

  Remember this: Credit cards don't extend your paycheck. In fact, they actually give you less money to work with because all they do is eat away at your income every month, preventing you from saving money.

- **Shop for better deals.** If you can't pay back the balances on your high-interest bank cards, shop for lower-rate cards and use those to pay off the more expensive ones. Even better, shop for the no-annual-fee bank cards. For information on how to apply, contact the nonprofit organization, Bankcard Holders of America. This is one of the largest consumer associations in the U.S. Annual dues are $24, and this entitles you to its newsletters and a wide variety of services. Perhaps of greatest value are its brochures identifying creditors around the country who market cards with low interest rates, no-annual fees, secured credit cards, etc. Contact: Bankcard Holders of America, 560 Herndon Parkway, Herndon, VA 22070. To order publications, call 800-553-8025.

- **Consider a home equity loan.** To consolidate your debts, consider applying for a home equity loan. Interest rates are not anywhere near those of credit cards, and at least the interest is fully deductible (provided your loan doesn't exceed $100,000). A strong word of caution before you do this: These loans put your home up as security. You cannot afford to further jeopardize your life by lavishing more things on your family. The only reason you should be borrowing against the roof over your head is to reduce and consolidate your debts. If all you can envision is packing for a Caribbean cruise, better pass on this option.

- **Get rid of the nuisance bills.** Try to pay off as many of your smallest debts as possible. They may not amount to much money in total, but at least you'll feel like you're making progress by scratching creditors' names off your list, and you'll also feel relief knowing there are going to be less threatening letters waiting for you in the future.

- **Pay with the green stuff.** Introduce yourself to the concept of "pay-as-you-go." It's one of the best bargains around. Start by making a promise that you won't charge anything that costs under $50. It's one way to cut back on the small, harmless impulse purchases that, bit by bit, eat away at your paycheck.

- **Keep track.** Get out of the habit of throwing away your credit receipts. Aside from the fact that they will come in handy if you return purchases, they will help you keep track of monthly spending. If you take each of your receipts, put them in an envelope for the month and then write down the amount of each of those receipts on the back of the envelope, you'll know exactly how much you owe before the bill shows up. Not only does that call immediate attention to billing errors or discrepancies, you'll know in advance if you're overdoing it for the month.

- **Pick up the phone.** If you feel that the only way to get out of your mess is to talk with your creditors, by all means do so. The key is to be upfront and honest with them, rather than waiting for them to turn you over to a collection agency. When you talk with them, tell them what you can realistically send them each month to reduce your debt. If they argue with you and threaten that your bill has to be paid in full, get to a supervisor or someone in management. In most cases, they will be happy to work out some kind of a payment plan with you rather than risk getting nothing back at all. Or, better yet, let your financial planner make the calls. I can tell you from experience that when creditors get assurances from a professional money manager who is supervising a customer's debts, it helps a lot.

- **Your second call should be to the nearest CFP.** Certified Financial Planners can make a big difference when it comes to getting back on track. A CFP can help you assess which are the best assets to sell off, which methods work best to create savings from tax deductions. They can help you set up a realistic budget, and develop a

total program for restructuring debt, setting up savings and reducing overhead and expenses. And don't procrastinate because you think the planner's fee will be too expensive. In the long run, it won't cost, it will pay.

I predict that once you make getting out of debt a top priority, you'll discover that even small steps will lead to more restful nights.

Good question!

Q. We'd like to work with a Certified Financial Planner (CFP), but don't think we can afford it. How do they charge?
A. If anyone can appreciate the subject of what things cost, it's going to be a financial planner. That's why the subject of fees should be an easy one to discuss, once the planner has a solid understanding of your case. As far as specific fees are concerned, sometimes it will be based on your income, net worth and assets under management. In most instances, however, fees will depend on how many hours it will take to generate your plan. The more complex a plan you need, the more it will cost.

Q. What's the difference between a fee-only planner and a fee-plus commission planner?
A. The largest sector of financial planning firms works on a fee-plus commission basis. They charge an upfront fee to develop financial plans and earn commissions from the sale of investments. Fees can range from $500 to $5,000, depending on the complexity of the case, and you are not obligated to

the planner for implementation. However, if you are satisfied with the planner's work, it can be very advantageous to have him or her manage your portfolio. This is because the planner will have a vested interest in how the investments perform.

A small percentage of planners work on a fee-only basis. They charge a flat amount for developing a financial plan and do not sell investment products or earn commissions. As a result, their fee structure tends to be much higher, with rates ranging from $1,000 to $15,000. With fee-only planners, their claims of total impartiality are valid, but the disadvantage is that they don't monitor or expedite their own recommendations. That means clients have to do their own legwork and decide from whom to purchase the investment products. Besides that, clients won't save any money with respect to commissions. At the point that the financial plan is implemented, they'll just pay commissions to the brokers. In the meantime, they've probably paid a higher price for a plan, just to get a supposedly unbiased opinion.

For these reasons, I strongly recommend working with fee-plus commission planners. It's the most cost-efficient approach, it's one-stop shopping, and you ultimately develop a relationship with one person who has an intimate understanding of your personality, your goals and the status of your portfolio.

Q. Does it really matter if you work with a CFP?
A. CFPs are the only experts who have gone through rigorous educational training to manage all aspects of a client's financial affairs. They do not replace your lawyer and accountant, they *manage* the team to insure that everyone is working toward common goals. When you work with a CFP, you will discuss your needs and goals and then he or she will develop a highly customized, detailed plan that will help you achieve those goals. In effect, financial planning is not a product, it is a *process*. And the result of the process is the potential to save thousands of dollars every year in income tax while creating a thriving portfolio through sound investment strategies.

Q. How do we get the names of the CFPs in our area?
A. Check the yellow pages or call the Institute of Certified Financial Planners for a referral at 1-800-282-PLAN (7526). Another source is the International Association of Financial Planners at 1-800-945-IAFP (4237).

Q. We've been in over our heads for so many years, I think the only way out is to file bankruptcy. How do we know if that is the right move?
A. Before you bring in the lawyers, I always urge people to exhaust every other possibility. Try to work with a Certified Financial Planner who can show you how to consolidate and pay back your debts. Or, get in touch with one of the 356 nonprofit consumer-credit counseling services across the country. Their advice is either nominal or free (they are supported by the government, creditors and even United Way). Plus, they can help you negotiate loan payments, show you how to consolidate your debts and stay out of debt. To find out about a nonprofit counseling center in your area, call or write the National Foundation for Consumer Credit, 8701 Georgia Ave., Suite 507, Silver Spring, MD 20910. 301-589-5600.

Q. What about the credit repair centers that advertise in the paper?
A. Stay away. Many are known to charge outrageous fees (how about $50 an hour?), make impossible promises about fixing your problem, and actually end up creating even bigger problems for you than the ones you originally presented.

Q. When I have extra money, what is better? To pay down a credit card or throw the money into my money market?
A. According to Bankcard Holders of America, paying off your credit card is like getting a 28-percent return on an investment! Here's the thinking: Hypothetically, if you put $100 in a bank account that paid 28 percent interest, you'd earn $28 that year. If you were in a 33-percent tax bracket, your net return would be about $18.50 ($28 X .33 = $9.24). Now suppose instead you took the $100 to pay your bank card, which coincidentally charges you 18.5 percent interest on your unpaid balance. Since you'd be using after-tax dollars to make the payment, you'd save about $18.50 in interest charges, which you could consider your return. The key, of course, is not to run up the credit card again.

Q. We're one of those couples in our late 50s who didn't take retirement planning very seriously until now. Is there anything extra we can do to make up for lost time?
A. Absolutely, provided you are willing to make retirement planning your number-one priority. For starters, all of the ideas discussed in this chapter are applicable to you, maybe even more so because of your age. So don't ignore the advice about doing a cash-flow analysis, creating a budget, reducing your debts, estimating your net worth, projecting the amount of income you'll need, etc. But in order to maximize the last years of working before you retire, there are a number of other strategies to consider:

- Get part-time and/or second jobs, do consulting or freelance work, or whatever you can to "heavy up" on your earnings for the next few years. Depending on the nature of the work and the income generated, you may discover you've created additional tax deductions for yourself (home office, travel, sales expenses, etc.).

- Make sure you are working with a good accountant, that you are itemizing if possible, taking every allowable deduction and basically getting the best possible advice on reducing your tax burden.

- If your employer offers incentive plans such as stock options, matching contributions, 401ks, I urge you to take advantage of those programs. To assure your participation, arrange for the employer to systematically deduct money from your paycheck. Otherwise your entire paycheck will likely be diverted to pay bills.

- If you are employed but not enrolled in a company pension or profit-sharing plan, you should take advantage of the fact that an IRA contribution is tax-free. But even if you are in a pension plan and can't deduct the contribution because your adjusted gross income exceeds the limit ($25,000 for singles; $50,000 for married couples), IRAs are still valuable.

Contribute up to $2,000 a year and your interest, dividends and appreciation will be tax-deferred until the funds are withdrawn at retirement. It sure beats a money market account or CD.

- If you have considerable equity in your home, consider selling it and trading down to one that is less expensive to own and maintain. This is best accomplished if you are 55 or older and can take advantage of the $125,000 capital gains exclusion (see Chapter 7). Invest the profits and earmark the amount you save every month on mortgage/maintenance for additional contributions to your investments.

- Work with a Certified Financial Planner to make sure you are getting the maximum rate of return on your portfolio. The closer you get to retirement, the more aggressive you need to be. Often, people become overly concerned about preservation of capital (understandably they don't want to lose what little they have). Instead they should move into safe investments that are better performers (See Chapter 5).

- Finally, you have to be willing to bite the bullet and cut back on all but necessary spending. At the same time, head to the library and check out the books and publications that feature money-saving ideas. One that has come to my attention is the *Tightwad Gazette*. This monthly eight-page newsletter is filled with everything from common-sense ideas (make your own popsicles from juice) to "you've

got to be joking" ideas (save on toilet paper by semi-flattening the role so you can only pull a few sheets at a time). But even if you get a few great ideas a month, the savings could be considerable. For a free sample issue, send a self-addressed, stamped envelope to *Tightwad Gazette*, R.R. 1, Box 3570, Leeds, ME 04263. Big spenders can *call* for a free issue (204-524-7962). Annual subscriptions are $12.

What I tell my clients

You're the boss, so pay yourself first. Don't wait to see what's left over at the end of the month to save or invest. Pay *yourself* every month, as though you were a creditor (pretend you're paying a utility bill). As long as you earmark a certain amount of every paycheck to pay your most important creditor—you—your nest egg will grow.

The best hedge your house offers is the one in the yard. If you believe your house's greatest value is that it gives you a hedge against inflation, think again. While houses will presumably escalate in value in the '90s, gone are the days where prices jumped by double digits. It's more likely values will increase by a modest 2 percent to 5 percent a year, if at all. That means you won't lose anything by keeping the house. But you do need to consider an older home's increased maintenance expenses as well as rising property taxes. These costs will go up every year, potentially offsetting any gains.

If you can preserve jam, you can preserve your money. As we'll discuss in in Chapter 5, you can't fall asleep at the wheel when it comes to managing your money. You must continually monitor your investments, analyzing the net rate of return (after taxes and inflation). Today, for example, most savings vehicles are not keeping pace with inflation. Thus, if you've got considerable funds tied up in money markets and CDs, the most prudent strategy is to convert a portion of those funds into equity investments, such as balanced mutual funds. These consistently outperform inflation.

Suddenly single. One of the saddest aspects of helping clients prepare for their retirement years is discussing the eventual loss of a spouse. No matter how painful, we can't overlook the financial implications when a spouse dies.

Because many couples plan on two Social Security benefit checks and possibly two pensions, and two paychecks from part-time work or consulting, it is essential to recalculate your financial projections in anticipation that one spouse will die before the other. For example, when a spouse dies, Social Security decreases the monthly benefit by the amount of the lower of your two benefits. As for pensions and annuities, depending on the terms, the benefits can stop completely when the pension owner dies. If the spouse was still employed at his or her death, obviously that source of income will be lost.

How to maintain the status quo when you are widowed. Ideally, the best strategy is to defer income until it is absolutely needed. By living on only what is necessary to be comfortable, you have the best possibility of preserving your assets for the greatest length of time. Secondly, continue "recycling" your money throughout your retirement so that your investments not only pay out, but continue to grow. It used to be that preservation of capital was a retiree's top priority. Today the most important goal is to make sure your capital is continually reinvested to keep up with taxes and inflation.

Another tactic is to have adequate insurance policies on each other so death benefits can replace the loss of income. The death of a spouse is enough of an emotional adjustment. Nobody needs the added burden of worring about keeping the house or paying the bills.

"Just do it!"

In his hit Broadway show, "The World According to Me," comedian Jackie Mason brilliantly summed up the human condition when he referred to the single biggest financial mistake people feel they've made. "Everyone I know *could have* bought a building 30 years ago for $9, but didn't. Now they cry, 'Do you know what that building is worth *today*? $187 million. They talked me out of it, those lousy SOBs!'"

It's funny, but true. We've all regretted passing on a stock or investment that would have yielded a tidy sum. Yet, in spite of the mistakes we have made along the path to financial freedom, it is never too late to learn from them. It would be even better if we could sell our mistakes for the same price they cost us!

But short of that, I say whatever the missed opportunities, poor judgments, and uneducated decisions took place, use this book as your guide to making a mid-course correction to beat the odds and retire with financial security.

Or as they say in those great Nike ads, "Just do it!"

2

Things your mother never taught you about Social Security

One of the first lessons of high school civics was that our government was founded on a system of checks and balances. Unfortunately, at the rate that Congress writes checks, one wonders if there will ever *be* a balance!

Yet in spite of what you may have heard, the runaway federal deficit did not bankrupt our Social Security system! To the contrary, Social Security operates more like a private corporation than a government agency—and business is booming! In 1992, it collected $47 billion more in revenue than it paid out. On top of that, last year its burgeoning $300-billion trust fund earned $25 billion in interest through investments in U.S. Treasury bonds.

That's quite a turnaround from only a decade ago when we were led to believe that this mammoth institution was insolvent and more akin to "Social Insecurity"!

Although there are an ever-increasing number of experts predicting that future generations will never see a surplus of this magnitude (or any at all), it is without question that Americans who retire in the 1990s are sitting pretty. According to Social Security, workers who are at retirement age today are assured of getting the highest level of payments in the history of the system. In 1992, the department wrote checks for $780 million *per day* to 41 million beneficiaries. In total, more than $145 billion in benefits were paid out to retirees.

Even with inflation, Americans are now getting 20 times more in retirement benefits than the first recipients received more than 50 years ago. In January 1993, the maximum monthly benefit at age 65 was $1,128 for individuals and $1,692 for couples (one worker, one nonworking spouse). As an equal opportunity institution, Social Security paid $2,256 a month to couples where both spouses are 65 and qualified for the maximum benefits based on their own employment records.

Furthermore, life expectancies are at an all-time high. The bottom line is that recipients who turn 65 this year are likely to receive between $151,826 to $203,000 in benefits in their lifetime. That's quite a return on their investment when you consider that their total contributions (employer and employee) probably amounted to no more than $24,000 to $47,000.

Who qualifies for Social Security benefits?

The original concept of Social Security was to provide supplemental income to retired workers who had earned these benefits through years of gainful employment. In effect, it was set up as an insurance program. If you paid your premiums in the form of Social Security taxes, at your retirement, it was payback time through monthly "dividend" checks. So, unlike Medicaid and welfare, taking Social Security benefits had nothing to do with *need*. However, what these programs do have in common is the confusion they create!

Whenever my clients are nearing retirement, I can count on a telephone call that goes something like this: "We can't make heads or tails of this Social Security stuff. Are we both going to get benefits? And how much will we get every month"? Because there are no clear and simple answers, I always suggest they come in to meet with me and to wear comfortable clothes. They're going to be sitting for a while!

In a nutshell, here is what I tell them:

First, to be eligible for Social Security benefits based on your *own* work history, you must have acquired a minimum number of "quarters of coverage" or "work credits" in your lifetime. For example, if you reach 62 any time after 1991, you will need *10* full years of employment/self-employment for a total of 40 credits (4 quarterly credits per year). If you reached age 62 prior to 1991, you would then need between 8 and 9 3/4 years of credits.

In addition, work credits are earned based on quarterly net earnings. In 1993, for example, workers had to earn a minimum of $590 per quarter to get one work credit. Prior to 1993, minimum quarterly earnings ranged from $250 (1978) to $570 (1992). Check with Social Security if you are concerned that your net earnings did not meet the minimum required for credit.

Anyone who meets the criteria for work credits and net earnings is considered a "fully insured worker."

Fully insured workers' spouses who never worked or did not earn enough work credits to be fully insured on their own are entitled to a percentage of their spouse's retirement benefits. The exact percentage depends on the age the working spouse retires (more on that to follow).

When does the Social Security clock start ticking?

Under the Old Age, Survivors and Disability Insurance Program (OASDI), nine out of every 10 Americans will receive Social Security benefits at some point in their lives. Essentially, Social Security writes checks when you and/or your spouse retire, become severely disabled or die.

In addition, since 1965, Social Security has also administered $900 billion in health care benefits through the Hospital Insurance Trust Fund, better known as Medicare. Today, Medicare has more than 35 million "customers." We'll discuss Medicare in greater detail in Chapter 3.

Here is a brief description of when benefits become available:

Should you become severely disabled: If you become severely disabled at any age before "normal retirement" and you meet all of Social Security's other eligibility requirements, you will receive disability benefits. Because of your disability, spouses and dependents may also be eligible for benefits if they are 62 and older, and/or are caring for 1) a disabled child or 2) a child under the age of 16. In addition, each disabled child, or a child under 18 (or 19 if still in high school) may also get benefit checks.

At your death: If your spouse is 60 or older when you die, he or she will qualify for Social Security benefits. If you are both widowed and disabled, benefits can begin at age 50. If age does not qualify your spouse, he or she can still be eligible to receive benefits if caring for a disabled child or one under the age 16. The child would also be eligible for his or her own benefits if under 18 (or 19 if still in high school).

NOTE: If you are 62 or older when your spouse dies, the surviving spouse is then entitled to his/her own or the widow/widowers benefit checks each month, whichever is higher.

At retirement: Again, if you have worked full-time for a *minimum* of 10 years, you are considered fully insured and are entitled to start receiving retirement benefits at 62. However, should you decide to begin collecting at this time, you will only receive 80 percent of your earned benefits. If you wait until age 65 before collecting Social Security, you will receive 100 percent of your earned benefits. For each year between 65 and 70 that you postpone applying for benefits, you'll receive an additional percentage increase in benefits. The percentage varies depending on your year of birth.

Spouses who are not fully insured based on their own employment are also eligible for benefits at age 62 or older, *provided the working spouse has retired.*

Example: A client turned 68 but continued to work in his dental practice. On her 62nd birthday, his wife, who had been a homemaker during their 40 years of marriage, applied for her Social Security benefits. She was declined because as a nonworking spouse, she could not receive her retirement benefits until her husband retired.

Nonworking spouses of retired workers who are under age 62 *can* receive retirement benefits if they are caring for 1) a disabled child or 2) a child under 16. In addition, each disabled child, or child under 18 (or 19 if still in high school) is eligible to receive his or her own benefits.

"How much will you get?"

After you have determined your eligibility for retirement benefits, the first thing that you will probably want to know is "How much money will we receive every month"? The answer is, "It depends."

The exact amount of benefits depends on three important factors:

1. The age of retirement: 62 to 64, 65, or 66 to 70
2. If you and/or your spouse were primarily average or maximum contributors
3. If one or both spouses worked

Age of retirement

If you were born in 1938 or before, then the normal retirement age (the age at which you are entitled to receive full retirement benefits) is 65. If you were born after 1938, the age you'll reach normal retirement age is 65 years and 2 months or beyond.

Age of retirement

Year of birth	Year you'll reach age 62	Normal retirement age will be (year/months)	Date you'll reach normal retirement age if birthday is January 2. (For later birthdays, add number of months after Jan. up to birth month)
1938	2000	65/2	March 1, 2003
1939	2001	65/4	May 1, 2004
1940	2002	65/6	July 1, 2005
1941	2003	65/8	Sept. 1, 2006
1942	2004	65/10	Nov. 1, 2007
1943-1954	2005-2016	66/0	Jan. 1, 2009-2020
1955	2017	66/2	March 1, 2021
1956	2018	66/4	May 1, 2022
1957	2019	66/6	July 1, 2023
1958	2020	66/8	Sept. 1, 2024
1959	2021	66/10	Nov. 1, 2025
1960 and after	2022 and after	67/0	Jan. 1, 2027 and after

Keep in mind that, although the normal retirement age is 65 or beyond, workers can opt to receive retirement benefits as early as one month following their 62nd birthday. Should you choose early retirement, understand that this will affect the amount of your monthly benefit checks. They will be smaller—not just until you reach the normal retirement age, but for the rest of your life. For example, workers that start collecting at 62 in 1993 will only receive 80 percent of the full benefits they're entitled to.

NOTE: As the official retirement age for baby boomers creeps up to 66, 67 and beyond, the reduction of benefits for early retirees will creep up accordingly. If the official retirement age for your birth year is 66, and you retire at age 62, you'll receive 75 percent of your total benefits. If the official retirement age is 67 and you retire at 62, you'll receive 70 percent of your total benefits and so on.

What's interesting, however, is that in spite of the 20-percent reduction in benefits, the majority of all new recipients are taking advantage of this early retirement offer. The reason is simple. They would prefer to get three years of benefits while they are more likely to be alive—even if the check amounts are somewhat smaller—than if they'd waited until age 65.

Moving on, if you retire between 62 and 65, Social Security prorates benefits, using a very complex table. Because most of us would rather get a cavity filled than try to figure out the bottom line, here is an easy-to-use table that illustrates the percentage of benefits that will be paid to both workers and spouses if they retire between ages 62 and 65.

Percentage of benefits paid based on age of retirement

	Age 65	Age 64	Age 63	Age 62
Worker	100%	93%	87.0%	80.0%
Worker's	50%	45%	41.7%	37.5%
Spouse (% is of worker's benefit)				

Here's what this means. If a worker retired at 64 and his spouse retired at 62, the worker would be entitled to 93 percent of his earned benefits. The spouse would then be entitled to 37.5 percent of whatever the 93 percent of benefits amounted to.

To help explain, we'll apply these percentages to some real people and some real dollars. Take the case of the Millers. Herb decided to retire on his 62nd birthday, which was in 1993. According to Social Security, based on his earnings and quarters worked since 1951, he was entitled to the maximum monthly benefit in 1993 of $901 ($1,118 X 80 percent). His wife, Elaine, who was also 62, had not worked long enough to earn Social Security benefits on her own, but was entitled to 37.5 percent of Herb's benefits ($1,118), or $419. Their total monthly benefit checks that first year was $1,320. For this example, the

figure is taken from a chart summarizing actual early retirement benefits by age, found on page 52.

In comparison, had Herb waited three more years to retire, he would have received 100 percent of his benefits, not just in 1993 but in every year until his death. Likewise, if Elaine had waited another three years to apply for benefits, she would have been entitled to 50 percent of Herb's full benefits until her death, instead of 37.5 percent. In addition, the annual cost of living adjustments favor the higher benefits (although the difference is marginal).

But here's the catch. Because Herb chose to start collecting benefits at age 62 and 1 month, it meant he would receive 35 more benefit checks than if he'd waited to 65. At the current benefit rate, that would amount to an estimated $31,535 (35 X $901). Had he waited to age 65, his monthly checks would have been in the range of $217 more, but he would have to collect for the next 13 or so years ($217 X 156 months = $33,852) to be even. Although everyone would hope to still be alive to do so, the conventional wisdom today is "take the money at 62 and run."

Will you receive average or maximum benefits?

Retirement benefits are based on your average earnings from 1951 through to one year prior to your retirement. *However, only the amount of income that was taxed for Social Security is considered.*

Each year since 1951, the maximum earnings level that could be taxed for Social Security has changed. This defined contribution has always been based on an index of average U.S. earnings for the respective year. In order to determine if you were contributing at average or maximum levels during your working years, and will subsequently receive average or maximum benefit checks, you would need to know what the ceiling was for each year you were employed.

Refer to this table to determine the maximum taxable earnings for the following years:

Maximum taxable earnings for social security

Year	Maximum taxable earnings
1951-1954	$3,600
1955-1958	$4,200
1959-1965	$4,800
1966-1967	$6,600
1968-1971	$7,800
1972	$9,000
1973	$10,800
1974	$13,200
1975	$14,100
1976	$15,300
1977	$16,500
1978	$17,700
1979	$22,900
1980	$25,900
1981	$29,700
1982	$32,400
1983	$35,700
1984	$37,800
1985	$39,600
1986	$42,000
1987	$43,800
1988	$45,000
1989	$48,000
1990	$51,300
1991	$53,400
1992	$55,500
1993	$57,600

What's the bottom line? If your contributions have fallen into the average range, the current monthly retirement benefit is approximately $653 in 1993. Workers' spouses of "normal retirement age" (65) would receive 50 percent of that amount for a total of $979.50.

If it appears that you consistently earned the maximum taxable amount, you should be eligible to receive the maximum benefit. If you retire at 65 starting in 1993, the maximum monthly benefit to fully insured workers is $1,128 per month. Workers' spouses of retirement age would be eligible to receive 50 percent of that amount for a total benefit of $1,692 a month ($20,304 annually).

If you would like to try to estimate your approximate benefits, use the replacement ratio method: If your career earnings were at an average level (below the maximum taxable), multiply your last year's gross income by 42 percent. For example, if your income that year was $25,000, your approximate annual benefit would be $10,500 (or $875 a month).

If your career earnings were at the maximum earnings level, then multiply your last year's gross income by 27 percent. For example, if the maximum taxable amount then was $57,600 (as it was in 1993), your estimated monthly benefit would be $1,555.20. Since that is in excess of the current cap of $1,106, at least you'd be confirming you were entitled to the maximum benefit.

One-, two-worker households

A spouse who didn't work long enough to meet the minimum 40-quarter requirement will receive 50 percent of the working spouse's benefits if both spouses are 65 or older at retirement. If the worker's spouse decides to collect at 62, he or she will receive 37.5 percent of the working spouses's benefits. In either case, the spouse must be married to the worker for one or more years to collect that worker's benefits.

In families where both husband and wife meet the working requirements, they will each receive their full share at age 65, or 80 percent of their share if they begin receiving benefits at 62.

Effects of early retirement on Social Security benefits

One of the most detrimental side effects of the recession has been the substantial job losses among older workers. According to the U.S. Department of Labor's Bureau of Labor Statistics, approximately 25,000 employees between the ages of 55 and 64 were laid off since 1990. The Bureau also projected that close to two-thirds of *all* jobs lost in this period would be permanent pink slips. In other words, tens of thousands of workers age 50-plus would most likely have to look to a new company if they wanted to stay in the work force.

But as any older job applicant can tell you, at a time when there's an endless supply of younger, less-costly talent around, age and experience are about as useful as typewriters and carbon paper. The older you are, the more you may feel like a relic ready for the junk heap.

Unfortunately, that's just the start of the bad news. Unemployed older workers have three serious problems: 1) They're likely to be losing out on the highest earnings of their lives. 2) Those high earnings are most likely to occur when family financial obligations are satisfied and there's finally a chance to save for retirement. 3) Without a job, there is no way to pay into Social Security. And if you don't pay into Social Security, particularly in the years when you are closest to receiving benefits, your monthly checks will subsequently be smaller than they would have been if you were still contributing to the system up to age 62 or beyond.

This last problem identifies a big misconception about Social Security. Many people believe that once they are "fully insured," they will automatically be entitled to maximum benefits. In reality, a fully insured worker's only guarantee is that he or she is entitled to benefits—period. The exact amount is still dependent on how much and when the benefits are paid in.

It's important for employees who are being enticed with early retirement offers to understand the consequences. They have to compare the amount of the bonus or incentive against the amount of monthly Social Security benefits they'll lose over their lifetime if they stop working with several years on the clock.

Below is a useful planning tool if you are offered early retirement (or are forced to retire). The chart shows how much your monthly benefits would be reduced if you stopped working at age 48 or later.

For sample purposes, this chart applies to fully insured workers who reached age 62 and one month in 1993 and who had maximum earnings in each year from 1951 through retirement.

Effect of early retirement on Social Security benefits
(Workers age 62 in 1993; the effect on future retirees will be similar)

How to use: Find the age you plan or are forced to stop working. Read across the columns to find the amount payable at age 65 vs. age 62 and 1 month. If you stop working before 62, the last column shows by how much your monthly benefits will be reduced if you receive them at age 62 and 1 month.

Stop work at age	Benefit at age 65	Benefit at age 62/1 month	Amount benefit is reduced if taken at age 62/1 month
62	$1118	$901	
61	$1107	$892	$9
60	$1097	$884	$17
59	$1087	$876	$25
58	$1077	$868	$33
57	$1067	$860	$41
56	$1057	$851	$50
55	$1046	$843	$58
54	$1028	$828	$73
53	$1010	$813	$88
52	$ 974	$785	$116

Paying taxes on your Social Security benefits

An estimated 23 percent of Social Security beneficiaries are presently affected by taxation. Of those, about 13 percent will pay a greater percentage of taxes on their benefits starting in 1995 (for tax year 1994) now that President Clinton's tax package has been signed into law. With this new law, the maximum percentage of Social Security income subject to tax went up to 85 percent (it was 50 percent). The way it will work is that individuals with "countable" income over $34,000 or couples with "countable" income exceeding $44,000 will be subject to paying taxes on 85 percent of their Social Security benefits. Although this higher tax will affect a small percentage of beneficiaries when it becomes effective, as income levels increase over the years, so will the number of retirees who will be subject to this higher tax.

To determine if your benefits will be taxed at all, add up your countable income.

Countable income

1. Adjusted gross income (before Social Security benefits)
2. Tax-exempt interest income (municipal bonds, etc.)
3. Half of your total annual Social Security benefits

Take this countable income and subtract one of the following base amounts:

Base amounts

1. $32,000 for married couples filing jointly
2. $25,000 for singles or those filing as "Head of Household"
3. "0" if you are married but filing separately

If your countable income is *smaller* than the base amount, your benefits will not be taxed. If your countable income is greater than your base amount, then the amount of benefits subject to tax will be the smaller of:

- Half the benefits, or
- Half the amount of combined income in excess of the base amount

---

Example: John and Mary Smith, who file a joint tax return

1.a) Adjusted gross income before Social Security benefits are considered		$30,200
b) Half of annual Social Security benefits		$6,300
c) Interest from municipal bonds*		$2,000
Countable Income		$38,500
2.a) Minus "Base amount" (for married filing jointly)		- $32,000
3.) Difference		$6,500

* Municipal bond interest is not taxable. However, the interest is included for the purpose of calculating Social Security benefits.

Since $3,250 (half the difference between their countable income and their base amount) is less than half their benefits ($6,300), Mr. and Mrs. Smith will include $3,250 of their Social Security benefits in adjusted gross income. Thus, their total adjusted gross income will be $33,450.

How much tax you owe depends on your personal adjusted gross income, as well as your taxable income, your deductions, exemptions and credits and other factors.

Social Security and inflation

In 1987, Congress passed a law that Social Security benefits must increase each year if there is any jump in the Consumer Price Index over the previous year. That way, recipients would not be penalized for inflation. So, for example, the Cost-of-Living Adjustment (COLA) for benefits payable in 1993 had an adjusted increase of 3 percent over 1992 benefits. In effect, each year Social Security determines the percentage that living costs have increased and adjusts benefits by the same percentage the following January. There is no cap on that increase.

Coming out of retirement to reenter the work force

Approximately 25 percent of all retirees end up "semi-retiring," or returning to the workplace, either on a full- or part-time basis. If you do plan to work, you must be aware of how your income after retirement affects your Social Security benefits. Here are some important facts:

1. There *is* a ceiling on earned income over and above your Social Security benefits. In 1993, if you are between the ages of 62 and 65, and you are collecting benefits, the maximum you can earn that year from outside employment or a business is $7,440. If you are between the ages of 65 and 69, you can earn up to $10,200 for the year.

   Incidentally, the maximum on earned income increases every year, so check with Social Security to find out what is the top salary for the year before you start earning it. Then continue to monitor your income throughout the year to insure that you don't penalize your benefits by going over the ceiling.

2. At present, there is no limit on earnings for people who are 70 and older. Apparently the government feels that if these seniors still want to earn a living, God bless them.

3. If your additional earned income does exceed the annual exempt amount, and you are between the ages of 62 and 65, for every $2 over that limit, $1 will be deducted from your monthly Social Security check. If you are between the ages of 65 and 70, for every $3 earned over the limit, $1 will be deducted. Dependent's checks will be reduced as well if they are collecting on your work record. Notify the Social Security office, not the IRS, if you have gone over the limit. Any benefits that are overpaid you will have to be returned to Social Security.

4. If you are self-employed, all of the rules regarding earned income limits apply to you as well.

The important thing is to make sure that taking a job will increase your income, not decrease it by jeopardizing your benefits. Check with your Social Security office to confirm that—before you go back to work.

Good question!

Q. I've worked for the federal government since 1970. Will I qualify for Social Security when I retire?
A. No. Federal employees hired before Jan. 1, 1984, are still covered for retirement, death and disability benefits under the Civil Service Retirement plan, or a similar pension plan. However, you will be eligible for Social Security's Medicare/Hospital Insurance benefits.

Q. I've been self-employed full-time for the past 20 years and my wife has never worked. Will we both receive benefits when I retire?
A. Yes, you will both be entitled to benefits. However, in spite of the fact that you've been contributing more each year than employed workers (you've been paying both the employee *and* the employer's portion), unfortunately, your benefits will be no higher than other workers.

Q. After 30 years of marriage, I am getting a divorce. I was a homemaker all these years. Will I lose out on Social Security benefits?
A. Anyone who was married to a fully insured worker for 10 or more years does not lose out on Social Security retirement benefits because of a divorce.

However, you must wait for two years after the divorce before applying, you must be at least age 62 and you must still be unmarried.

Q. My husband passed away five years ago and I plan to remarry. Whose benefits will I get? My first or second husband's? I only worked for a few years, so I'm not eligible on my own.
A. Actually, it depends on your age when you remarry. If you are 50 or over, you'll receive benefits from the husband whose earnings were greater. In other words, if your new husband's benefits are greater than your first husband's, you are entitled to receive 50 percent of your second husband's benefits. If you remarry before you turn 50, you lose all entitlement to your first husband's benefits.

Q. I lied about my age to get this last job. Now I'm 65 and they think I'm 60. This company has mandatory retirement at 65, but I'm not ready to retire. What happens to my Social Security benefits if I don't file at my 65th birthday.
A. There is no penalty for applying for benefits after 65. In fact, you'll receive 3.5 percent more for every year you wait up until your 70th birthday. Be sure to check with Social Security concerning your Medicare coverage, even though you elect to continue working.

Q. If I want to retire at age 70, will that increase my benefits when I do start to collect?
A. Yes. You'll receive a percentage increase for each year you delayed benefits until your 70th birthday. These are called Delayed Retirement Credits

(DRCs). If you retire at 71, you will accrue no more additional credits.

Q. Both my husband and I worked over 20 years and paid in the maximum. Are we each entitled to the maximum benefit, or does Social Security have a cap on the total they'll pay per family?
A. What you're really asking is if there is a "marriage" penalty. The answer is no. Each worker is entitled to receive benefits based on his or her own contributions, even if that means Social Security ends up paying you both the maximum benefit each month.

Q. How do I let Social Security know I'm ready to start receiving my benefit checks?
A. Contact your nearest Social Security office approximately three months before you are ready to start receiving benefits. At that time, you'll need to complete the necessary application form as well as provide proof of your age. If you have been employed for the past two years, bring your W-2 forms from that period. If you've been self-employed, bring your federal income tax returns. You must also provide proof of your current marital status. If you are married, divorced or widowed, bring your marriage certificate with you. If you prefer, Social Security will take your application over the phone. You can call the toll-free number at 1-800-772-1213. Then, just mail copies of the necessary documents proving age and marital status and you'll be all set.

Q. When will we get our checks?
A. Benefit checks are scheduled to be received on the third of each month for the preceding month. In other words,

you'll receive your check for May on June 3. If the third turns out to be a weekend or federal holiday, the check should be in your hands on the business day immediately prior to the third.

Q. Will my spouse and I get separate checks?
A. If you each have your own earnings records, you'll get separate checks. If one of the spouses is receiving benefits from the other spouse's earnings, the total amount may be combined in one check. It's a good idea for you to arrange for automatic deposit into a checking or savings account.

What I tell my clients

Forced retirees may be entitled to benefits. Employees who are forced into early retirement and who continue to receive termination pay for a period of time often assume that they're not eligible for Social Security benefits because they're still receiving a "paycheck." That is not the case. Termination pay is not viewed the same as a salary earned while working. As long as you are not on the job but are age-eligible, you are entitled to Social Security benefits.

Ditto for mid-year retirees. People who retire mid-year and who have subsequently earned more than the maximum earnings allowed by Social Security ($7,680 for those under age 65, $10,600 for those 65 to 69), often assume that they are not entitled to benefits until the new year. But they'd be wrong. Social Security's clock doesn't start ticking until *after* you retire. So, whether you retire in February or November, whatever income you earned is not counted against you.

Don't be a late check-in. Many people procrastinate and don't get around to requesting a summary of their estimated benefits until a few months prior to retirement. That can be a big problem if there are major discrepancies in the report. It can take months to resolve the errors or omissions, causing a headache when you start to collect. The more lead time you give yourself to review your file, (one to two years is sufficient), the more likely everything will be in order when you're ready to receive benefits. As it is, Social Security is about two years behind in reporting your employment history.

Pay as you go. Don't forget that any income earned after retirement is not only taxable, it is subject to Social Security taxes as well. In addition, you'd be taxed at the same rate as a full-time employee, without any corresponding benefit to you. That means you could be collecting benefits at the same time you're paying into the system.

False alarms. In this uncertain economy, it is not unusual for workers in their 60s to lose their jobs, apply for Social Security benefits, only to get rehired at a later time. While getting a second chance to work full-time for a few years may be great (more time to save for retirement), remember that once you've begun collecting, there will be a permanent reduction of benefits when you reapply. That's why, ideally, you should wait 6 months after you've lost your job to apply for benefits. In this interim, you may be eligible for unemployment benefits—and if you do get rehired you'll be glad you didn't notify Social Security. Check with Social Security to find out how you'd be penalized.

Fair shares. To stay one step ahead of greedy ex-spouses who refuse to retire so their former mate cannot collect on their benefits, Social Security enacted the Independent Entitlement clause. This allows the worker's spouse who has reached 62 or older to receive benefits even if the worker has not retired. The only stipulation is that the worker's spouse cannot apply until two years after the divorce (to prevent couples from voluntarily divorcing so the worker's spouse can get benefits without the worker retiring).

Dodging the tax bullet. Now that President Clinton's tax package has passed into law, retirees who pay income tax on their Social Security benefits will have up to 85 percent of their benefits subject to taxation. One way to minimize the bite will be to alternate the years you withdraw your investment and retirement income. For example, if you can keep your income under the $32,000 cap one year, you won't pay income tax on Social Security benefits that year. Then the next year, you can withdraw more income by scheduling your T-Bills, CDs, IRAs, bonds and other income sources to come due. Now, of course, you'll have to foot a higher tax bill in that year, but the amount saved in the alternate years could very well be enough to offset the years you do pay more to Uncle Sam.

Contacting Social Security

One of the first things you need to do before you retire is to get in touch with your local Social Security office or call its toll-free number for details on estimated benefits owed you and your spouse.

Until 1988, you had to be at least 55 or older in order to request this information. Now any worker has the right to review his or her file.

To get your Request for Personal Earnings and Benefits Estimated Statement (Form #SSA-7004), stop by any Social Security office or call 1-800-772-1213. Once you have completed and submitted the short questionnaire, a Personal Earnings Statement will come back to you with a complete breakout of your annual income for every year you worked, Social Security taxes paid in and number of quarters that have been credited to you and/or your spouse's accounts, among other data. It generally takes up to six weeks to receive this report.

This is a very important document and one that should be scrutinized with a fine-tooth comb for inaccuracies. Please don't assume that Uncle Sam's colleagues at Social Security keep perfect records. It's not unusual to find some very serious discrepancies. In fact, that's why you should make a point to review your file *every three years*.

Specifically, there is one very important area you'll want to check. When you get your Summary, compare it to your tax returns or W-2s to determine if you ever *overpaid* Social Security taxes. It would not be unusual to find that an employer did not stop deducting taxes even after you had already paid in the maximum amount for the year. Often this happens when you change jobs during the year and earned in excess of the maximum taxable amount. If you discover that you did overpay even one year, you are entitled to a credit on your next federal income tax return.

Other common mistakes found are the omission of years of military service,

omission of one or more employers, employment under a maiden name not reported correctly, even an incorrect Social Security number.

Should you find any errors in your Personal Statement, call your local Social Security office for instructions on how to set up a case review. If you are still not satisfied after your inquiry has been reviewed, you have the right to a hearing, a review by an appeals court and an appeal through a federal court (in that order). Fortunately, taking such extreme measures is rare.

When you are ready to apply for benefits, there are two ways to notify Social Security. To apply by phone, call 1-800-772-1213. You'll then need to follow up by mailing the necessary documentation that proves your age and marital status. You'll also need to send your Social Security card and proof of the worker's death if you are applying for survivor benefits. If you prefer not to mail important documents, you can go to your nearest Social Security office and apply in person. In either case, it will take approximately three months to activate your benefits.

NOTE: Hours of operation of the 800-number are weekdays, 7 a.m. to 7 p.m. (regardless of time zone). However, if you don't want to hear those annoying busy signals, the best times to call are from 7 a.m. to 9 a.m. or 5 p.m. to 7 p.m. The best days to call are Thursday and Friday. The worst days to call are Mondays and the third of each month (when Social Security checks arrive).

Looking ahead

In these uncertain financial times, the need to plan ahead for retirement has never been greater. To help

Americans with the process, Congress recently mandated that starting in 1995, the Social Security administration is to send every worker over the age of 60 the complete details of their estimated benefits on an annual basis until they retire. Beginning with the year 2000, every worker over 25 will receive an annual statement of estimated benefits.

From a financial planner's perspective this is landmark legislation.

But what is really amazing to me—and I'm sure to you—is that workers who first started contributing to the Social Security system in 1951 only paid taxes on the first $3,600 of income. In 1993, earnings up to $57,600 are now taxable.

Back then, in your wildest imagination, could you have dreamt of making that kind of living legally? Ironically, today $57,600 is how much you *must* earn before the government will stop taking FICA taxes out of your paycheck. Even more astounding, the Medicare tax portion now applies to the *first $135,000* of annual earnings!

Yet in spite of our ever-increasing contributions, the majority of Americans who will retire in the 1990s are likely to receive two-and-a-half times what they paid into Social Security. That's the good news.

The bad news is that there are many knowledgeable people in both government and the private sector who predict the Social Security sky is going to fall on future generations unless changes are not made soon. And they may very well be right! Which is why in the coming months and years, you'll be hearing an awful lot about higher taxes on benefits (part of President Clinton's economic package), delaying the official retirement age by the end of the decade (Congress has already passed a bill to raise the normal retirement age to 67, but it's not in effect until the year 2027), removing the income cap (so six-figure earners pay more) and many other steps that could permanently alter the flow of Social Security revenues and benefits.

It's anyone's guess what will actually transpire, but one thing is for sure. The times they are a changin'. Not too long ago, former House Speaker Tip O'Neill said of Social Security, "It's the third rail of politics—touch it and you die." But with President Clinton's tough stand on deficit reduction and the American people begging for the government to be fiscally responsible, that may no longer be true.

3

For the health of it: Examining your medical coverage at retirement

Can you guess one of the most popular topics of conversation among seniors? It's not the weather or where to find the best early-bird specials. It's health. As much as we promise ourselves we're not going to become one of those people who dwells on what ails us, it takes a lot of willpower not to jump in when everyone else is lamenting about aches and pains. Sadly, while talk is cheap, health care is not.

While it is comforting that the Clinton Administration is trying to wrap its arms around what's been described as a "Rube Goldberg-type health care system," there is no immediate relief in sight for the millions of older Americans who have been financially crippled by the high cost of medical attention.

Currently, healthy people over 65 spend an average of $3,300 a year, out of pocket, on medical bills not covered by Medicare or private insurance. It may not seem like much until you realize that this represents an estimated 17 percent of the average retiree's income. It is also a shocking revelation when you consider that only 30 years ago, the average person over 65 spent $347 a year on medical expenses not covered by Medicare.

The bottom line is that while inflation has been rising at about 3 percent to 4 percent a year, the cost of health care has been going up at a rate of 9 percent to 10 percent annually. By the year 2000, it's projected the average, healthy 65-year-old will have an estimated $5,500 a year in out-of-pocket medical expenses. The average 62-year old will pay an estimated $7,500 a year.

It's getting so that when someone shouts "Oops," it's not because they're clumsy. It's because they're upset about all the *Out Of Pocket Sacrificing!*

Aside from discovering that Medicare is no panacea, another major misconception people have is that eligibility is a "group" deal. In other words, they assume that, as with Social Security, marriage entitles a spouse to benefits. But this is not true. The *only* way to qualify for Medicare is to turn 65 (the exception is if you have certain disabling diseases).

Now, because it is highly unlikely that you and your spouse were born on the same day *and* year, one of you is going to reach 65 before the other. And that means that there will be a period of time, depending on your ages and employment status, when the sources of your health care coverage will differ.

So, in preparation for landing, no matter if you retire at age 55 or 65, this chapter will help you understand the types of medical coverage you'll need at the various stages of your—and your spouse's—retirement. Whether you'll be shopping for private health insurance or a Medicare supplement (Medigap), you'll learn how to buy a policy without breaking the bank. We'll also get into the differences between Medicare and Medicaid and take a look at the need for long-term care policies.

In the meantime, I urge you to get some valuable free booklets on these subjects. These include: "The Medicare Handbook," "The Guide to Health Insurance for People With Medicare," "Medicare Q & A" (60 commonly asked questions) and "Medicare Secondary Payer." Pick up copies at any Social Security office or write to: Medicare Publications, Health Care Finance Administration, 6325 Security Blvd., Baltimore, MD 21207.

Staying covered when you're under 65 and not working

You can't pick up a newspaper today without reading about yet another company that is struggling under the weight of the recession. Their knee-jerk reaction is to lay off workers, cut back hours so employees are only part-time, and/or dangle early retirement offers as a way to keep payroll and benefits costs to a minimum. At the same time, more and more Americans are opting to retire early. This way, they can play offense instead of defense.

Aside from the emotional shock of being retired, ready or not, one of the hard facts you'll face is the realization that if you are a young retiree (ages 50 to 65) and are not covered under a spouse's plan, you are going to need comprehensive medical insurance until you are eligible for Medicare. Without an employer to provide and subsidize a plan, what do you do?

The government thought about that back in the 1980s and passed landmark legislation referred to as the COBRA law, for Consolidated Omnibus Budget Reconciliation Act. The basic gist of the law was that companies that employed 20 or more people could not discriminate against workers because of their age. For example, they could not force workers to drop out of the company's group medical plan once they turned 65 (provided the worker had not retired). Nor could they force those under 65 to drop out of the plan if their employment status changed (if they were laid-off or became a part-time worker).

COBRA laws also stipulated that to be eligible to continue individual coverage at the company's group rates, workers could not be covered by any other group health insurance plan and could not be leaving the company because of gross misconduct. The other significant caveat was the employee must be willing and able to pay not only their share of the premiums, but the employer's share in addition to a 2 percent administrative fee.

Under this 1986 law, employers must inform workers of their rights to continue coverage within 44 days after the coverage has been terminated. Workers would then have 60 days to decide if they wanted to continue the coverage and another 45 days to pay the first premium. In the event of a 44-day lapse in coverage while the employer was getting its act together, generally the worker's coverage would be reinstated retroactively and the worker reimbursed for covered medical expenses incurred during this period. Coverage under the COBRA laws must be extended for a minimum of 18 months.

Insofar as family members (dependents) are concerned, they are protected under the COBRA laws as well. Coverage must be extended to spouses (even if they separate from or divorce the covered employees), widowed spouses, and even children of former employees who have lost their dependent status because of age.

Although continuing your coverage in a group policy can be a costly proposition, it will never cost you as much as *not* being covered for even one day. In a worst-case scenario, the consequences for leaving you and your family unprotected could bankrupt you. In fact, the reality is that paying for your own coverage at group rates will be significantly cheaper than going out and buying your own private policy, and at the same time, it will provide better coverage.

The other advantage of staying on the company plan is that there is no need for you and your family to pass physical exams. This is of major importance if you or a family member have a pre-existing condition or are considered high risk.

In terms of what happens when the coverage runs out (anytime after 18 months), you can generally opt to convert from the group coverage to an individual policy. While it's a comfort to know that coverage will be available, this option will unfortunately result in higher premiums and yet provide fewer benefits.

Regardless of whether you stick with the company plan or immediately buy your own policy, be sure to hold on to all your medical records and correspondence with the current insurance carrier, especially any outstanding claims. You never know when questions or problems will arise that can be resolved through your copies of paperwork.

Shopping for private health insurance

If you or your spouse do not have access to a group plan and are not yet eligible for Medicare, you will need to shop for coverage. Before you consider an individual policy, which will likely be expensive and probably not very comprehensive, I suggest you look at some alternatives.

First, make a list of all the organizations and associations you are members of, such as industry trade associations, civic groups, national charitable or religious organizations, etc. Next, you should inquire as to whether they offer group medical insurance as a benefit to members. I can honestly say that some of these plans are so suitable and affordable, it would be worth it to join the organization, just to have access to the insurance.

For example, AARP now sells long-term care policies, group hospital insurance and Medicare supplements through Prudential. While I don't endorse AARP's plan or any other insurance products, I believe it can be helpful to compare their benefits and prices with those of other national competitors.

Another option is if you are doing business as a consultant or a salesperson, and can demonstrate all the characteristics of running a business, such as filing a Schedule C on your income tax, receiving independent income on a 1099, having business stationery, etc. In this case, you can apply for group medical coverage, even though you are only a one-person business.

Both strategies will save you money and allow you to get as comprehensive a policy as possible at a price you should be able to live with. Regardless of which way you go, you want to make sure that, at a minimum, your personal coverage includes 1) major medical and 2) hospitalization. Here is a brief description of what they offer:

Major medical policies

Major medical insurance generally covers the cost of the following: doctors (in-hospital/outpatient), x-rays, lab tests, anesthesia and possibly prescriptions and private-duty nurses. Typically, most major medical policies require a deductible and offer an 80/20 co-payment (they pay 80 percent, you pay 20 percent). In addition, there is a cap on the benefits paid over the life of the policy.

Hospital/medical/surgical

Basic hospital/medical/surgical policies pay a certain portion of hospital room-and-board costs each day (the amount is equal to the cost of a semi-private room in the city where you live), for at least 31 days of any one hospital stay. Coverage also includes hospital services and supplies, such as lab tests, medicine, x-rays and other items in an amount equal to at least 10 times the amount the policy pays for daily room-and-board.

The medical expense portion of the policy pays a set daily amount for doctor's visits during the hospital stay, and provides this type of coverage for a minimum of 21 days. The surgical expense portion typically pays 75 percent of reasonable charges for a surgeon's fees, or up to a set amount for certain operations listed in your policy. When reviewing this schedule, you'll find coverage information for anesthetic services and operating room charges as well.

As with major medical, hospitalization requires a deductible, the amount of which is set by the policyholder. The policy provides coverage for a certain length of time or in a certain dollar amount, and you are responsible for anything over and above that.

Other types of plans

When you start shopping for health insurance, you may discover that you are being encouraged to consider a variety of other plans, such as hospital indemnity, accident or catastrophic policies. These "special-interest" plans are important profit centers for the insurance companies, but do very little for the insured. In the majority of cases, they don't end up paying benefits and may even duplicate your coverage, particularly if you are covered by Medicare and a Medicare supplement (Medigap plans).

The two exceptions might be purchasing a catastrophic policy (often purchased as a safeguard against paying the astronomical cost of cancer treatments), if you cannot afford a comprehensive medical plan. We will discuss this on page 67.

The other exception might be a dental plan, which would cover you for office visits and treatments, periodontal work and other services. Both could be invaluable if you are not covered under a major medical plan.

15 Steps to buying the best possible coverage

It used to be said that the best part of getting old was that insurance agents would finally leave you alone. But times being what they are, the right agent and the right medical coverage can be lifesavers. Here are the steps to take so you buy what's in your best interest.

1. Shop, shop, shop. Take the time to carefully compare policies. Sure, this will be time-consuming, and even boring. But the time spent will invariably lead to substantial savings and better coverage.

2. How's the service? Rates aren't everything. Compare how companies are set up to service claims and how long it takes for them to process the paperwork and reimbursements.

3. Get the facts straight. Talk with several agents and make sure you're getting the same story with respect to the laws and other general information. If this is all foreign to you,

ask a trusted friend or family member to help you sort out the facts from the fantasy.

4. Your license, please. Ask every agent to provide proof that their agency is licensed by the state.

5. Coverage summary. The best way to comparison-shop is to get a summary of the policy benefits from each agent you talk to. Before you compare price, you want to be sure that any policy you are considering has all of the benefits you're looking for.

6. Tell the whole truth. Don't jeopardize your coverage by making false statements and claims on your application. If the truth is ever uncovered, you'll have big troubles. Any agent who tells you it's OK to alter the truth a little has probably altered the truth a little about what he or she is selling!

7. Pay by check. Never pay for insurance premiums with cash. Pay only by check or money order and make them payable only to the insurance company—never the agent or agency.

8. When the policy arrives. Don't throw anything out, including the envelope. The postmark will verify the approximate time you received it. If you haven't gotten the policy after one month of making your first payment, get on the phone *pronto*.

9. Get out your best reading glasses. Do not stash the policy when you get it. Read it immediately to make sure that you've bought what you've been promised. That means reading all the fine print and comparing the policy to the summary of coverage the agent originally gave you.

10. Keep your policy safe. Store one copy of your policy in an easy-to-find place in your home and store extra copies in a safe-deposit box or with an attorney.

11. Free looks are OK. Ask each agent about a free-look period. This entitles you to review the policy before committing to it.

12. No obligations necessary. If you decide against a policy after your free-look period, just return the policy to the company by certified or registered mail with return receipt requested within the allowed time frame. This entitles you to a complete refund.

13. Beware of ads that promise the world. If something sounds too good to be true, it probably is. Look out for newspaper ads that make big claims but have little asterisks next to them. When you read the fine print, that's where you'll find the real story.

14. Put your foot down. If you find yourself up against high-pressure tactics, "just say no." If you are undecided, sign nothing and commit to nothing. If you are uncomfortable with the agent's tough-sell approach, insist that he or she leave. Report any harassment or other unprofessional behavior to the State Department of Insurance.

15. Don't stop thinking about tomorrow. Insurance policies are not set in cement. Keep your eye open for information on companies offering potentially better coverage at lower rates. Publications for seniors are excellent sources of ads that may be worth following up on. If you learn about a plan that appears to be more competitive, ask your agent to review the information and to prove to you why you should stick with what you've got.

Questions you'll never be sorry you asked

When reviewing a prospective health insurance policy, gather the following information and compare notes for each one:

1. What are the waiting periods before certain illnesses are covered?
2. What is the deductible, and is it for each treatment or on an annual basis?
3. What is the co-insurance? In other words, what percent of the claim must you pay after the deductible has been met?
4. What are the renewal conditions?
5. Under what circumstances can the company raise your rates?
6. What is the maximum amount the policy will pay for each illness and for the entire time you hold the policy?
7. What types of services are covered under the policy, and what is not?
8. Will the policy cover routine doctor's-office visits? What about house calls?
9. How do the benefits compare with actual costs for doctor's visits, hospital care or surgery in your area?
10. What are the limits on the amount paid for daily hospital room and board, medicine, tests, surgery, doctor's visits, etc.?

11. What are the limits on the maximum number of hospital days paid for and the number of doctor's visits during a hospital stay?

Low-cost health care options for seniors

If you don't choose to stick with a former employer's group policy and can't afford private insurance, there are four other possible options to consider. None offer perfect solutions, but if it's a matter of these or nothing, they may be just what the doctor ordered.

If you are in relatively good health, you can buy a private insurance policy but *agree to a higher deductible*. Although it will require laying out more money up-front until the deductible is met, it will keep your premium costs down. The major advantage is if you are fortunate enough to have minimal claims during the year, you'll have saved yourself a bundle.

Secondly, as mentioned earlier, you can opt to buy a *catastrophic policy* only. This is a high-deductible, low-premium cost policy that covers you only for a major illness (such as cancer or a stroke) or accident. All other medical costs are out-of-pocket. But again, if you are in good health, it's possible that your annual medical bills over a couple of years will be much lower than the premiums you'd pay for a comprehensive policy.

The third option is to join a *Health Maintenance Organization (HMO)*. Of course, it helps to know what this is. (I asked a client if she had looked into HMO and she said, "No, we don't spend a lot of time watching television.")

As a member of an HMO, you must use the physicians and facilities under contract with that particular health organization. Although you can usually choose the doctor at the HMO that you would like to see on a regular basis, you cannot select a doctor in private practice and then expect your HMO to pay the bills.

There are many advantages to being part of an HMO. First, they often provide prescription drugs, eye exams and other services not typically covered by private health insurance plans. Most important, HMOs usually result in less out-of-pocket expenses for members. Instead of paying deductibles, participants pay nominal costs for doctor's visits, usually at a substantially reduced cost. And because HMO services are prepaid, members don't fill out and submit claim forms.

Conversely, there are disadvantages, too. One drawback of an HMO is being limited to HMO physicians. Sometimes you will not even be seen by a physician, but by a nurse practitioner or physician's assistant. In addition, HMOs generally pay for medical treatment outside their service areas *only in emergencies*. If you travel out of the area, routine medical care will not be covered. But back home, the biggest complaints are often about the long lead time needed to schedule appointments, long sitting spells in the waiting room with, ironically, short visits when they finally get to see the doctor. This is certainly not true with every HMO (some take painstaking efforts to avoid these problems), but you definitely want to find out if the HMO you are considering is an offender.

Finally, as a fourth option, some states allow insurance companies to sell *mail-order health care policies.* These direct-mail agencies do not necessarily have offices in the state or any local agents. Although they are licensed to do business in the state and must maintain a registered agent within the state, these programs can only be purchased by mail. Offerings are generally advertised on radio, TV and in print media, and, of course, through direct-mail campaigns.

The obvious advantage of mail-order insurance is the low-cost premiums. Because they do not have to pay agency commissions, their biggest expenses are mailing and advertising.

However, you must be careful when examining mail-order policies. They are very cleverly worded to give the impression of offering comparable coverage to private health insurance. In truth, they generally offer reduced benefits. In fact, in many instances, the benefits are so unrealistic in terms of deductibles, pre-existing conditions, waiting periods, etc., that they are of little or no value. If you are seriously considering a mail-order plan, have a knowledgeable person review the details.

Your state department of insurance is there to help

Before you buy *any* policy, if you have any questions or concerns, it is wise to contact your state's insurance commission. It can be very helpful in securing information and advising you about your particular insurance needs. In addition, while it cannot recommend a particular company, it can advise you regarding a carrier's reliability and integrity based on any files of customer complaints.

65 and still working? What about your medical benefits?

Let's say you just turned 65 and the company you work for doesn't have mandatory retirement. You've made the decision to work for one or two more years before retiring, but are concerned that you won't be allowed to continue participating in the group medical coverage because you are now eligible for Medicare. Can the company force you out of its group plan?

If your firm employs 20 or more people and provides comprehensive medical coverage, then they must continue coverage for workers who stay on after 65. Under the federal COBRA law of 1986, age discrimination in the work place is illegal.

However, when you become Medicare-eligible, it does have a direct bearing on how your total health care coverage is coordinated. If you are working at 65, and are still covered under your group medical plan, your employer's plan will still be your primary payer, Medicare will then be your secondary payer. Nevertheless, the combination of Medicare and the group plan *cannot result in reduced coverage* for you. It still has to be comparable to what other employees receive.

NOTE: If you continue to participate in a group plan (either yours or your spouse's), you are allowed to delay enrolling in Medicare's Part B (comparable to major medical) until such time when you are no longer eligible to be in the group plan. You have up until seven months from that point to enroll. If you do not enroll within that seven-month window, and instead enroll maybe a year later, Medicare will bill you for a

10-percent surcharge for every 12 months you delay enrolling.

For more information, get a copy of the booklet, "Medicare Secondary Payer" (see page 62 for details).

Younger spouse not eligible for Medicare?

As we discussed earlier, since it is unlikely that you and your spouse will reach age 65 at the exact same time, many couples have to walk down different paths insofar as medical coverage is concerned.

For example, once you officially retire from your company, if you are 65 or older, your employer is no longer obligated to continue insuring you under the group plan. Nor does the company have to convert the coverage to an individual policy for you. In fact, even if the company wanted to continue your health care benefits at retirement, it's possible that its insurance carrier's contract would stipulate that your coverage be automatically terminated at age 65.

However, if you are 65 at retirement, but your spouse is younger and has been covered under your company health plan to this point, the spouse *must* be given the option to stick with the employer's group coverage. This ability to remain covered under a spouse's former employer is allowable for 36 months after the worker's retirement. If, at 36 months, the younger spouse is still not 65, he or she must be allowed to convert the employer's policy to an individual plan.

Obviously if you do choose to either continue or convert coverage, you must agree to pay the premiums. The employer does not have to pay a dime. And,

of course, as soon as the spouse turns 65, the employer is no longer obligated to provide coverage.

One last but very important point. When you convert from a group policy to an individual policy, don't expect to receive identical benefits. In all likelihood, the benefits will be less comprehensive while costing more than the premiums you paid at the group rate.

On the positive side, however, if you have a pre-existing condition, the insurance carrier cannot drop you until age 65. In other words, once you have been protected under a group policy, you cannot be deemed ineligible to participate for any reason other than turning 65.

If you or your spouse have any problems getting coverage under the company's group benefits because an employer contends you are no longer eligible to participate, you can call the Department of Labor's COBRA office in Washington, D.C. This government agency protects people from age discrimination and will provide assistance in determining your rights, and see to it that your employer complies with the law. Call 202-219-8776.

If eligible for Medicare, here's what to expect

Have you heard the one about the Medicare patient who woke up from surgery with a note taped to his incision? It read: "Your federal tax dollars at work."

Well, maybe the note wasn't there. But when it came time to settling the bills, the message was clear. Medicare spends $140 billion a year on hospital/surgical charges for more than

32 million seniors. This federal health insurance program, administered by the U.S. Department of Health and Human Services, Health Care Financing Administration, is offered to any citizen 65 or older, regardless of income and assets. Here is an overview of Medicare coverage and benefits, as of 1993.

Medicare: Hospitalization

With Part A, or Medicare Hospital Insurance, seniors are covered for 1) inpatient hospital care, 2) some post-hospital care in a skilled nursing facility, 3) home health care under the supervision of skilled nursing care, 4) hospice care and 5) blood transfusions.

Each time the hospital, nursing home or hospice submits a bill to Medicare for your treatment, you will get a Medicare Benefit Notice explaining the decision made on the claim. If Medicare approves the bill, the hospital or home will be paid directly. If Medicare does not approve the bill, you will be responsible for payment.

Under Part A, you also have a lifetime reserve of 60 days for inpatient hospital care. This can be used whenever you need more than 90 days of inpatient care during one benefit period. When a reserve day is used, Part A pays for all covered services except for co-insurance of $338 a day (1993). The co-insurance is still your responsibility and, once used, reserve days are not renewed.

In terms of your out-of-pocket costs, if you are 65 or older, and are receiving Social Security benefits, the only time you pay for Part A is when you are admitted to the hospital. Then you are required to pay for deductibles and co-insurance payments. The current annual deductible for Medicare Part A is $676 per benefit period. A benefit period begins on the first day you become an inpatient at a hospital, and ends after you have been out of the hospital for 60 consecutive days.

If you are 65 or older, but not eligible for Social Security retirement benefits (because you were a municipal or federal employee or did not earn enough work credits), you can apply to be covered under Medicare Part A and then pay a monthly premium of $221 (as of 1993).

Medicare: Medical bills

Part B, or Medicare's Medical Insurance program, is an *elective* program that is intended to take the place of your major medical policy. It helps pay for 1) medically necessary doctor's services, 2) outpatient hospital services, 3) home health care (skilled care only) and 4) blood transfusions.

After you pay a $100 deductible for covered medical expenses (the 1993 deductible), Part B will generally cover 80 percent of your approved charges. The Medicare patient is responsible for the other 20 percent. In addition, there is a monthly premium, which currently costs $36.60 (1993). Effective in 1994, the premium will cost $41.10 and in 1995, it will run $46.10

Now, although Part B is optional, don't even *think* of passing up this low-cost plan.

The charts on the next two pages show a breakout of Medicare coverage, Parts A and B.

Medicare (Part A): Hospital Insurance-Covered Services Per Benefit Period (1)

Services	Benefit	Medicare Pays**	You Pay**
HOSPITALIZATION Semiprivate room and board, general nursing and miscellaneous hospital services and supplies.	First 60 days	All but $676	$676
	61st to 90th day	All but $169 a day	$169 a day
	91st to 150th day*	All but $338 a day	$338 a day
	Beyond 150 days	Nothing	All costs
POSTHOSPITAL SKILLED NURSING FACILITY CARE You must have been in a hospital for at least 3 days, enter a Medicare-approved facility generally within 30 days after hospital discharge, and meet other program requirements. (2)	First 20 days	100% of approved amount	Nothing
	Additional 80 days	All but $84.50 a day	up to $84.50 a day
	Beyond 100 days	Nothing	All costs
HOME HEALTH CARE Medically necessary skilled care, home health aide services, medical supplies, etc.	Part-time or intermittent nursing care and other services for as long as you meet criteria for benefits.	100% of approved amount; 80% of approved amount for durable medical equipment.	Nothing for services; 20% of approved amount for durable medical equipment.
HOSPICE CARE Full scope of pain relief and support services available to the terminally ill.	As long as doctor certifies need.	All but limited costs for outpatient drugs and inpatient respite care.	Limited cost sharing for outpatient drugs and inpatient respite care.
BLOOD	Blood	All but first 3 pints per calendar year.	For first 3 pints.***

* 60 reserve days may be used only once.   ** These figures are for 1993 and are subject to change each year.

*** To the extent the blood deductible is met under one part of Medicare during the calendar year, it does not have to be met under the other part.

(1) A benefit period begins on the first day you receive service as an inpatient in a hospital and ends after you have been out of the hospital or skilled nursing facility for 60 days in a row or remain in a skilled nursing facility but do not receive skilled care there for 60 days in a row.

(2) Neither Medicare nor Medigap insurance will pay for most nursing home care.

Medicare (Part B): Medical Insurance-Covered Services Per Calendar Year

Services	Benefit	Medicare Pays	You Pay
MEDICAL EXPENSE Physician's services, inpatient and outpatient medical and surgical services and supplies, physical and speech therapy, diagnostic tests, durable medical equipment, etc.	Medicare pays for medical services in or out of the hospital.	80% of approved amount (after $100 deductible); 50% of approved charges for most outpatient mental health services.	$100 deductible,* plus 20% of approved amount and charges above approved amount.** 50% of approved charges for mental health services.
CLINICAL LABORATORY SERVICES	Blood tests, biopsies, urinalysis, etc.	Generally 100% of approved amount.	Nothing for services.
HOME HEALTH CARE Medically necessary skilled care, home health aide services, medical supplies, etc.	Part-time or intermittent nursing care and other services for as long as you meet criteria for benefits.	100% of approved amount; 80% of approved amount for durable medical equipment.	Nothing for services; 20% of approved amount for durable medical equipment.
OUTPATIENT HOSPITAL TREATMENT Reasonable and necessary services for the diagnosis or treatment of an illness or injury.	Unlimited if medically necessary.	80% of approved amount (after $100 deductible).	Subject to deductible plus 20% of billed amount.
BLOOD	Blood	80% of approved amount (after $100 deductible and starting with 4th pint.	First 3 pints plus 20% of approved amount for additional pints (after $100 deductible).***

*   Once you have had $100 of expense for covered services, the Part B deductible does not apply to any other covered services you receive for the rest of the year.

**   The amount by which a physician's charge can exceed the Medicare-approved amount is limited by law (see page 6).

***   To the extent the blood deductible is met under one part of Medicare during the calendar year, it does not have to be met under the other part.

As you can see from these charts, Medicare coverage offers a decent head start on medical bills. However, the costs that fall into the "nonapproved category" can be staggering. On average, Medicare only pays for an estimated 40 percent of the beneficiary's health care bill.

Equally as disconcerting is that there is a tremendous disparity between health care costs around the country, while Medicare premiums, deductibles, and co-insurance rates are identical whether you are living in Ohio or California.

What that means is that if you live in a part of the country where 1) office visits, hospital costs are at the top of the scale, 2) the majority of doctors don't accept Medicare assignment and/or 3) there are patterns showing that doctors in your area consistently treat certain medical conditions with excessive amount of testing, your Medicare benefits aren't going to take you as far as they would if you lived in a place where medical costs were in line with national averages.

Regardless of where you live, seniors are discovering that out-of-pocket health care costs are increasing at almost twice the rate of fixed incomes. That leaves people shouldering some enormous costs at a time in their lives when they are most prone to accidents, illnesses and catastrophic disease.

That is why the only way to buy sufficient protection against runaway medical bills that are not Medicare-approved is to contract for a private supplementary health insurance policy, referred to as Medigap coverage. Although this strategy still might not guarantee you 100-percent protection against out-of-pocket costs, at least you'll be assured that the largest portion, and presumably the most expensive bills, will be covered by insurance.

Before you can start shopping for a policy, it is important to know what Medicare does not cover. Here is a breakout of the current gaps:

Gaps in Medicare coverage

Inpatient hospital coverage

Patient pays: 1) $676 deductible per benefit period on admission, 2) $169 daily coinsurance for days 61 to 90 and 3) $338 daily coinsurance for each of the "lifetime reserve days."

There is no coverage for: 1) The first three pints of blood used, 2) a private hospital room (unless medically necessary) or a private-duty nurse, 3) care that is on a nonemergency basis in a non-Medicare hospital or that is not medically necessary and 4) care received outside the U.S. and territories (there are some exceptions throughout Canada and Mexico).

Skilled nursing facility

Patient pays: 1) $84.50 daily co-insurance for days 21 to 100 per benefit period.

There is no coverage for: 1) Any days after 100th day per benefit period, 2) care in a nursing home or a skilled nursing facility not certified by Medicare, or for just custodial care in a Medicare-approved skilled nursing facility or 3) the three-pint blood deductible.

Home health coverage

Patient pays: 1) 20 percent of the Medicare-approved amount for durable medical equipment (DME), plus charges in excess of the approved amounts on unassigned claims.

There is no coverage for: 1) Full-time nursing care, 2) drugs, 3) meals delivered to your home or 4) homemaker services to assist in meeting personal care or housekeeping needs.

Medicare hospice coverage

Patient pays: 1) Limited charges for inpatient respite care and outpatient drugs and 2) deductibles and co-insurance amounts when regular Medicare benefits are used for treatment of a condition rather than a terminal illness.

Doctors and medical supplies

Patient pays: 1) $100 annual deductible, 2) 20-percent co-insurance, 3) legally permissible charges in excess of Medicare-approved amounts for unassigned claims, 4) 50 percent of approved charges for most outpatient mental health treatment and 5) all charges in excess of Medicare's $600 yearly limit for independent physicals or occupational therapists.

There is no coverage for: 1) Self-administered prescription drugs and immunizations, 2) routine physicals and screenings (except pap smears and mammograms), 3) hearing aids or exams to measure hearing loss, 4) dental care or dentures, 5) routine foot care, 6) routine eye exams or eyeglasses, 7) the first three pints of blood and 8) any services not deemed reasonable and necessary for an illness or injury.

Get the picture? Medicare coverage has more holes than a golf course! That means Medigap insurance is a true necessity, and by no means a luxury item. Thanks to congressional intervention, it is now possible to purchase an inexpensive policy to cover the most basic Medicare gaps.

Medigap insurance: Don't leave home without it

Medicare supplements, or Medigap, have come a long way. If you were in the market for a policy before July 1992, when Congress stepped in, you might easily have been a victim of the insurance industry's questionable marketing tactics. Tens of thousands of retirees were each sold several expensive policies that still provided inadequate coverage. Today, policies have been standardized so consumers can compare apples to apples.

For example, each state has the right to allow insurance companies to sell as many as 10 different plans, but each plan must offer a minimum level of benefits established by the National Association of Insurance Commissioners. Furthermore, each company's plans must use the same format, language and definitions to describe the benefits. In the end, then, all they're competing on are service, reliability and, of course, price.

Under the law, all plans must have a loss ratio of at least 65 percent for individuals. This means that, on average, 65 cents of each premium dollar must go for benefits.

As far as actual benefits are concerned, Plan "A" provides the most basic coverage, Plan "J" the most comprehensive. To better understand the benefits, the definitions on the following page should clarify terms often referred to.

- **Deductibles and co-payments.** A *deductible* is the out-of-pocket cost you pay before Medicare will pay. The *co-payment* is the actual percentage of the bill you'll be responsible for. For example, with your major medical policy, you may have been accustomed to paying 20 percent of a bill, with the insurance company covering 80 percent. Medicare revises the deductibles and co-payments every year, so be sure you have current information before you submit bills.

- **The difference between actual charges and Medicare's "reasonable" charges.** Every year, Medicare determines the highest amount it'll pay for physician's fees, services, tests, hospitalization, etc. They call this Medicare-approved charges or "reasonable" charges. As you would expect, its view of *reasonable* is often less than what health care actually costs, leaving the patient to pay the difference.

- **Medical assignment.** An arrangement whereby a physician or medical supplier agrees to accept the Medicare-approved amount as the total charge.

The chart below provides an overview of the benefits available in the 10 standard plans. Again, not all plans are available in every state (at a minimum, Plan "A" must be available).

10 Standard Medicare Supplement Benefit Plans

CORE BENEFITS	Plan A	Plan B	Plan C	Plan D	Plan E	Plan F	Plan G	Plan H	Plan I	Plan J
Part A Hospital (Days 61-90)	X	X	X	X	X	X	X	X	X	X
Lifetime Reserve Days (91-150)	X	X	X	X	X	X	X	X	X	X
365 Life Hosp. Days-100%	X	X	X	X	X	X	X	X	X	X
Parts A and B Blood	X	X	X	X	X	X	X	X	X	X
Part B Coinsurance-20%	X	X	X	X	X	X	X	X	X	X
ADDITIONAL BENEFITS	A	B	C	D	E	F	G	H	I	J
Skilled Nursing Facility Coinsurance (Days 21-100)		X	X	X	X	X	X	X	X	X
Part A Deductible		X	X	X	X	X	X	X	X	X
Part B Deductible			X			X				X
Part B Excess Charges						100%	80%		100%	100%
Foreign Travel Emergency			X	X	X	X	X	X	X	X
At-Home Recovery				X			X		X	X
Prescription Drugs								1	1	2
Preventive Medical Care					X					

How much protection is enough?

If your cash assets are sizable and you are in reasonably good health, you might not need a Medigap policy at all. The deciding factor would be: Could you afford to pay your out-of-pocket medical costs without jeopardizing your financial well-being?

For those who are on fixed incomes, which are hard enough to live on as is, Medigap can be a lifesaver. It's entirely possible that the $550 to $1,400 you'd pay for a policy could save literally thousands in that same year. But if your budget is stretched and you need to cut costs somewhere, eliminate the benefit that provides for skilled nursing care beyond the Medicare-approved allotment of 150 days. The vast majority of patients never exceed this need.

Although the federal laws standardizing Medigap policies are so new, expert opinion is that Plans "C" through "F" meet the vast majority of people's needs. According to industry experts, at a minimum you want coverage for the 20-percent co-insurance you are responsible for as well as coverage for long hospital stays (anything in excess of 60 days). In combination, these two coverages could prevent bankrupting you from an unpredicted accident or illness.

The ins and outs of buying a Medicare supplement

I recommend you consider the following list of suggestions when shopping for a Medigap policy:

All you need is one. It's unnecessary to buy an assortment of policies so you're covered for everything under the sun. You'll be wasting money on duplicate benefits that will never pay out. Just buy one affordable, comprehensive policy that covers as much as possible.

Renewable for life. Newer policies now require that Medigap plans be guaranteed renewable unless you stop paying or were found to have lied on the application. (Incidentally, policy renewal does not mean that premiums can't be raised.) If you bought your policy a few years back, double-check to make sure you can't be dropped in the future

Read between the lines. Confirm your understanding of the policy with the insurance agent before you buy. Make sure your contract's conditions are ones you can live with, such as the specific benefits, limitations, pre-existing conditions, waiting periods, etc.

Free trial period. Make sure that the agent informs you of your right to have a "free-look" period for 30 days. That will give you enough time to decide if you want to keep the policy after you've bought it. Should you decide you've made a mistake, you can return the policy within the allotted time and get a complete refund.

"Whadja-say"? There's so much lingo and verbiage in the insurance industry, it's no wonder that most people don't know what they're buying. However, Medigap policies must now include a summary of the plan in plain English so that it is easy to compare different policies.

Seal of approval. The U.S. Government does not sanction, approve, sponsor or otherwise have anything to do with private supplemental insurance. If you see a policy that boasts government symbols or logos, giving the appearance of an endorsement, it's a hoax. Let the buyer beware.

Is "Best" the best judge? Although policies are now standardized, the prestigious "A.M. Best" ratings can tell you a lot about an insurance company's history, its current solvency and other important factors. However, when it comes to buying a Medicare supplement, there are three issues that could be even more important to you as a policyholder:

1. Are you getting the greatest number of benefits?
2. Will you be paying the lowest possible premiums for those benefits?
3. Are you assured that the company will pay benefits promptly and with a minimum amount of hassle and paperwork?

Pay your premiums annually. Ideally, There should be a discount for paying for the year's premiums up-front, rather than paying quarterly. Even better, if a rate increase takes place during the year, you won't be responsible for the higher rate until your next premium comes due. *But regardless of when you pay, never pay cash!* As for rate increases, be aware that a company cannot raise premiums because of a person's age or condition.

If you are still hesitant about the need for buying a Medicare supplement because you think that Medicare coverage will be greatly improved by the time you really need it, there's something to consider: No matter how much its benefits increase, Medicare will 1) never pay more than 80 percent of approved charges and 2) will never pay for the difference between approved charges and actual costs. There will always be a limit on how much they will allow for a service, procedure, surgery, etc. And you can bet that with medical costs rising as they are, and the most sought-after physicians charging top dollar, a Medigap plan will always provide you that much-needed protection.

Please read on

Given the page constraints in a resource book that addresses a large number of topics, it's impossible for this book to serve as the definitive source on everything. With such important issues as Medicare, supplements and long-term care, you can only be doing yourself a favor by getting more information.

First on the recommended reading list is a brochure entitled, "The Guide to Health Insurance for People with Medicare." Write to Consumer Information Center, Dept. 515Z, Pueblo, CO 81009.

AARP also has a helpful handbook entitled, "Medicare: What It Covers, What It Doesn't" (Bulletin #D13133). Write to AARP Fulfillment, 601 E St., NW, Washington, DC 20049.

Finally, one of the finest resources you could ask for insofar as in-depth details on all of these (and dozens of others) issues is a book called, *American Guidance for Seniors* by Ken Skala (distributed by Career Press). This 540-page, easy-to-understand guidebook is indispensable for getting quick answers to very complex questions. To order, call 1-800-227-3371.

If you have general questions about Medigap coverage, Medicare has a toll-free hotline to help you. The number is 1-800-638-6833.

Long-term care: The life support system of the '90s

For many American families, growing old in this country is fast becoming a tragedy. Every year, tens of thousands of elderly die penniless—or as wards of the state. And I'm not just referring to the indigent and the homeless. More and more middle-class Americans are discovering that they cannot afford to take care of the most important people in their lives. Spouses. Parents. Grandparents. These are hard-working individuals whose biggest "mistake" is becoming too ill or too senile to care for themselves.

Even those who scrimped and saved their whole lives never expected that they'd need such an extraordinary amount of money to pay for long-term care. More to the point, they never expected that they would *need* long-term care. The "this-could-never-happen-to-me" syndrome is the mindset that still prevails.

But, statistically speaking, it does *happen*! Almost 2 million of our elderly will be living in this country's 17,000 nursing homes this year. This represents two out of every five people over 65. If you are around age 65 today, there is a 40-percent to 50-percent chance that you'll spend time in a nursing home, and a 23-percent chance of spending a year or more. Because of longer life expectancies, the odds of a woman going into a home are greater.

In spite of the fact that putting someone you love in a nursing home is a deeply emotional and heartbreaking decision, it's actually a small part of the problem. The real dilemma occurs among families who expected that the costs would be covered by Medicare.

In fact, nothing could be further from the truth.

There are hundreds of thousands of people going to the bank every day in order to pay for a loved one's long-term care. When a patient is placed in a nursing home, more than 50 percent of the time it's the family who ends up paying the bills. In comparison, Medicare pays a paltry 2 percent of the country's long-term care bill.

When you consider that the average cost of being in a home runs $30,000 a year (there are plenty of homes that charge $70,000 to $100,000 a year) and that it is not unusual for someone to remain for one to two years, the economic impact of this obligation is devastating. The typical middle-class patient exhausts his or her life savings in a little over a year. Last year, nursing home costs exceeded $50 billion, $18.3 billion of which was paid for by private citizens.

The role of Medicare and Medicaid in long-term care

Again, Medicare was created to pay for health care for those who are 65 and older, regardless of income or assets. Medicaid, on the other hand, was established in 1965 as a medical assistance program jointly financed by the state and federal governments to pay for health care for low-income individuals, the blind and the disabled.

But neither agency was ever set up with the intention of paying for long-term care. And yet, with an annual budget of over $100 billion, Uncle Sam and his cosponsors at the state levels are finding that their fastest-growing expenditures are nursing home costs. Currently, almost half of all nursing home patients in this country are Medicaid beneficiaries.

The majority of people are not poor when they check in, but they certainly are after the first year or two. What is so tragic is that taking Medicaid reduces these individuals' status to "impoverished," making them wards of the government. This has an immediate and direct impact on the finances of the healthy spouses who are still living at home, and are being forced to "spend down" their life's savings to qualify for Medicaid. In doing so, they are forced to sell their assets or transfer them to family members.

For these once-proud people who may never have taken a dime from anyone, living off the government and being forced to accept their minimal benefits is debilitating.

In other words, first the cost of long-term care breaks these persons' banks, then it breaks their hearts.

"OK," you say. "Maybe Medicaid is a last resort, but at least someone can enter a home without placing a huge financial burden on the family." Unfortunately, that is not true, either.

It is extremely difficult to place a person into a home if he or she needs Medicaid support from the onset. Remember, these facilities are for-profit businesses. They are not government-owned, so there is no obligation to take everyone who applies. Those who are not able to pay for at least the first year or two will find it near-impossible to be admitted to a private nursing facility.

In fact, in some areas of the country, facilities are over 90-percent occupied. Since it's a seller's market, Medicaid patients are going to be the last to be accepted in a facility. The bottom line is that just because a senior is approved for Medicaid coverage doesn't mean there will be a bed for him or her.

In addition, even those facilities that accept Medicaid patients offer no lifetime guarantees. It is not unusual anymore for facilities to decide to withdraw from Medicaid, and to then give patients a deadline to find another home. There is also evidence of a growing trend for homes to set up "Medicaid wings." The level of care is not supposed to differ from those of privately subsidized patients, but go prove it!

"I never dreamt this could be such a nightmare"

There's no question that life-preserving techniques and medicine are keeping people alive much longer than they would have expected. In fact, it seems to me that the "Today" show's Willard Scott has yet to miss a day of wishing another 100-year-old a happy birthday. But the other side of the coin is that over the past few years, I've worked with an increasing number of clients who are living proof that this nightmare is a genuine atrocity when a parent or a spouse needs long-term care.

What's the answer to this living hell? While the Clinton administration is grappling with the issues, the only realistic strategy is to purchase a private long-term care policy. There are two excellent reasons to do so.

1. You will insure that you will not have to burden your family with the exorbitant costs of long-term care.

2. Your spouse will not have to divest your assets or "spend down" to be eligible for Medicaid.

If you are in your late 50s or early 60s, it's a good time to explore some long-term care options for yourself and your spouse. Remember, just as with auto, fire and casualty insurance, you can't buy a policy after there's been a fire or an accident. While it's true that the earlier you buy, the more you'll end up paying in premiums, perhaps years before you'll ever need the benefits, you'll be grateful that the policy is in place when the need arises. Secondly, the earlier you buy, the more likely that the policy will offer a guaranteed lifetime renewal. In other words, you won't run the risk of being dropped or closed out when you most need the coverage 20 years from now.

As with most other insurance, the closer you are to needing the benefits, the more costly it is. For example, a 50-year-old who buys a long-term care policy today will pay approximately $850 in annual premiums. If he or she waits until 65, the cost is projected to jump to over $1,800 a year. And after age 70, you might not even be able to touch a policy for under $3,000 a year.

The basics of long-term care policies

At present, more than 130 different companies market long-term care coverage and, because the concept is still relatively new (less than 3 percent of all Americans 65 or older have policies), there is no telling what these insurance products will look like even a few years from now. At best, we can discuss the types of coverage that are available, as well as the typical limitations.

Basically, long-term care policies pay a fixed daily amount for a certain length of time. The newer policies also recognize that the elderly would 1) prefer to be cared for in their own homes and 2) in most cases only require custodial care and therefore need benefits to cover the cost of being helped with daily tasks.

That's why the best policies today are the ones that offer the greatest flexibility. Basically, you buy a maximum benefit per day for a certain number of years and that gives you a pool of money to tap into as needs arise.

For example, if you bought a policy that paid $100 a day for three years, that would give you a total benefit of $109,000. If you needed a home health aid for six months at a cost of $50 a day (180 days X $50 = $9,000), you would deduct the $9,000 from your benefit amount ($109,000). Some policies even go as far as providing "disability" benefits where you can actually pay a friend or family member to provide services for you if you become disabled (as confirmed by the insurance company).

With so many possibilities, it's essential to be diligent about comparison-shopping companies and policies. Here are the most important features to look for:

- **All levels of care.** You want a policy that covers skilled, intermediate and custodial care facilities. And you want the beneficiary to be able to enter at any level. *Skilled facilities* provide care that is ordered by a physician, given by a trained nurse and is available around the clock. *Intermediate facilities* provide care that calls for nursing skills, but not at the same level you'd need in a skilled facility. *Custodial facilities* provide assistance with daily tasks such as taking medication, eating and bathing, walking, etc.

- **Waiting periods.** A 90- to 100-day period is the most you want to wait before benefits are available. Or, you can opt for a 0-, 20- or 30-day deductible. To keep your costs down, extend the waiting period for as long as you could realistically pay for care without jeopardizing your entire financial structure. Also, keep in mind that Medicare will pay for 21 to 100 days of skilled care if you are in an approved facility.

- **Daily benefits.** Don't buy less than a $60 daily benefit (some policies start at $20 a day). The best policies will pay over $100 a day and cover you for an adequate period of time (3 to 5 years). The maximum coverage you can buy today is $200 a day for life.

- **No prior hospitalization.** You absolutely want a policy that *doesn't* require a hospital stay before long-term care benefits can be available. Approximately 60 percent of all patients who enter nursing homes were not hospitalized immediately beforehand.

- **Check the benefit triggers.** The better policies pay if the patient is unable to perform two or three of five daily tasks: eating, bathing, walking, dressing and standing

- **Guaranteed renewable.** Your policy should be guaranteed renewable for life and should not be cancelable by the insurance company. The premium should also be based on the age of the person when the policy was bought.

- **Alzheimer's disease.** Make sure your policy covers Alzheimer's and that it allows for as many types of home health care arrangements as possible.

- **Waiver of premiums.** Be sure you can stop paying the premiums after the benefits begin.

- **Home health care and adult day-care.** Try to get a policy that does not require skilled nursing care as a pre-condition. Otherwise, people with Alzheimer's or who are senile will not be protected.

- **Inflation riders.** If you are a "young" senior, don't buy a policy without one. The only predictable thing about nursing home costs is that they will continue to rise every year. Make sure your policy can keep up.

- **Pre-existing conditions.** If a policy has more than a six-month pre-existing condition limitation period, don't buy it.

If you are still unsure about what you are looking at, find out the company's policy's ratings from *A.M. Best Company, Inc.* If it has an "A" rating or better, you're buying a decent policy. Other sources are *Moody's Investors Service, Inc.* and *Standard and Poor's Corp.* Most local libraries have these guidebooks in the reference section.

Talk to your financial planner

Let's face it. Nobody in their right mind wants to think about being old or ill enough to go into a nursing home. But if you are already retired, or are in the retirement planning stages, I can't urge you enough to start considering the permanent impact that long-term care will have on your savings and your assets, should the need arise. Today, the biggest financial threat a retired person faces is an extended stay in a nursing home. There's nothing like a $5,000 bill every month to erode your life savings.

The best person to speak to about this matter is a Certified Financial Planner. One of the most important functions of a planner is to help clients preserve their estate so they can enjoy a comfortable retirement and have the satisfaction of passing on a war chest to their heirs.

A Certified Financial Planner is trained and prepared to set up a comprehensive insurance program for you, taking your personal needs and circumstances into consideration.

For more information

You can call and order some helpful booklets, including "Long Term Care Facilities" from the American Health Care Association (202-842-4444), "Home Care and Nursing Homes" from the Council of Better Business Bureaus (703-276-0100) and the "Consumer's Guide to Life Care Communities and Long Term Care" from the National Consumer's League (202-639-8140). For general questions on any insurance question, call the National Insurance Consumer Helpline at 1-800-942-4242.

Good question!

Q. My husband and I were both hospitalized this year for different reasons, but one thing we had in common was that when we got the bills, there were charges for tests that were never performed (one was dated the day before I was admitted). What gives?
A. According to the General Accounting Office of the federal government, an estimated 99 percent of all hospital bills have at least one overcharge. So when you get the bills, read them (don't assume they are completely correct), and, even better, don't hesitate to pick up the phone and ask questions of the hospital billing office. Odds are, the time spent on this will save you money.

Q. We stuck with my former employer's health care plan when I retired at age 62 because we were afraid to be without coverage. Now we've shopped around and can do better. Can I cancel the policy?
A. Absolutely. Just stop paying the premiums and I assure you they'll drop you like a hot potato. However, be sure that you have already been approved by the new company and have started paying premiums before you dispose of your old policy.

Q. How important is it to have Medigap coverage that pays over and above Medicare assignment?
A. That depends on whether you are willing to be treated by only those physicians that accept Medicare assignment. When you enroll in Medicare, you can get a copy of a bulletin called "Provider Assignment Rate List," which identifies the doctors in your area who accept Medicare assignment. If a doctor bills over and above the Medicare assignment, he or she is not supposed to charge more than 115 percent of the allowable amount.

Q. When I got laid off at 63, I was told I could stick with my employer's group health insurance for up to 18 months if I paid the premiums. But my wife, who never worked there, could get coverage for up to 36 months. Why the discrimination? It doesn't seem fair.

A. You're right, and that's why more and more companies are willing to extend coverage to former employees for up 36 months now. Since they can charge you the 2 percent administrative fee, and you are responsible for both yours and their share of the premium, it's no skin off their nose to let you stay.

Q. When I retired, I was promised comprehensive medical coverage for the rest of my life. Now I just got a letter that they're sorry, but high costs have forced them to terminate my benefits. How can these big companies get away with this?

A. One hard lesson we've all learned from the recession is that big companies are no less immune to economic downturns than small ones. In fact, a recent study by Arthur Andersen & Company (the accounting and consulting firm) showed that an overwhelming 95 percent of all companies (large and small) were planning to significantly reduce, terminate or require the retiree to pay their full premiums for medical benefits at some point because of the exorbitant costs. You could point fingers all day long, but it won't change the fact that an estimated 13 million retirees are currently receiving health care benefits from their former employers and they are vulnerable. This is particularly true of those whose documents gave the company an escape plan (at least 4.5 million people are in this position). There have

been many instances of class action suits against companies that dropped the health care benefits of retired workers, but no decisions have sided with the employees as of yet.

Q. We're very happy with our HMO. Do we have to drop out when we go on Medicare?

A. As long as the HMO has a contract with Medicare, that you still live in the plan's service area and you are already enrolled in Part B, you don't have to drop out. Of course, you would still have to pay your Part B premiums in addition to any monthly premiums and/or copayments the HMO charges. If, at any time, you do want to change HMOs or leave the system, you can cancel by providing written notice to either the HMO or Medicare.

Q. I'm a diabetic and am concerned that I won't qualify for a Medigap plan when I retire. Will I likely be turned down?

A. Thanks to a new law (effective November 1991), you are guaranteed that for six months following enrolling in Medicare's Part B, you cannot be denied Medigap insurance because of your medical history, health status or previous claims experiences. Obviously, that means you don't want to delay applying for coverage.

Q. If I buy a cheaper Medigap policy today and decide to buy a better one five years from now, am I going to have any problems?

A. Probably not, if you stick with the same company. But if you do want to switch coverage to another insurance company, count on being asked for information on your health status, and count on the possibility of being turned down if your condition is considered risky. However, if the company does accept your application, there would be no waiting period to get coverage for what might be considered a pre-existing condition.

Q. I've heard about a new law that protects the elderly from having to dispose of their assets to go on Medicaid, if they own a long-term care policy. How does it work?
A. New York state residents are getting first crack at a pilot program in which residents who buy a qualified long-term care policy will be eligible for Medicaid assistance when the benefits from their policy have been exhausted. The difference is that under this Long Term Care Security Demonstration Program, policyholders won't have to "spend down" their assets to become Medicaid beneficiaries. The premiums are competitive with other policies but there are a number of minimum-purchase requirements that could drive prices up. While I applaud this breakthrough legislation and feel confident that other states will follow suit, there are still a lot of kinks to work out before consumer acceptance will be widespread.

Q. We're thinking about relocating to North Carolina and are wondering what to do with our Medicare supplemental and long-term care policies. Are we better off keeping them or letting them lapse and buying different policies down there?
A. According to AARP, if your insurance carrier is licensed to do business in both your old and new state, you can certainly request to transfer your policy and get hooked up with a local agent. As

for dropping one policy in lieu of another, you have to weigh the risk of being turned down because of your medical history with the benefit of saving money if you can buy a less-expensive policy in your new home state. The best advice is to call the insurance company and see what they can do for you. Otherwise, it probably doesn't pay to make a change.

Q. I know that you have to be poor to be eligible for Medicaid, but how does the government define "poor"?
A. Actually, each state has its own definition of what is considered "impoverished," and these definitions can be quite complex. But what all states have in common is a two-prong test for eligibility based on assets and income. Most say that your assets can't exceed $2,000, but that is only on "countable assets." Countable assets would exclude life insurance, personal property, one car, your home and others. The income test is more complex. Many states allow that the patient's annual income not exceed the annual cost of the nursing home—and that they surrender that income to pay for the home, except for a small personal needs allowance ($30 a month). I recommend that you consult with an eldercare attorney at least once to get up to speed on the most current laws and to work out a strategy for transferring your assets if necessary.

Q. What do you think about the mail-order pharmacies? Do they really save you money on prescription drugs?
A. Absolutely. In fact, I've found the savings to be anywhere from 10 percent to 40 percent for the same exact drugs, and the discounts are even deeper for

the generics. However, there will be instances when the big retail chain prices are still lower, so keep comparing prices. Some of the largest mail-order pharmacies are Medi-Mail (800-331-1458), AARP Pharmacy (800-456-2277) and Action Mail Order (800-452-1976).

What I tell my clients

Are you sure you've been admitted? Recently *U.S. News and World Report* made a horrifying discovery that many hospitals across the country were keeping elderly patients under observation for days, but were not officially admitting them as inpatients—unbeknownst to the patient! What difference does it make? Plenty. As an outpatient, you are billed under Part B and are responsible for 20 percent of all hospital expenses (ironically, including room charges for however many days you are being "observed"). But when you are admitted as an inpatient, you are covered under Part A, and are only responsible for the $676 deductible (it probably takes less than two hours to spend that during a hospital stay).

The motive of the hospitals is clear. Medicare sets no limits on hospitals for outpatient billing. When billing Medicare for inpatients, hospitals are only entitled to flat fees for services and the charges are scrutinized by a Peer Review Organization (not so for outpatient billing). The other Catch 22 for the patient is that if, after "observation," it is determined that he or she needs to be in a skilled nursing care facility, Medicare won't pay a dime for the nursing care facility. The rule is you must be an inpatient for three days to be eligible for a skilled nursing facility. So a word to the wise: If you or a loved one are in a

hospital—demand to know if you've been officially admitted!

Overpaid. States and Medicare are starting to focus attention on doctors who overcharge Medicare patients. As of 1993, by law, a doctor is not supposed to charge Medicare patients more than 15 percent of Medicare's allowable fee (Pennsylvania and Massachusetts don't allow doctors to charge Medicare patients anything over the allowable fee). Although some doctors are becoming more aware of the allowables in their area, it appears that the majority are crying ignorant. And even when you do discover you've been overbilled, asking the doctor for a refund takes a lot of courage.

What to do? Generally speaking, the best strategy is to work with doctors that accept Medicare assignment (about 50 percent do). If your doctor of choice does not, ask if he or she will consider Medicare assignment on a case-by-case basis, or allow you to pay after you've received your Medicare statement (benefit statements now indicate the maximum you can be charged for a procedure covered by Medicare) so you can determine the exact balance due (and, more importantly, not overpay). But even in a case where you have signed a consent form to pay what Medicare does not (some doctors require this), legally you still cannot be charged more than 15 percent of the Medicare allowable.

Oversold. One of the biggest mistakes I see retirees make is overbuying Medigap insurance, no doubt a reaction to the problems discussed in the previous section. Understandably, seniors are so fearful that medical expenses will wipe them out and so confused about their coverage, they err on the side of buying more than one policy, "just in case." The truth is Medicare, in tandem with one comprehensive Medigap plan, will provide excellent protection.

Undersold. Conversely, the problem with long-term care policies is that too many people are avoiding the purchase all together. Admittedly, people have had good cause to be skeptical. The original plans were very costly and based on useless premises. For example, most required that the patient be released from a hospital stay before long-term care costs would be paid. The problem was, at least 60 percent of patients who enter nursing homes had not been hospitalized. Another obstacle is that many people feel that buying one of these policies is like buying a computer. Growing competition is creating better products at lower prices—the longer you wait to buy, the better off you'll be. However, there is a certain point at which you need to take the plunge. I urge you not to delay.

Going coach is cheaper than first class, but you still get where you're going. One possible strategy for people who cannot afford a long-term care policy with lifetime benefits is to buy one with only a three-year benefit period. It is much cheaper and at the same time, if you or your spouse are admitted to a home, you'll be readily accepted because you are a private-pay patient. Furthermore, more than half of all stays are less than three months and 75 percent are less than a year, so you'd be guaranteed coverage in the most likely of circumstances. As for transferring your assets, you are required to do so within 30 months of becoming a

long-term care patient to qualify for Medicaid when the policy lapses. However, for a number of complex reasons, it is best to arrange for the transfer prior to being admitted to a home.

For the health of it

One thing I've discovered about health insurance is that, unlike life, auto and home insurance, most people don't have to sweat the details—decisions about what to buy are made by employers. The only thing employees need to be concerned with are what the plan covers and how much they have to kick in (if anything). It's like being a passenger in a car. You don't pay attention until it's your turn to drive.

Unfortunately, that has left a lot of people approaching retirement without a clue about the intricacies of health care coverage. And, as you now know, not only is it complex, it can also be outrageously expensive. It seems everyone knows someone who has faced enormous medical bills that would have wiped 'hem out if not for insurance protection.

I can't urge you enough to make health insurance, medical supplements and long-term care a number-one priority as you approach retirement. Not only do you need to become knowledgeable, you have to do everything within your power to allocate a part of your budget toward health care expenses. Until such time when there is a federal health care plan, the only thing you can count on is increasing out-of-pocket expenses.

In the meantime, it never hurts to step back and count your blessings. The best gift we get in this life is the ability to get out of bed in the morning. Just ask anyone who can't.

4

What your retirement plans are really worth

I will never forget the client who retired as a vice-president from a manufacturing company he had joined in 1961. On his last day of work, the head of the benefits department handed over the proceeds from his pension and profit-sharing plans. The checks totaled almost a *half a million dollars*. My client was so nervous just holding the checks, he called his wife to pick him up. She was so nervous having the checks in the car, she hit a parked car on their way home.

"It didn't matter that I'd earned that money over 30 years. It still felt as though I'd won the lottery and it scared me," he said.

It's understandable to be nervous when you are handed the single biggest paycheck of your life. I've had many otherwise rational people throw their lump sum settlements at me, as if they were hot potatoes. They say, "You decide where this goes—just make sure I keep every last penny I'm entitled to."

You see, it's not only the amount that makes people uneasy, it's knowing that the wrong move could result in dire consequences. For starters, there is the potential to lose thousands of dollars to taxes—unnecessarily. Secondly, because some of the maneuvers with the settlement are once-in-a-lifetime opportunities, taking the wrong turn means living with your decisions the rest of your life.

But let's start from the beginning. It's important to remember that settlements from retirement plans represent both your savings over the past 20 to 30 years as well as the compounded interest on those savings. This money has been flourishing without having to pay its respects to Uncle Sam or his colleagues at the State Department of Revenue. At retirement, however, the funds are removed from this protective womb, and there is the imminent threat of substantial taxes and penalties if the proceeds are not properly transferred. And once the funds are withdrawn and not properly distributed, watch out for the domino effect. The added income may push you into a higher tax bracket, which may trigger an ever *bigger* tax liability on all your income. The more taxes you pay, the less you have to put into your retirement nest egg. Naturally, the less money you have set aside for your retirement, the more difficult a time you will have meeting your obligations as you grow older. And so it goes.

It's like watching a standoff in a Western flick. Make one wrong move and you're dead. Who wouldn't be nervous?

And yet, at least the people who are concerned about their pensions have retirement funds to worry about. What about the millions of Americans who have worked for many years, but because of periods of unemployment, job-switching and other circumstances, have not stayed with a company long enough to get vested in a pension? According to the Pension Rights Center in Washington, D.C., 60 percent of American workers are not participating in any type of company-sponsored retirement plan.

How is this possible? Because these plans are sponsored by the company, and the vast majority have been expertly designed to insulate the employer from paying out unless an employee has met the most stringent, and often unrealistic, requirements. In other words, when employees leave or are laid off before certain minimum commitments are met (i.e., number of years of service), it is the employee who will lose out, not the company.

In fact, one of the biggest mistakes people make is assuming they are entitled to "X" amount, only to discover

that vesting requirements were not met. Or that the plan was designed to prevent them from withdrawing before a certain time...or at all.

Because of the complexity of all these issues, as well as the bushel of tax laws governing the participation in and disbursement of funds from retirement plans, this chapter will provide an overview of the different types that have become widely available—defined-benefit pensions, profit-sharing, IRAs, 401ks, simplified employee pensions (SEPs), and other plans. We'll review their advantages and disadvantages, so that if you are presented with a choice, you'll have a good sense of what best meets your needs. Then we'll take a look at your options when it comes time to withdraw the funds at retirement. Should you take a lump-sum distribution and roll over the money into your IRA or should you annuitize the benefits? Should you start withdrawing before, at, or after age 59½ (the first year you are able to withdraw without a 10-percent penalty)? These are just some of the decisions we'll grapple with.

A short course on retirement plans

Today, it seems there are as many kinds of tax-deferred retirement accounts as there are Heinz varieties. Unfortunately, this may be of no benefit to the average person who is only eligible for one or two types of plans, depending on his or her employment, income and/or marital status. In fact, in some cases, once you are determined eligible to participate in the plan that is offered, there is little else for you to decide. Still, any plan is better than no plan, and what is of greater importance than the type of plan you are in, is that you contribute the maximum allowable each year.

Here is a brief overview of the most commonly used plans so that if you have the opportunity to enroll, you'll have a sense of how they work and what are their advantages and possible drawbacks.

Defined-benefit plans

How they work: In these plans, the employer makes 100 percent of the contributions and subsequently gets to "define" how much you will be entitled to at retirement. Ultimately, you'll receive a set amount each month, regardless of how the pension performed over the years (rates of return) or how much the company actually contributed on your behalf.

To determine how much you'll be owed, the company refers to a special table (when you get a copy of the summary plan it will be in there) that outlines a benefits formula. Two of the most important factors considered are your average salary and length of employment (years of service). Average salary can be determined by looking at your highest-paid five years (consecutive) or the highest-paid five years (out of 10).

Other companies simply average your salary out over your career, which is less beneficial because your starting years will bring down the average. In terms of a payout, if you are 100-percent vested at retirement, your pension might be 50 percent of your average salary over the last three years. If that amounted to $50,000, your annual pension would be $25,000.

What else you should know: Until recently, defined-benefit plans were

the only game in town. If you wanted to be in a pension plan, it was take it or leave it. But the biggest problem was that, because these plans did not require employee contributions, they didn't consider an employee's needs or desires. For example, the company's formula for establishing the payout may have been contingent on employees retiring at age 65. Employees who wanted to retire early would likely have their benefits reduced by a certain percentage for every month they retired prior to 65.

Furthermore, once the national economy soured and the cost of contributions started choking companies' bottom lines, employers started scrambling for inexpensive alternatives to funding the pensions, such as annuities and employer stock, or even trying to eliminate their pension obligations altogether. Not surprisingly, with both plan sponsors and employees looking for a way out, *defined-contribution plans* or *employee-funded retirement accounts* have fast become the pension of choice.

Defined-contribution plans

How they work: Defined-contribution plans are actually a broad range of programs, including profit-sharing, stock option plans, 401k plans and others. You may have the option to participate in more than one. But regardless of which type of plan you choose, they essentially work the same way.

You and/or your employer will make the contributions (generally a percentage of your annual earnings). And, unlike defined-benefit plans, the final payout at retirement will depend on how much was contributed in your name as well as how well the pension funds performed in their various investments.

Each year, your company must provide you with a summary of your current balance.

What else you should know: The government sets a limit on how much can be contributed in your name each year. The amount is no more than 25 percent of your annual earnings, or $30,000 (whichever is the smaller amount). This is the total amount you can contribute whether you are participating in one or several types of retirement plans.

1. Profit-sharing plans

How they work: Initially conceived as a way for employers to encourage hard work and loyalty, profit-sharing plans contributed money in employees' names when the company showed a profit. Today, not only does the company not have to show a profit to make contributions, they can change the amount they contribute every year. In most cases, there isn't a minimum amount the employer can contribute, but there is a ceiling amount. The maximum contribution cannot exceed 15 percent of the company payroll. As with most company-sponsored plans, decisions on how profits are invested are made by the employer.

What else you should know: If a company normally contributes 10 percent of its earnings in a profit-sharing plan, and it has a phenomenal year one year, it may be prevented from making that 10-percent contribution that year. This would be the case if 10 percent of the profits exceeded the amount equal to 15 percent of the payroll. However, the company may elect to roll over the contribution to the following year.

2. Money-purchase plans

How they work: Unlike profit-sharing plans, where the employer may or may not contribute each year, in money-sharing plans, the employer is obligated to contribute even if it didn't show a profit one year. The company calls the shots on how the money is invested, using a formula that is based on a percentage of its payroll.

What you should know: Again, the employer has no minimum contribution of profits to make, but the maximum can't exceed 25 percent of the combined earnings of the employees who are participating in the company's defined contribution plans.

3. 401ks

How they work: Another type of defined-contribution plan is an employee savings plan called a 401k (the name was adopted from the IRS Code that established the plan). It happens to be one of the best, most effective retirement savings plans available today, because it offers a variety of advantages. First, 401ks give employees a chance to reduce their current tax bill for every year because the contribution comes from pre-tax income. Secondly, 100 percent of the contributions (including interest, dividends and earnings) are tax-deferred until withdrawn at retirement, allowing the more rapid growth in value of the nest egg. Third, many companies match the employee contributions, with typical employer contributions ranging from as little as 3 percent or 6 percent of the employee's contribution to 50 cents for every dollar invested by the employee.

What else you should know: Unlike all the other plans discussed, with a

401k, you get a menu of investment options to choose from so that you can pick one that is most in line with your financial goals. In addition, when employers kick in 50 cents for every dollar you contribute (for example), that's as good as getting a 50-percent return on your investment before you start counting the *growth* of the investment (interest, dividends, etc.). However, because the investment selection is now the responsibility of the employee, the proper investment decisions are of vital importance. If you opt for the most conservative selections rather than the aggressive investment choices, you are likely to see a tremendous disparity in rates of return when you look ahead 20 years from now. The key to maximizing the return of your 401k is to diversify as much as possible, leaning more heavily toward long-term equities and other aggressive inflation-fighting vehicles.

4. ESOPs

How they work: Employee stock ownership plans (ESOPs) give employees the opportunity to invest in the potential growth of their employer (company). If the company expands and prospers, theoretically, the stock will follow in suit. But conversely, the stock can decline in value if the fortunes of the company take a turn for the worse. Obviously, with retirement benefits tied to performance, there is risk involved for stock owners.

What else you should know: Because of the potential risk, the government says that, at age 55, employee stock owners can invest a portion of their account in other investment vehicles that may offer more predictable returns.

5. Deferred-compensation plans

How they work: Unlike other company-sponsored plans, deferred-compensation plans do not need IRS approval and are, therefore, most likely offered as a special bonus or perk to a company's key employees or top executives. Basically, the company invests additional earnings into an account on behalf of an employee, over and above his or her profit-sharing and pension benefits. The funds are to be made available at retirement or when the employee leaves (arrangements vary by company).

What else you should know: There are two types of plans: With a *funded* plan, the company opens an account in the employee's name and makes contributions as stipulated in a contract. The terms of withdrawal are also established in the contract. In the case of an *unfunded* plan, the company agrees to pay an established benefit amount at retirement, regardless of where the funds are taken from. The risk to the employee is that this assumes that the company will have the assets and the ability to pay out on the promise at the appropriate time.

Small business owners, the self-employed and others

Thanks to changes in the tax laws, company-type pensions are no longer the exclusive domain of employees of large corporations. Self-employed individuals, small business owners, private practitioners, employees of small businesses/private practitioners, and individuals who are working but not participating in a retirement plan now have a number of options to turn to when it comes to setting up tax-deferred retirement accounts.

1. SEPs

How they work: One of the new kids on the block is the simplified employee pension (SEP), which permits self-employed people or business owners/private practitioners to contribute up to 15 percent of their net business income or $30,000 (whichever is less) into a tax-deferred retirement account. With a SEP, employees select how the money is invested, although most accounts are opened at banks or at mutual fund companies (it takes one application and about $10 to $30 per employee to set up). All employees are immediately vested, so if they leave, the money is theirs. (Naturally, withdrawals will trigger taxes and possible penalties).

What else you should know: With a SEP, you can change the level of contributions every year to be commensurate with your earnings, or you can even miss some years. If you are a business owner with employees and you do contribute to a SEP, you must contribute the same percentage of earnings for employees that you do for yourself. In other words, if you contribute 5 percent of your annual earnings into a SEP account one year, you must also contribute 5 percent of your employees' salaries into the account. All of the money contributed is deductible as a business expense.

2. SARSEPs

How they work: The Salary Reduction Simplified Employee Pension (SARSEP) permits companies with 25 or fewer employees to set up individual accounts for employees who want to defer a portion of their salary by contributing to a retirement plan. Then the employee's salary can be reduced by as much as 15 percent of his or her annual earnings, or $8,725, whichever is less (rates as per 1992). To set up a SARSEP, at least half the employees must agree to participate.

What else you should know: Unlike a SEP, where employer/employee contributions must be equal percentages, with SARSEPs, employers may defer a higher percentage of their income, provided the total contribution doesn't exceed 25 percent of the average contribution made by employees.

3. Business retirement plans

How they work: Similar to profit-sharing plans set up by large corporations, small businesses can establish such plans, originally called KEOGHs. These plans allow businesses to contribute up to 15 percent of their net business income or $30,000 (whichever is less) into a tax-deferred retirement account for employees. As with other profit-sharing plans, employers can change the level of contributions every year to be commensurate with earnings, or they can even miss some years. If you are a business owner with employees and you do contribute, you must contribute the same percentage of earnings for employees that you do for yourself.

What else you should know: Unlike a SEP, 100 percent vesting is not automatic. Companies are permitted to set up a vesting schedule that serves as an inducement for employees to stay.

Employees who leave before they are fully vested must bequeath the contributions in their name to the remaining participants. The other big difference between business retirement plans and SEPs is the paperwork. Unless there are no employees and/or the business retirement plan account has less than $100,000 invested, the IRS requires the filing of a lengthy financial statement every year along with the distribution of an annual report to employees.

4. Individual Retirement Accounts (IRAs)

How they work: IRAs are like personal pensions, with contributions coming from your earnings (this explains why you must be an income earner to open an account in your name). The maximum contribution you can make each year is $2,000, plus an additional $250 if you are married to a nonworker.

What else you should know: Any worker can contribute to an IRA, but not every IRA owner can get a tax deduction. For example, the only way to deduct 100 percent of your contribution is if neither you nor your spouse are actively participating (contributing to) in a company-sponsored retirement plan. Once you or your spouse are active participants in such a plan, the amount you are entitled to deduct will depend on your *adjusted gross income*. The following chart indicates which portion of your annual contribution is deductible, based on your adjusted gross income and whether you are single or married.

Single AGI	Joint AGI	Individual Deduction
$25,000 (or less)	$40,000 (or less)	$2,000
$26,000	$41,000	$1,800
$27,000	$42,000	$1,600
$28,000	$43,000	$1,400
$29,000	$44,000	$1,200
$30,000	$45,000	$1,000
$31,000	$46,000	$ 800
$32,000	$47,000	$ 600
$33,000	$48,000	$ 400
$34,000	$49,000	$ 200
$35,000 (or more)	$50,000 (or more)	Non- Deductible

Keep in mind this schedule of deductions is applicable only if you or your spouse are active participants in a company-sponsored pension plan. Otherwise your IRA contributions are 100-percent deductible. Regardless of whether you can deduct partial or full contributions, IRAs are still advantageous because the growth (interest) on the money accrues on a tax-deferred basis until funds are withdrawn at retirement.

NOTE: If you choose to contribute to a nondeductible IRA, it is advisable to keep this account segregated from an IRA account that has deductible contributions, so that your record-keeping is kept separate and you have more rollover options down the road. We'll discuss this in greater detail later in the next chapter.

Disbursement of retirement funds

The day will eventually come when you retire and have to make decisions about what to do with the money sitting nicely in a pension and/or other retirement funds. With the threat of the tax man hovering at your door, which way do you turn? (Out the back is the wrong answer.) Do you have your company write a check for the lump sum? Or do you annuitize your benefits (keep the money in the plan, but the company sends you a check every month)? Do you start to draw down on your IRA at 59½, or do you wait? What about forward-averaging the benefits to minimize the tax bite? We'll discuss these and other options so you are aware of the pros and cons of each.

Annuitized benefits

The single biggest advantage of having your pension funds annuitized is that you are then guaranteed of receiving a set amount of money every month. It's a sure thing, no matter the state of the economy, market conditions or if something ever happens to the company you worked for. The money is safe and it all belongs to you.

When your pension funds are annuitized, you have several options for withdrawing the funds, starting at age 59½. You can choose to receive the maximum annual payout, which results in leaving nothing for a beneficiary at your death, or, you can name a beneficiary, which guarantees a monthly income for him or her upon your death. However, naming a beneficiary reduces the amount of your monthly benefit from the first check.

Here is a description of the most widely used options:

Maximum benefit. This option allows you take the maximum monthly allowance because you are electing not to continue payments to your beneficiary at your death. Also, payments stop at your death, regardless of whether you had already received one payment or 100 payments. If you are married and take the maximum benefit, by law you must provide a notarized signature from your spouse, indicating that he or she has consented to receiving no monthly payments at your death.

Lifetime payments to a beneficiary. If you do name a beneficiary, you can opt for one of four different methods for him or her to receive benefits after your death. Once the beneficiary is named and once your retirement starts, you cannot change the beneficiary. That is because the age and sex of your beneficiary will determine the monthly allowance. For example, when a husband names his wife as beneficiary, the younger the wife, the smaller the monthly payments because of a woman's longer life expectancy. Given the importance of age and sex in calculating the monthly payment, you will be required to prove the date of birth of your beneficiary.

Joint and survivor options. There are four basic options if your beneficiary survives you, but essentially the more your beneficiary is scheduled to receive after your death, the less you will receive each month while you are still alive: 1) He or she receives the same monthly allowance you did for life, 2) he or she receives three-fourths of your monthly allowance for life, 3) he or she receives half of your monthly allowance for life, or 4) he or she receives a quarter of your monthly allowance for life.

NOTE: Some annuities offer a pop-up feature, which allows the pensioner to revert to the higher benefit amount if his or her beneficiary dies first.

Guaranteed payments for certain periods. With this option, age and sex are not a factor in determining the amount of the monthly payment. Instead, the actuaries work out a formula in advance that determines the exact amount you receive each month based on the length of the guarantee. For example, a 10-year certain would pay a specified amount each month for 10 years even if you died within that period. However, if you outlive the 10 years, you will receive benefits until your death.

Why annuitized benefits can be a disadvantage

When you annuitize your pension benefits, you must realize it's an irrevocable decision. That is because once you retire, you immediately start to receive checks. So even if a better investment opportunity comes along five years from now, you are under contract to continue receiving your monthly checks. You cannot suddenly decide to request a lump sum payout. Secondly, if you buy an annuity today, when interest rates are the lowest in 20 years, you will be locking in this rate and will be unable to take advantage when interest rates start to climb. In addition, not having access to the principal means you can't benefit from certain tax choices, you can't control how the assets are invested, nor can you pass the assets to

your heirs. Finally, most annuities don't have cost-of-living increases built in. That means you can expect that the monthly benefits payments will eventually lose their value as inflation diminishes their purchasing power.

For these reasons, when given the option, it is generally advisable to take the lump sum distribution.

Lump sum distributions

The biggest reason that a lump sum distribution is so advantageous is that it gives you the flexibility to invest the money as you see fit. It also allows you to take advantage of certain tax breaks (such as deferring the tax on the entire amount by rolling over the money), have access to the money and incorporate the remaining funds into an estate plan. You can even buy an annuity from an insurance company at a later date, should you decide it is advantageous. In effect, you can control the destiny of the funds.

The biggest downside of taking the money in a lump sum is that it must be properly invested or you will be at great risk for depleting the funds before you ever have a chance to make use of them. But by their own admission, most people are not financial wizards. What if they select the wrong investment? What if interest rates keep dropping?

The obvious solution is to consult with someone who is trained in pension benefits, a Certified Financial Planner or CPA, so that you don't have to take matters into your own hands. Once you have found the right person to advise you, you'll probably find that taking the lump sum distribution is more advantageous than annuitizing your pension funds.

What to do with a lump sum distribution

If you plan to take a lump sum distribution, the first question is "What do I do with it?" There are two options that allow you to defer or reduce your tax liability on this money. But before we discuss those, it is important to understand the one thing *not* to do! You do not want to keep your pension proceeds in a savings or money market account for more than the allowable 60-day rollover period. This seemingly harmless move spells trouble with a capital "T."

For starters, if the amount of the lump sum is over the insured limit established by FDIC or its counterparts, the portion that is not under the insurance umbrella is at risk of being lost if the bank closes.

But a much bigger problem if you don't roll over the money within 60 days, is that the lump sum will be counted as ordinary income and tagged on to your final year's pay. This amount may already be at the highest level of your career, which means the combination of your salary and pension could result in your being taxed at a higher rate, reducing your payout by thousands or *tens* of thousands of dollars. Worse still, not taking advantage of special rollover opportunities at the start of your retirement means losing out on some very favorable tax benefits *forever*.

Further complicating matters, as of January 1993, there is a new wrinkle. It's called the 20-percent withholding tax (Congress enacted it as a way to pay for the extension of unemployment benefits it approved). Here's how it works: Before you receive your lump sum pension check, 20 percent of the proceeds will automatically be held on account by the IRS in anticipation of a tax liability when you file your return. Whatever portion of the withholding is not used for tax purposes will be refunded to you. But what this means is that, right off the bat, you'll automatically lose the right to make use of 20 percent of your benefits until you file your tax return and settle with the IRS.

There *is* a way to avoid the withholding, but you might not like it. If you immediately turn over your pension benefits to a custodian or escrow agent at a bank, mutual fund company or brokerage firm, for example, this is considered a trustee-to-trustee transfer—and 100 percent of the proceeds will be transferred without being subject to the 20-percent withholding. The reason some find this unsatisfactory is that it doesn't allow them to take advantage of the period of 60 days they're not subject to taxes. Mind you, the 60-day rollover period is still allowed, it just doesn't protect you from the withholding tax. It's like discovering that even if you land on "Free Parking," it will cost you.

To give you an idea of the potential cost of each of your lump sum distribution options, the chart on the next page shows the taxes and penalties for an employee who is under 59½, in a 28-percent tax bracket, and getting a $100,000 lump sum benefit check.

As you can see from this chart, unless you play by the government's rules and immediately sign over your pension distribution through a trustee-to-trustee transfer, you will lose the use of 20 percent of the proceeds until you file your next income tax return and determine what portion of that withholding (if any) wasn't subject to taxes and can be refunded to you.

Lump sum distribution and their related costs

Distribution options (1)	Rollover amount	Mandatory 20% withholding tax	28% income tax (2)	10% penalty tax for early withdrawal (3)	Net cost of decision (4)
Take lump sum in cash and rollover no portion of distribution	0	$20,000	$28,000	$10,000	$38,000
Take lump sum in cash and rollover the entire amount within 60 days (5)	$80,000	$20,000	$5,600	$2,000	$7,600 plus the lost (6) investment opportunity
Take lump sum in cash and rollover amount equal to entire distribution within 60 days (7)	$100,000 (using $20,000 from another source to make up for the amount being held in escrow)	$20,000	0	0	Lost investment opportunity (8)
Transfer full amount directly into IRA on a trustee to trustee basis	$100,000	0	0	0	0

Source: Kemper Financial Services, 1993

Explanations:

1. These options may not represent all of the available choices available to participants.
2. Represents taxes due on portion of cash distribution not rolled over, based on a 28-percent tax bracket.
3. A premature distribution tax applied to portion of cash distribution not rolled over if recipient is under age 59½.
4. This is the total tax liability, including actual taxes and penalties due on distribution, based on a 28-percent tax bracket.
5. In this case, the recipient rolls over the distribution amount, less the 20 percent withheld.
6. The recipient has lost the tax-deferred growth on $20,000 until retirement and the opportunity to invest this amount until the refund is received.
7. In this case, the recipient rolls over the $80,000 received after the withholding tax, along with $20,000 from other personal income sources.
8. The recipient has lost an investment opportunity to invest the $20,000 until the refund is received.

Obviously if it is more important to you to have access to the remaining 80 percent for the 60-day rollover period, that is your choice. But the majority of recipients only want one thing—to hold on to every last dollar they are entitled to. The section that follows will tell you how to do just that.

Basically you have two choices when it comes to handling your lump sum distribution. The first is to take advantage of *forward-averaging*, which eliminates the annual tax burden from your pension disbursement by calculating a one-time, up-front settlement. The second option is to use an *IRA rollover*.

Forward tax-averaging

With forward-averaging, often referred to as 5-year and 10-year averaging, you'll pay the tax on your entire retirement distribution when you retire and then never have to pay tax on this money again. If you don't use averaging, the pension proceeds will be counted as ordinary income and taxed accordingly each year you withdraw funds. Basically, the IRS taxes you at a reduced rate because it is getting use of your money earlier than it would otherwise. Once you pay the taxes, the balance of the distribution is free and clear.

Here's how forward tax-averaging works: When you file your tax return for the year, you take the pension distribution, you'll calculate the tax on your lump sum payment, which is at a special rate (hopefully lower) than your earned income. For example, if you received a $100,000 lump sum settlement and took 10-year averaging, you'd divide $100,000 by 10 years, which is $10,000. If, according to the special tax table, the rate on $10,000 was $1,500, you would

multiply the $1,500 times 10 (years), which would equal $15,000. Your total tax liability for the $100,000 lump sum would then be $15,000. The same formula would apply for 5-year averaging. After you've determined the tax on the pension benefits, you'll add it to the tax on your other earned income, and that is the total amount you'll owe for the year.

The one catch is the new 20-percent withholding tax. If your lump sum settlement is $100,000, for example, you can still forward-average, but you'll be taxed on the entire $100,000 even though $20,000 is being withheld. It may all work out in the end because you may have owed the $20,000 anyway.

Who is eligible to forward-average?

There are two ways to qualify to forward-average your retirement distribution. To be eligible for 5-year forward-averaging, you must 1) have participated in your company pension plan for at least five years, 2) have taken the distribution in a lump sum and 3) be 59½ or older when you receive the distribution. To be eligible for 10-year forward-averaging, you must meet all of these requirements, and have been born prior to 1936.

The benefits of forward-averaging

Naturally, if there were no major advantages to forward-averaging, there would be no takers. So the IRS has created a special tax rate for pension benefits, which, in most cases, is lower than the normal tax rate for earned income. However, this is dependent on the size of the payout. The larger the lump sum, the closer the tax rate is to the rates used for ordinary income. Generally, 10-year averaging is slightly more favorable in reducing your tax liability than 5-year averaging, unless your distribution is more than $473,000.

For example, on a $200,000 lump sum, you could save close to $7,500 in taxes with 10-year averaging. With a $473,700 distribution, there would be no difference between 5-year and 10-year. This next chart illustrates the differences in tax savings.

5-year vs. 10-year forward-averaging

Lump-sum distribution	5-year averaging One time tax liability	10-year averaging One time tax liability
$50,000	$6,900	$5,874
$100,000	$16,398	$14,471
$200,000	$44,398	$36,922
$473,700	$132,636	$132,736
$1,000,000	$280,000	$280,000

Note: The special rate table the IRS created to calculate forward averaging tax rates is based on ordinary income. It is the same whether you earned $10,000 a year or $100,000 a year.

If you are considering forward-averaging, the main advantages are:

1. One-time tax. Lump sum distributions can be sizable amounts of money, which can represent an enormous tax obligation, particularly when calculated at the rate of ordinary income. With forward-averaging, you pay taxes one time and up-front in the first year, and the money is free and clear.

2. It's less of a bite. Not only is the tax bite a one-time obligation, but the bottom line is that you should end up paying much less that one time than if you had paid taxes on that same lump sum over 5 or 10 years.

3. Freedom of choice. Once you pay the IRS, the money is yours to do as you see fit. You can invest it, buy a home and/or a business, buy an annuity,

etc. These options would be not allowed with annuitized benefits or an IRA rollover.

4. Purchasing power. If your pension fund involves a large amount, a lump sum payment will give you enormous purchasing power. With annuitized benefits, the amount of the monthly payment may be too small to be of any consequence should you have special financial needs (starting a business, caring for a parent, buying a home, etc.)

5. Win again with tax-frees. You can throw good money after *good* by reinvesting in tax-free bonds or tax-free annuities. This continues the process of sheltering the pension benefits from current tax rates.

6. Freedom to pass it on. With a lump sum, you can elect to include the assets in a living trust that will benefit your heirs. If your money is in a company pension or IRA, this is not possible.

Annuity and lump sum distribution

It is possible to enjoy the benefits achieved by both annuitizing and taking a lump sum distribution. This strategy is called taking a *partial distribution*. In this case, you withdraw a lump sum amount (a minimum of 50 percent of your pension benefits) and the balance is annuitized.

This still enables you to take advantage of the forward-averaging methods assigned to lump sum distributions, provided you meet the eligibility requirements of 5-year and 10-year averaging. If you do use forward-averaging on the partial distribution, understand that it is a one-time-only privilege. Any further distributions you take after this would not be eligible for averaging.

Taking a partial distribution is a very good way to simultaneously reduce and postpone paying taxes. At the same time, you'll be assured of receiving a pension check every month while having a certain amount of cash to reinvest, buy a home or business, or do whatever you see fit.

IRA rollovers

In our initial discussion of lump sum distributions, I mentioned that there are two basic options. The first is forward-averaging, and the other is an IRA rollover. As the name indicates, with a rollover, you literally roll over your pension

benefits from one tax-advantaged pension into another. In other words, you go from a company-managed pension to a personally managed pension, or Individual Retirement Account (IRA).

After you receive your benefit check in a lump sum amount, you have two choices. You can take 60 days to roll over the money and put it in a separate IRA account—and be subject to the 20-percent withholding tax. Or you can have your employer directly transfer the money into the IRA and avoid the withholding tax. Either way, as long as the money is put into an approved retirement plan, the money will not be subject to income tax until funds are withdrawn at retirement.

As far as investment flexibility is concerned, you can opt for any instrument that regular IRAs invest in: stocks, bonds, mutual funds, etc.

And similar to other IRAs, the funds are not to be taxed until they are withdrawn, which is possible starting at age 59½. Should you withdraw prior to that, there could be a penalty, in addition to the amount withdrawn being taxed as ordinary income. However, there is a way to avoid the penalty for early withdrawal, and we'll discuss that later in this chapter.

The thing to keep in mind is that with an IRA rollover, your money can grow tax-free until you're 70½, at which point you must begin withdrawing funds and paying taxes on the amount withdrawn each year. This is called taking the maximum tax deferral. The thinking is that your earned income at this age should be less, and subsequently the tax bite smaller.

In past years, tax experts recommended that people hold off until age 70½ to withdraw IRA money, if possible.

Today, however, with the threat of higher taxes looming over us, the maximum deferral may not be as advantageous because the older taxpayer may be in a higher bracket anyway. Consult with your tax advisor to determine the best strategy for you.

Portability

An obvious question people have is whether they are allowed to have more than one IRA. The answer is yes. There is not a limitation on the number of accounts or different IRA investment vehicles you can own. There is only a limit on the total amount you can personally contribute or roll over each year.

Another common question is about combining IRA accounts. Let's say you retire or leave a job with a $60,000 pension that is yours to take. Can you roll over those funds into your personal IRA (the one only you contributed to—not your company)? Yes, this is permissible. However, there is one possible drawback. If you ever went back to work, started a business, etc., and had the opportunity to participate in another company-sponsored plan, the IRS would not allow you to remove the $60,000 you had deposited in your personal IRA and roll it back into the new pension plan. The reason is that once personal and company pension dollars are mingled and interest has accrued, there is no easy way to tell which portion of the money came from after-tax dollars, etc.

That is why it may be beneficial to keep your personal IRA and your IRA rollover (the pension money you rolled over into an IRA) segregated. This way, you always have the option to roll over pension proceeds from one company-sponsored plan into another plan. This strategy is called *portability*. And by taking advantage of it, you can benefit from the compounded interest and growth of the combined sums.

IRA rollover distributions

The question everyone wants answered is, "When can I get my money out of my IRA?"

To most people's surprise, it is possible to withdraw from your IRA rollover without a penalty before retirement age. However, it is most advantageous to either start withdrawing at age 59½, which is considered normal retirement age, or to postpone withdrawals until age 70½. We will discuss each of these options.

Tapping into your IRA before 59½

Many people are troubled by IRAs because they can't withdraw funds prior to retirement without paying a stiff penalty. Not only would the money be taxed as ordinary income, but they would also be liable to pay a 10-percent fine on the total withdrawal.

Recently, however, a provision in the tax code (Section 1.72-9 of the IRS regulations) was put to a test by a 45-year old man who wanted access to the $750,000 sitting in his IRA rollover. With the help of his attorney, he was able to prove that he had a right to annuitize the money in his pension and receive an annual income of $60,000, starting now. The decision went in his favor because, based on the amount he had sitting in the IRA, coupled with his life expectancy, he had accumulated enough money to receive annual payments throughout his retirement.

If you are taking early retirement or would like to annuitize your IRA roll-over account before you turn 59½, there are three ways you can set up the payment schedule.

1. Determine the balance in your IRA at the first of the year, and divide that by your life expectancy (or the combined expectancy of you and your spouse). That's the amount you should be allowed to receive on an annual basis.

2. Simply amortize the benefits over your life expectancy, calculating interest at the rate you've been told you'll receive.

3. With the help of an actuary, and the use of mortality tables and interest rates, you can establish an annuity factor. This will allow you to annuitize your pension benefits and receive a set amount each month starting at an age before 59½.

NOTE: Regardless of the amount you start to withdraw, it cannot be changed for the first five years. This is called the *substantial equal payments over a minimum of 60 months rule.*

Although it may be a comfort to know you can take an early withdrawal of your pension benefits, it can also be a dangerous temptation. Remember, if you start to deplete funds at an early age, you'll be touching the money you were going to live on at retirement. And wasn't the whole point of starting an IRA to put away money after you stopped bringing home a paycheck? Another

thing to consider is that the earlier you remove funds, the smaller your monthly payments will be.

NOTE: There is no penalty for premature distribution if the funds were withdrawn to pay your beneficiary at your death, or to provide income in the event you become disabled.

Starting your distributions at age 59½

Once you turn 59½, you can begin to withdraw funds from your IRA rollover. However, before you request a distribution, you need to be aware of the following ramifications:

1. If you made non-deductible contributions to your IRA, that portion of your distribution would not be taxed when you withdrew the money. The reason? That would be double taxation, as the income you originally contributed came from your after-tax earnings.

2. That means when you receive a distribution from your IRA, the portion that is attributable to your *deductible* contributions is taxed as ordinary income. Therefore, if you don't need the money one year, you may be triggering taxes unnecessarily.

3. Until you turn 70½, the IRS cannot dictate the size of your distribution each year, nor can it require that you take a distribution each year. You can take a distribution on an "as-needed" basis. The ability to decide how much and when you withdraw funds will help you control your annual tax liability.

Postponing IRA withdrawals until age 70½

Now let's say that you've reached age 70½, and you've got a total of $100,000 sitting in your IRA. This is the age where the government requires you to start withdrawing funds or pay a penalty for every year you delay a withdrawal. How much do you need to take out?

The IRS bases the required annual withdrawal on your life expectancy or the joint expectancy of you and your beneficiary. At age 70 today, a man's life expectancy is 16 years. If his wife is also 70, their combined expectancy is 20.6 years. This means that one of them will presumably live another 20 years and the yearly withdrawals are calculated accordingly.

If you want to further reduce the withdrawal amount, it is possible to name a child or grandchild as a beneficiary. This further extends the maximum deferral by establishing a combined life expectancy to a maximum limit of 26.2 years. Now, although you would still have to withdraw funds at the age of 70½, the amount would be smaller than if you didn't have a younger beneficiary named. And, naturally the smaller the amount, the less taxes you'd pay.

Based on all these life expectancy figures, here is the amount that would have to be withdrawn each year starting at age 70½:

Yearly required withdrawal for maximum deferred IRAs
($100,000 Account)

	Husband	Husband/Wife	Child/Grandchild
Life expectancies	16	20.6	26.2
Yearly required withdrawal	$6,250	$4,854.50	$3,817

Benefits of IRA rollovers

To summarize, these are the main advantages of IRA rollovers:

1. Tax-free decision. Because you are only transferring your pension benefits and not withdrawing them, no taxes are taken out. They are totally deferred until you withdraw funds.

2. Pension continues to grow. By transferring or rolling over your pension, it will not only stay intact, it will also continue to grow. Thus, you are assured of accumulating an even larger amount by the time you're most in need.

3. Tax planning options. Because you can predetermine how much you will withdraw each month and at what age, you can establish an arrangement that will reduce the tax bite. In other words, you can be scheduled to take out enough to live comfortably, but not so much that you end up in a higher tax bracket.

4. Portability. If you ever go back to work again and start another pension, you can combine these funds with your IRA rollover at retirement, thus giving you the ability to consolidate your retirement investments, making the task of managing your finances easier and more efficient.

Other important considerations

In weighing the pros and cons of all of the options we've discussed, it's easy to lose perspective and only consider the tax implications. However, there are numerous other issues to consider at retirement than just trying to figure out how to keep Uncle Sam away from your retirement fund.

What about your lifestyle? How do you want to live? What about your medical care needs? What about helping your children while you're alive and/or leaving a legacy when you die? What about the desire to invest or pursue a new career? Maybe you've always wanted to open a small business. Before you can make a final decision about disbursing your pension benefits, you must take these and other important factors into consideration.

Staying liquid

For example, to what extent will you need this money to be available to you? If you don't have savings and money market accounts or other cash investments, then annuitizing your pension could be harmful. What if one day you absolutely needed cash to meet an emergency? If all of your money was tied up in your company pension plan, you'd be out of luck.

On the other hand, if you took the lump sum distribution and put a portion into mutual funds, all you'd have to do is write a check from the account.

Major purchases

Similarly, what if you wanted to buy a new home or business or make a big investment in real estate? That would require a large amount of money, which might be unavailable to you if your retirement fund was tied up in an IRA rollover or annuity. Depending on how much you had accumulated in pension benefits, it might be possible to take a partial distribution and still have enough in the lump sum to accomplish your goals.

Additional income

On the other hand, you may not need a lump sum at retirement because other investments are providing the necessary income. In this case, you might welcome the idea of getting a check every month out of your pension plan so that you had more discretionary dollars to spend on vacations, hobbies, etc. In that case, annuitized benefits would meet your needs.

Did you hear the one about the three retirees in a boat?

Regardless of your financial priorities for retirement and the decision you ultimately make about disbursing your benefits, you are probably curious as to which route would lead to the largest bottom line.

To answer this question, we'll compare stories of three retirees who had each accumulated $250,000 in pension benefits. One retiree took an IRA rollover, one took advantage of 10-year forward-averaging and the other retiree dumped the money into a liquid investment.

During the 10-year period following their retirement, none of them had withdrawn any money, they were each in a 28-percent tax bracket and their interest earnings had averaged 10 percent over a number of years.

How did they fare? The one who opted for the IRA rollover ended up with a retirement account totaling $487,267. Although this was a larger amount than the other two retirees had accumulated, he was the only one who was required to withdraw his funds as ordinary income (by age 70½) and pay tax accordingly. However, at least up to this point, his money was growing on a tax-deferred basis.

The one who took a lump sum and then 10-year forward-averaged, ended up with an account valued at $410,004, all of which was free and clear of taxes. If this person then went on to invest in tax-free and tax-deferred vehicles, the money would be working at an optimum level insofar as generating income while minimizing taxes.

As for the third retiree, the one who opted to put the money in a liquid account, she ended up with $369,003. After taxes, her rate of return didn't even keep up with inflation.

But again, the total amount accumulated is not the only priority. This is not a race to see who can create the largest nest egg. What may be more important is knowing that your money was meeting as many different needs as possible for as long as possible while preserving your assets to leave as a legacy.

Good question!

Q. I just started working for a company that offers a 401k plan. I have no experience with this type of pension and don't feel like I know what I'm doing. Where should I go for help?

A. Participating in a 401k will definitely make the average person feel as though he or she'd better become a professional pension manager overnight, or else. You must enroll in the plan yourself, contribute your own money, and then oversee your investment selections to make sure they are performing to your expectations—all without the help and advice of your company's pension experts. So, the first step is to get an education. Attend seminars, read up on current trends in magazines, newsletters and books. Insofar as investment strategies, ideally, you don't want your 401k to be too heavily invested in employer stocks. This retirement fund is too important to take more of a chance than necessary on your company's feast-or-famine periods. As with any sound investment strategy, the more diversified you are, the better.

Q. What happens to the money in my 401k if I leave the company?

A. The beauty of the 401k plan is that all the money is yours! Unlike the defined-benefit pensions, the company can't deny you access to it or claim you aren't 100-percent vested. Instead, you can move the money into your new employer's plan or put the money into an IRA rollover account at a bank, mutual fund or brokerage firm.

Q. We have retirement accounts valued at close to $250,000. The problem is the accounts are in our

local savings and loan, and FDIC no longer insures an amount this high. What should we do?

A. You are referring to the December 1992 federal ruling that the maximum insurance coverage a bank can offer on a customer's retirement account(s) is $100,000. Mind you, this is not per account, but per *depositor*. So if you have an IRA, a 401k, and a KEOGH, for example, your total FDIC insurance is still $100,000. (Prior to this, the maximum insurance was $400,000 per depositor). To overcome this, you can always spread your accounts out over as many banks as it takes to insure the total value of your retirement funds. However, the real issue is, if you have this much money put aside, why is it sitting in a bank earning 3 percent to 5 percent interest? The majority of your assets should be converted to long-term equity investments because that is the only way to potentially achieve enough growth to outpace inflation.

Q. Isn't it too risky to invest something as important as your retirement account in the market?

A. Precisely because your retirement accounts are so important is the very reason you need to be in long-term equity and other investments. In fact, the greatest risk you can take is taking no risk at all by putting all of your funds into one "basket"—such as a CD. Actually, the greater the diversity, the lower the risks and the better chances you'll have that the rate of return will be higher. Let's say, for example, that you invested a $100,000 IRA rollover offering an 8-percent fixed rate of return. After 25 years, the account would be worth $684,850. But, what if you took that same $100,000 IRA rollover and

put it into four or five different investments, perhaps cash funds, bond funds, stock funds, company stock, etc.? If these vehicles ranged in performance from a 15-percent return, all the way to a 100-percent loss, after 25 years you could have accumulated an estimated $962,800. Admittedly this is a hypothetical example, but the concept is dead center!

Q. I plan to take early retirement in two years. My company will then give me a lump sum settlement from my pension and profit-sharing. I was thinking of using the proceeds to buy into a quick-print franchise. Is this a good idea?

A. While I can't respond specifically to the merits of this particular business proposition, I can tell you that in order for it to be viable, the profit potential would have to be substantial. To start, the profits on the franchise would have to compensate for the hefty state and federal income tax you'd owe when you withdrew the pension funds.

Furthermore, since you wouldn't be transferring the money to another retirement plan, the funds would be subject to the 20-percent withholding tax. That means you'd lose access to 20 percent of the proceeds up-front (the money would be held by the IRS on account against the potential tax liability), and at the end of the year, possibly be subject to a balance of taxes not yet paid. All told, taxes could reduce your takeaway by as much as one-third.

In addition to compensating you for the tax liability, the business would also have to return an amount in excess of what the investment was earning in the retirement fund. In light of high start-up costs and an uncertain income stream in the first year of business, that is an awful lot to expect. I would recommend leaving your pension benefits intact and going to the bank to apply for a business loan. The rates for borrowing are at a low 7 percent to 10 percent, and are deductible to the business.

Q. I am a retired teacher with a pension who occasionally works as a substitute. Can I deduct my new IRA contributions, even though I am already receiving pension benefits?

A. Yes, you would be allowed to deduct 100 percent of your IRA contributions (up to $2,000) since you're not an active participant in a company-sponsored plan. An active participant is defined as someone who currently contributes to a plan, not someone who receives benefits as a former employee. The only thing that would prevent you from deducting 100 percent would be if your spouse was an active participant. Then the percent you could deduct would be based on your adjusted gross income.

Q. I work part-time and earn about $13,0000 a year. Is that enough to be eligible to open an IRA account?

A. Since there is no minimum earnings required to open an IRA, you would certainly be eligible. It is also important to point out that the government does not impose a minimum contribution amount. That is up to the bank, mutual fund company, brokerage firm, etc., with whom you open the account.

Q. I'm a computer consultant. What is the best type of retirement account for me since I'm the only "employee" in my firm?

A. That depends on how much money you want to put aside every year. If you anticipate that you won't be contributing more than 15 percent of your net income, then a Simplified Employee Pension (SEP) will be fine. Or as an alternative, if you expect that you can put away more than this, you might consider a business retirement plan. With this plan, you can set up both a profit-sharing plan and contribute as much as 15 percent of your income, as well as a money-purchase plan, where you could deposit an additional 10 percent of your income.

Q. I own a small chain of kids' clothing stores. I've had one manager with me for seven years, but there is tremendous turnover with my other employees. Would it be to my advantage to offer retirement benefits, or should I just set up a business retirement plan for myself?

A. There are no simple answers, but in many cases, small business owners who have a high rate of employee turnover need to choose a plan that allows them to require minimum years of service in order to participate. This is known as a *vesting* schedule, which generally phases in over a six-year period. After six years, an employee is entitled to 100 percent of the employer contributions. Typically, after one year of employment, the employee might only be entitled to 20 percent of those contributions if he or she were to leave the company. Many of the profit-sharing and money-purchase plans can be designed to incorporate this schedule, including a SEP.

Q. My husband and I started a small health care company and we now have seven employees, half of whom are at executive levels. We want to set up a retirement plan,

but aren't sure which is the best way to go.

A. In this case, I might recommend going with both a SEP and a SARSEP. Anytime you have high-level employees, they are likely to want to defer income to reduce their tax burden, which is what a SARSEP does. You should confer with your employees and determine the percentage of income they'd want to defer and contribute to the retirement fund. If the average contribution would be 8 percent, you could contribute 10 percent for yourself. Then, you could set up a SEP and contribute 5 percent of the firm's net income for you and your employees. By going with this strategy, you'll have contributed the 15 percent maximum allowable for yourself, without having to contribute an equal amount for your employees.

Q. Is it possible to borrow money from your pension plan before you turn 59½?

A. Most companies do allow you to take a loan (five years is the maximum), provided you agree to pay back the money through payroll deductions. The maximum you can borrow is 50 percent of the vested value of your account, or $50,000 (whichever is less). Interest rates are typically 1 percent above the prime lending rate, which is a bargain compared to credit-card interest, but may not seem as desirable when compared to the cost of borrowing from the equity in your home (interest rates are typically lower and there are tax advantages). On the other hand, taking a loan from your pension account won't require any applications, fees, nor will your pension turn you down—unlike borrowing from the bank. Plus, the interest you pay goes right back into your account!

Q. What are the deadlines for participating in the various retirement plans?

A. If you wanted to enroll or contribute to a 401k, profit-sharing plan, defined-benefit plan or money-purchase plan, you must do so by the last day of the employer's tax year. If you want to enroll or contribute to a SEP or SARSEP, you must do so by April 15 (unless you apply for an extension). If you want to open or contribute to an IRA, you may do so by April 15 of the next tax year, which would allow you to take a deduction for the previous year. You cannot get an extension beyond April 15.

What I tell my clients

Beware the excise tax when you "overdraw" your retirement accounts. Thanks to the Tax Reform Act of 1986 (the gift that keeps on giving from former President Reagan), you now have to be concerned about the excise tax on excess distributions from your retirement accounts. Originally, the law was thought to be a problem of the rich. But as the years have passed, we've seen it become more of a detriment to the middle class. The law stipulates that if you take out any amount over $150,000 a year from your retirement accounts, you'll be liable for a 15-percent excise tax on that excess withdrawal. While $150,000 sounds like a big number, keep in mind that it represents the total withdrawal from your combined accounts: IRAs, KEOGHs, pension distributions, 401ks, profit-sharing, etc. And let's say one year you need a large amount to buy a home or a business, you are going to meet that tax head-on. It would be nice if your former employer could warn you, but they have no way of knowing what you're taking from other sources, so it's up to you to keep track. One way to avoid the tax is to try to split up your distributions by taking one part in December and the balance in January.

GICs 'R Us. Although companies give employees options when it comes to making investment decisions for their 401ks, those choices may still be somewhat limited. Typically they include employee stock ownership, trustee-managed pools for fixed-rate securities, and the new darling, GICs (Guaranteed Investment Contracts).

A GIC is an agreement between the employer's pension plan and an insurance company that offers a fixed rate of return on the funds invested for the duration of the contract (some banks and private firms also offer these contracts). People are gravitating toward them because, with guaranteed fixed rates, they seem as secure as CDs. Let the buyer beware. A guarantee from some insurance companies and banks today may only be one step above a handshake.

Other serious drawbacks of GICs? They are often riddled with high fees, the fixed rates aren't inflation-proof, and the government doesn't provide a security net. Optimally, you want your retirement funds to be invested in tax-deferred vehicles that are well-balanced between growth and safety.

Speaking of choices. The defined-contribution pension (401k, profit-sharing, etc.) used to be called the wave the future. But the future is here. Today, more than 100,000 pension plans in this country, covering 20 million employees, are now defined-contribution plans. With more than $600 billion in assets, the U.S. Department of Labor has stepped in to insure that workers participating in these plans are guaranteed greater choices and flexibility.

Starting Jan. 1, 1994, companies are going to be urged to comply with something called the 404(c) rules. These rules dictate that plan sponsors must offer participants 1) at least three core investment alternatives that vary insofar as risks and returns, 2) adequate information about each of the investment options so that the employee can make informed decisions and 3) the option to change their minds and move into different investments, at least on a quarterly basis. The incentive to companies/sponsors to comply with this regulation is the promise that plan trustees and managers will not be held liable for losses or other problems associated with the investments' performance. In light of all the pension shenanigans going on today, not having fiduciary responsibility is what most companies want!

The overlooked retirement account. Many of my clients are homemakers who have held part-time jobs at the local mall, or who earned money through baby-sitting and other off-the-books type of work. So the only retirement benefits they may have are their husbands' Social Security, pension, IRAs, etc. When they ask if there is anything they can buy so they have a retirement account in their name, they are always surprised by my response. I tell them that, believe it or not, one of the most overlooked "retirement accounts" is a life insurance policy.

Aside from the fact that it will pay out upon your death, it can provide tax-deferred savings every time you pay a premium. In addition, there are no limitations on the amount you can "contribute" (you can buy as big a policy as you can afford), you can withdraw the money at any time without any restrictions (you can even take a tax-free loan), and when you retire you can convert the policy to an annuity so it provides income for the rest of your life.

Even the paperwork is easier. There are no costly annual fees or special tax forms to fill out. Plus, you can arrange that if you become disabled or seriously ill, your premiums will be paid for you until you recover—and the IRS won't consider those payments taxable income. Similarly, when you retire and take the income from the policy, it won't be added into the amount the government considers when calculating the possible taxes on your Social Security benefits. All in all, a life insurance policy is an excellent way for a "nonworker" to save for his or her retirement.

Join the club. As we were going to press, we learned of a brand-new association called the 401k Association, run by none other than Ted Benna, the man who created the 401k. As this is a new organization, I cannot speak to the quality of its services. But from what I can tell, it has the potential to provide a tremendous service to the legions of people who are investing in 401ks. The organization will focus on lobbying for more favorable legislation (its first order of business will be to try and do away with the 20-percent withholding tax), offering investment recommendations and basically keeping members apprised of matters that have a direct bearing on 401k maintenance. Annual membership for the first year is $95. For more information, contact The 401k Association, 1 Summit Square Rd., Doublewoods and Route 413, Langhorne, PA 19047. Or call 1-800-320-401K.

It's 10 p.m. Do you know where your 401k is?

It is projected that, by the year 2000, American workers will have more than $1.2 trillion invested in 401k accounts, up from $600 billion today. This is a wonderful revelation in that it means that today's generation has gotten the message about saving for retirement and is really trying to put its money where its mouth is. The other major stride made as a result of the acceptance of the 401k plan is that employees are no longer subject to the whims and decisions of the employers and plan sponsors. Now, 401k accounts are self-directed, meaning the individual investor decides where, when and how much to invest. It is a dream-come-true after decades of living and dying by a company's vesting rules, its funding strategies and, most importantly, its possible decision to raid or disband the plan all together.

On the other hand, you know what they say about getting what you wish for. For the first time, millions of investors must take fiduciary responsibility for their retirement benefits, and the employer gets to wash his hands of the decision-making, or even offering advice. As a result, books, magazine articles and even companies are proliferating to help individual investors make the best, most informed decisions about their 401k plan.

If you find yourself suddenly thrust into the job as your personal pension manager, the best decision you can make is to do your homework. And don't be concerned that your investment choices are irrevocable. The new trend is to give investors as much flexibility as possible to change strategies or investments, even on a daily basis, if that's what it takes.

One thing has not changed. The bottom line now, as then, is that regardless of what type of plan you participate in, you owe it to yourself to contribute the maximum allowable amount as many years as you possibly can before you retire. Forget about all the twists and turns in the laws and the possible wrong moves. The very biggest mistake you could possibly make is not saving enough for your retirement. The key today is to get informed about your choices, stay informed, and watch the account as if it were a golden goose. The truth is, if properly invested, your retirement plans have the potential to lay the grandest retirement nest egg you ever saw!

5

Investing for income: There's more to life than CDs

The two most important rules, when it comes to your income, are: Make it first, and when you retire, make it last. With more people retiring in their late 50s and early 60s, average life expectancies are prolonging retirement for an unprecedented 20 to 30 years.

Although the prospect of seeing your grandchildren grow up is a wonderful dream, there is a potential nightmare. Many Americans are deeply concerned that they won't be financially prepared to maintain their current lifestyles when they retire, let alone when they reach their 80s and 90s.

As a dear aunt remarked at her 75th birthday party, "I think I could handle just about anything now, except out-living my money." She's not alone! As most people approach retirement today, the burning question is, "How *will* I support myself?"

According to a variety of government and financial sources, personal investments provide the major source of income. Other sources, such as Social Security and wages, are important but represent a much smaller piece of the income pie. The chart on the following page shows how the percentages break down.

When I share this chart with a new client, it's an eye-opener. Here's the proof that a comfortable retirement isn't going to be a gift from Uncle Sam. It's going to be a direct result of aggressive savings and investing. Invariably, the next thing I'll hear are the "Yes, but's":

"Yes, but the market is so unpredictable. Investing is nothing more than a crapshoot today."

"Yes, but the idea of all our money being tied up in investments is a problem. The last thing we want is to be retired and cash poor."

"Yes, but we've always been conservative investors. Now it looks like we'll have to take a lot more risks if we want to have enough money to retire."

Sources of retirement income

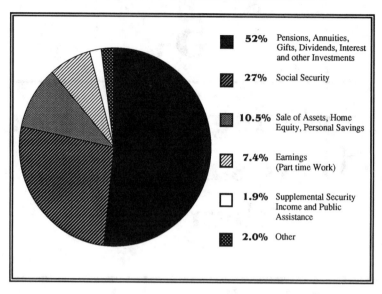

■	**52%**	Pensions, Annuities, Gifts, Dividends, Interest and other Investments
▨	**27%**	Social Security
▦	**10.5%**	Sale of Assets, Home Equity, Personal Savings
▨	**7.4%**	Earnings (Part time Work)
□	**1.9%**	Supplemental Security Income and Public Assistance
▨	**2.0%**	Other

An even more common reaction comes from honest, hard-working people who have paid for braces, bar mitzvahs, college, weddings and everything in between: They throw their hands up and say:

"We did the best we could, but we didn't put away as much as we should have. Now we worry when or even if we'll be able to retire."

I don't take any of these concerns lightly, particularly the issue of being able to afford to retire. But as hopeless as the situation seems, I assure you that there are many things that can be done right now and in the future to achieve financial security.

That's why this chapter is an important starting point. You'll learn about today's most viable investment options as well as about the ones that can hurt you. Just as important, I'll tell you how to structure your portfolio at certain ages so you'll get the maximum return

at retirement. Even late-starters will learn how to make up for lost time.

Don't try this at home

In spite of the fact that this book devotes a large chapter to investment strategies and that I am constantly after my clients to stay informed, here's an important warning: Just because you gain insight into different investments doesn't mean you should proceed alone.

In today's highly complex world, the task of managing your financial affairs is a daunting responsibility. If your life is anything like my clients', you have enough going on without suddenly trying to be a student of high finance.

Think of it as finding out you need surgery. Would you read up on the techniques, rent an operating room and perform the procedure yourself? Hardly. You would go to the best surgeons available and let them do what they were trained to do. The same is true with handling your retirement planning.

Furthermore, the investment strategies we'll be discussing are general in nature. And yet, each of us has our own set of circumstances, financial philosophies and unique goals, all of which can impede our ability to do what is "textbook" simple.

That is why I strongly urge each of you to work with a Certified Financial Planner. CFPs are the only experts who have gone through rigorous educational training to manage all aspects of a client's financial affairs. They do not replace lawyers, stockbrokers and accountants, they manage the team to insure that everyone is working toward common goals.

The greatest benefit is that financial planning is not a product, it is a process. A CFP will meet with you, discuss your needs and objectives and then develop a highly customized, detailed, financial plan that factors in all of your personal goals and circumstances. The cost of a plan will vary with the extent of the work that needs to be done. But ultimately it won't cost you, it will *pay* you. With a financial plan, there is the potential to save thousands of dollars every year in income tax while generating a thriving portfolio through sound investment strategies.

Check the yellow pages or call the Institute of Certified Financial Planners for a referral at 1-800-282-PLAN (7526). Another source is the International Association of Financial Planners at 1-800-945-IAFP (4237). Ask for the free booklet, "Consumer Guide to Comprehensive Financial Planning."

The wise investor

One of the first things I tell clients is that I don't care whether they have $10,000 or $10 million to invest. Either way, they need a *diversified portfolio* and they have to know their *risk tolerance*. In fact, I tell them that investing is a lot like cooking. If you want your investment recipe to be a masterpiece, just mix the ingredients well and decide how hot you want the oven.

The benefits of a diversified portfolio

Everyone likes a sure thing. It's why so many investors put money into one investment that consistently performs well. But with the unpredictable world we live in, sure things have gone the way of nickel candy bars. And besides, no single investment, no matter how effective, is going to meet all your objectives. Furthermore, regardless of how safe an investment is, the riskiest strategy in the world is putting all your eggs into one basket.

The stock market crash of October 1987 was an important reminder of that, particularly to retirees who were counting implicitly on their investments to produce income.

Let's pretend that in September 1987, the largest segment of your portfolio was tied up in stocks, with about $200,000 sitting in your favorite blue chips. A month after the crash, the market was down by a whopping 22 percent. That would have left you with a net loss of $44,000, or a balance of $156,000. Three to six months later there was even further erosion. In a very short time, you lost a year's worth of income.

Now let's take your know-it-all brother-in-law who believed in putting his eggs in more than one basket. He also had a $200,000 portfolio but it was divided equally between blue-chip stocks, U.S. Treasury bonds and a money market account. A month after the crash, he had only suffered a 6-percent loss even though stocks had plummeted by 22 percent. That's because bonds rallied and money market funds remained stable. His portfolio still had $184,000 and was continuing to hold its own several months later.

Please don't interpret this to mean that the stock market is too risky for retirees. To the contrary, later in the chapter I'll be proving to you why it's actually one of the safest, most profitable places for you to invest—as long as it's not the *only* place you invest. The point is, the backbone of any sound financial plan is "asset allocation," or just good old-fashioned *diversification.*

And by diversification I do not mean an assortment of savings and money market accounts. Rather, a diversified portfolio includes the widest possible range of liquid, growth, tax-free and income-producing investments.

The advantage of this "balancing" act is that it is the best way to insulate your assets from a particular category that may be weathering a storm. And let's face it. Between the ever-changing investment environment, erratic interest rates and the yo-yo effects of inflation and recession, up-and-down cycles are all part of the process.

Unfortunately, one of the biggest misconceptions about diversified portfolios is that the strategy applies only to big spenders. Small investors argue that it's better to be strong in one investment than weak in several. In reality, small investors have the most to lose if their one investment choice flounders.

That's why my premise is, regardless of the amount you have to invest, the strategy remains the same.

Do you know your risk tolerance level?

When it comes to deciding the degree to which they can tolerate risk, most people react emotionally rather than intellectually. It's like the kid who can't wait for his turn on the roller coaster and then begs to get off the first time it plunges. If he would just stay calm and hold on tight, he would be there to enjoy the ride when it climbed back up again.

Even though it is *common knowledge* that investments are like roller coasters and either rise, coast or plunge, it's not always *common practice* to hang on for the whole ride.

Human nature being what it is, most people hate to lose money more than they like to make it. In other words, they worry more about the return *of* their money than they do *on* their money. So, all too often, inexperienced investors pull out before an investment has had a fair amount of time to perform.

In the same vein, it's human nature to want to stay with the pack. This is particularly true of investing. For example, the vast majority of people buy when prices are rising and sell when prices are falling. Suggest the reverse and the typical investor's comfort level plummets. Yet often, that's the very best approach.

These are just some of the quirks that get in the way of making the best investment decisions. To summarize, successful investors 1) have established their comfort level, 2) diversify, 3) are patient, 4) stay calm and 5) take risks only when the potential for gains is greater than the potential for losses.

How to evaluate investments

Before we explore the various investment vehicles that are available, it's important to have a basis for evaluating them. With virtually thousands of investment products on the market, how can you be sure you're making the right choices?

What's important to remember is that you're not just trying to build a retirement nest egg, you're trying to reduce your tax burden, preserve your assets, find safe havens, stay ahead of inflation and so on. If your portfolio includes a variety of investments, each designated to accomplish something different, then not all your investments have to deliver high yields. It's actually more important for an investment to serve its intended purpose.

For example, interest rates on savings and money market accounts are at a 20-year low and are the last places to invest for growth. Yet you still need them for liquidity and for short-term parking. If an emergency arises, you want money that is ready and waiting—not to have to pay a penalty for early withdrawal on a CD or a bond. Show me a portfolio without liquidity and I'll show you an investor who's got *too* high a tolerance for risk!

The point is, there are a number of ways to judge the value of an investment. The following list identifies the attributes to look for, along with the important questions you want your financial advisor to answer:

Safety. Is the principal safe? What kind of market conditions will cause the values to decline? Can I bail out before the losses are substantial?

Liquidity. Will I have immediate access to my money or will I be locked in? For how long? What are the penalties for early withdrawal? How easy is it to get to my money? Are phone and wire transfers available? Will I have check-writing privileges and, if so, with any limitations?

Insurance. Is either the yield or the principal guaranteed? What about FDIC-insured?

Terms. How long am I committed for? Will I have any problems holding on for that amount of time and, if not, can I live with the penalty for early withdrawal? Have the important terms and conditions been explained to me?

Yields. What are the anticipated returns and what guarantees are built in for the future? To what extent will the yield be reduced by commissions, service charges and fees? Are there any hidden costs when I sell? What will be my annual tax liability based on my tax bracket?

Inflation. Is this investment expected to at least keep pace with inflation? What is the anticipated rate of return annually and over the lifetime of the investment?

Taxes. What is the real rate of return after taxes and inflation? If the after-tax return has reduced my purchasing power over the life of the investment, are my other investments able to meet the shortfall?

History. How has the investment performed in good economic times—and bad? Is it still considered a solid investment after the one-two punch of taxes and inflation?

While each one of these questions is important, there is one other consideration that is even more essential to a retiree, and that is the *preservation of capital*. More than anything, you only want to be investing where your principal is not at risk. You simply can't afford to be losing ground at this point of your life.

Think about it. When you retire, you will have all the assets you are ever going to have. If your investments suddenly start eroding rather than flourishing, how and when will you make up for the loss? As you get older, returning to work may no longer be an option. Ultimately that's why the rate of return on your investments can't be at the expense of risking your capital.

Debunking the worst investment myths

When I start to do retirement planning with clients, I ask if they could make their investment dreams come true, what would they wish for? In so many words they say they'd want their portfolio to be in safe, reliable investments that showed consistent growth and that always outpaced inflation. And because they cherish a good night's sleep, the last thing they'd want is a portfolio that went up and down like an elevator.

In response, I'll show them a chart that illustrates the performance of a very popular investment over a 20-plus-year period. When I ask if they'd want their money there, they immediately say no. In fact, after seeing the tremendous volatility in yields every year, one client swore that if this were his portfolio, he'd probably have ulcers again.

I believe him, because I know many people who put all their money into this single investment, certain it was a reliable source of income at retirement. And now they don't feel so terrific. But at least they're in good company. Currently, investors have over $3 trillion sitting in this investment. We're talking about 6-month CDs. Yep, old reliable.

It's a harsh reality, but not only have CDs teeter-tottered for decades, their performance after taxes and inflation has consistently showed a net loss. Even in 1981, a virtual heyday for CDs (they paid 15.79 percent), investors *still* took a loss of 2.43 percent after factoring in the 8.9-percent inflation rate and the 50-percent tax rate. See for yourself when you examine the chart on the next page.

I'll never forget the client who studied this chart and said, "When you show this to people my age, maybe you should have a paramedic standing by." I'm happy to tell you that that's never been necessary because people are just happy they've been enlightened. They finally understand the risk of counting on one single investment and realize that their hard-earned money needs to be parked elsewhere.

But where? If CDs aren't engineered to outpace inflation and taxes, what investment is? In one form or other, the answer is stocks and bonds.

I know what you're thinking. "Stocks and bonds? But what about the risks? The market is so volatile and unpredictable." Not true. For proof, take a look at the graph appearing on page 120, which shows the growth of dividends during the same 20-year period in which we examined the CDs on page 119.

Overall performance of 6-month CDs
(1970-1991)

Year	CD rate	Federal tax rate	Inflation rate	Real rate of Return
1970	7.65%	50%	5.6%	-1.78%
1971	5.21%	50%	3.3%	-0.70%
1972	5.02%	50%	3.4%	-0.89%
1973	8.31%	50%	8.7%	-4.55%
1974	9.97%	62%	12.3%	-8.51%
1975	6.89%	62%	6.9%	-4.28%
1976	5.62%	62%	4.9%	-2.76%
1977	5.92%	60%	6.7%	-4.33%
1978	8.61%	60%	9.0%	-5.56%
1979	11.44%	59%	13.3%	-8.61%
1980	12.94%	59%	12.5%	-7.19%
1981	15.79%	59%	8.9%	-2.43%
1982	12.57%	50%	3.8%	2.49%
1983	9.28%	48%	3.8%	1.03%
1984	10.71%	45%	3.9%	1.99%
1985	8.24%	45%	3.8%	0.73%
1986	6.50%	45%	1.1%	2.48%
1987	7.01%	38%	4.4%	-0.05%
1988	7.91%	33%	4.4%	0.90%
1989	9.08%	33%	4/6%	1.48%
1990	8.17%	31%	6.1%	-0.46%
1991	5.91%	31%	3.1%	0.98%

Source: Oppenheimer Funds (Federal Reserve, Consumer Price Index, Bureau of Labor Statistics)

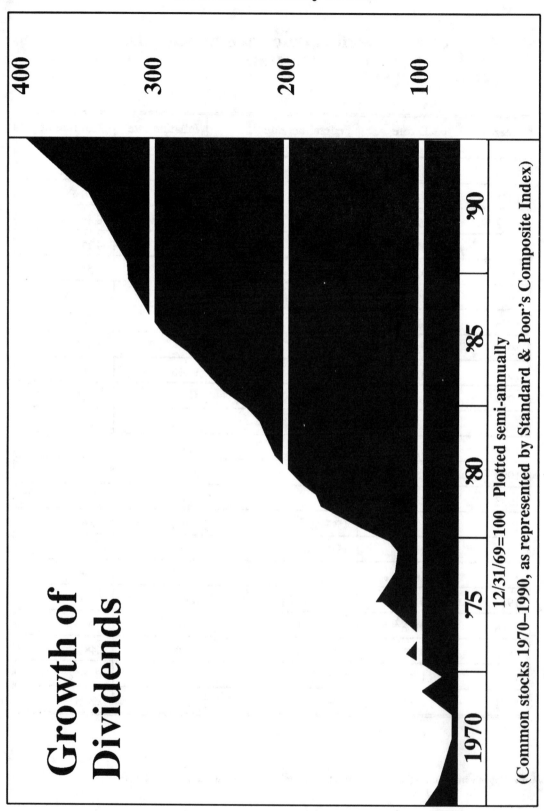

Growth of Dividends

400

300

200

100

1970   '75   '80   '85   '90

12/31/69=100   Plotted semi-annually

(Common stocks 1970–1990, as represented by Standard & Poor's Composite Index)

This illustrates that since 1970, common stock dividends have grown by 400 percent without a single downturn, not even in 1987. More importantly, for the past 66 years, the market has consistently outperformed all other investment categories in terms of growth, which is a retiree's main artillery against inflation—as you'll see in this next chart.

Average annual total returns

Dec. 31, 1925 - Dec. 31, 1991	
Stocks (S&P 500 Index)	10.38%
20-Year U.S. Treasury Bonds	4.79%
30-Day U.S. Treasury Bills	3.70%
Consumer Price Index	3.14%

Source: Ibbotoson Associates, Chicago, IL (Consumer Price Index is a measure of annual change in consumer prices)

Now, mind you, on an individual basis, not every stock performed so admirably. Over the years, there have been hundreds, if not thousands, of stinkers.

However, as an investment entity, the stock market doesn't owe anyone an apology because when it comes to outpacing inflation, nothing has compared as favorably. Those who were loyal to the market and didn't jump in and out depending on how the wind was blowing, surely discovered this, as this next chart shows.

December 31, 1925- December 31, 1991			
Holding periods	% of time beating inflation		
	Stocks	Bonds	Bills
1 Year	67%	59%	62%
5 Years	77%	50%	58%
10 Years	88%	42%	53%
15 Years	92%	35%	62%

Source: Ibbotson Associates, Chicago, IL

Two different retirement stories make these numbers come to life.

In 1978, the Gardners retired and put $250,000 into a balanced fund, which invests in the stocks and bonds of established companies. How did they do? This year, their interest income was $30,000, or 123 percent more than they earned the first year in the fund. Even better, although they've taken all their dividends in cash, as of Dec. 31, 1992, their original $250,000 investment had grown to $624,183. Had the Gardners opted, they could have reinvested their dividends, making their holdings worth more than $1.5 million.

Compare this to the case of the Browers, who also retired in 1978. They invested their life savings of $250,000 into CDs, hoping to live on the interest. The first year they got a respectable 8 percent return and were even able to take a cruise. They were feeling really good about their decision because the yield was strong while the principal was insured. But when we fast-forward to December 1992, we see that inflation ate up 56 percent of this investment's purchasing power. In other words, their 1992 dividend check, which was $10,475, bought only as much as $4,585 would have bought 15 years ago. In effect, although their total income from their original $250,000 investment was $344,554, its actual value in today's dollars was exactly $250,000.

I hope all of this will whet your appetite for a variety of investment options you might never have considered because of your fear of losing your principal. And although CDs still play an important part in a retirement portfolio, it is clear that they were never intended to stand alone. Again, no one investment, including stocks, should. As we've seen, the misplaced fear that leads people to put all their money into one "safe" investment can actually erode their income and purchasing power over the years.

Investment income options for retirees

What follows is an overview of the 25 most popular investment products for retirees, because they are most likely to provide safety and/or income. They are presented in order of complexity.

NOTE: Because interest rates are so volatile, it would be impossible to include the current yields of these investments. Check with your banks, CFP or other investment advisors for the latest available rates of return. In addition, because the fates and fortunes of companies are always changing, no attempt is made to recommend specific investment products. To keep abreast of potentially good investments, I recommend that you become a frequent reader of your newspaper's business section as well as financial publications such as *Money* magazine, *Kiplinger's Personal Finance* magazine and others of that nature. For stock tips, there are dozens of newsletters, such as "Value Line Investment Survey," "Standard & Poor's Stock Guide" and "Moody's." Most offer a trial subscription, but before you send your money (annual subscriptions range from $17 to $450), check to see what your local library keeps on file. A few hours of "free" research could well be one of your better investments.

The 25 most popular investments for retirees

1. Money market accounts

How they work. Money markets buy shares in taxable funds that invest in the short-term debts of major corporations and banks. For parking your money without fluctuation of principal, you get monthly "dividends" (interest). The amount of interest depends on the prevailing yield being paid on short-term debt instruments such as short-term Treasuries, federal funds, bank lending rates, etc. As a liquid account, there are no penalties for withdrawals, making money markets ideal for emergencies and unexpected bills.

How they pay. Money markets guarantee monthly interest earnings based on their current values.

2. Certificates of Deposit (CDs)

How they work. Bank CDs require a low initial investment (denominations vary from hundreds to thousands) with maturities ranging from one month to five years or longer. The money is not liquid and there are stiff penalties for early withdrawal, with some banks charging up to six month's interest. Similar to bank accounts, the interest on CDs is subject to state and federal taxes. And if your deposit is in a member FDIC bank, it is insured up to $100,000 (per depositor, not per account). CDs remain attractive because of their safety. The principal never fluctuates, only the interest.

How they pay. CDs pay either at maturity, or you can take out the interest at quarterly or semi-annual intervals. The yields are generally higher than money markets or comparable to U.S. Treasury securities of equal maturities. However, I must point out that in today's economy, neither CDs, money markets or government securities are stealing the show.

3. U.S. Treasury bills

How they work. Putting money into a Treasury bill is today's equivalent of Grandma putting money under the mattress. The money is safely tucked away, but T-bills beat mattresses because the government guarantees both the principal and the interest. Further, because the terms are short (13, 26 or 52 weeks), you won't feel handcuffed if interest rates take off. Finally, your interest is exempt from state and local taxes. The minimum denomination is $10,000 with additional $5,000 increments. If you don't have $10,000 to invest and you still have your heart set on T-bills, look to some of the money market funds that hold short-term Treasuries. Then it's possible to invest as little as $1,000.

How they pay. The idea is to buy T-bills below face value ($10,000) and to receive the face value at maturity. For example, if you pay $9,600 for a 26-week T-Bill, you'll get a check for $10,000 when the bill matures.

4. Stocks and stock (equity) funds

How they work. People often compare the stock market to riding in a speeding Porsche up a mountain in a rainstorm. They'd simply feel safer somewhere else. But the numbers contradict that. The market has consistently outperformed all other investment categories over the long term. (In the past 50 years, it averaged a 9-percent compounded annual return). It's why the stock market is the one place you can go for growth, which is what you need to do battle with inflation. As a stockholder, you become an equity owner of the company and share in both the profit potential or losses, so choose wisely. *Stock funds (equity funds)* are mutual funds that invest in stocks. Another option is to look at the global and international stock funds. These take advantage of very profitable companies abroad or ones that invest in particular regions of the world that are experiencing rapid industrial or techno-logical development.

How they pay. If the stock is pay-ing dividends, you'll receive your earn-ings quarterly (of course the real payout is the growth potential over a period of years). Check the stock exchange list-ings in the newspaper for details.

5. Preferred stocks

How they work. A preferred stock is like a hybrid. It offers the safety of a bond because it pays fixed dividends, but, as a stock, it has the potential for growth and appreciation. However, be-cause of the guaranteed return, prefer-red stock prices don't rise in value as fast as common stock prices for the same corporation. Many are cumulative pre-ferred stocks, which means dividends accrue quarterly but pay at a later time.

How they pay. Because preferred stocks pay fixed dividends, shareholders get first crack at the profits (common stockholders don't get their dividends until preferred stockholders are paid). Generally, dividends are paid quarterly.

6. High dividend paying stocks

How they work. There are approx-imately 65 stocks in the Standard and Poor's index that have a history of pay-ing dividends on a regular basis, al-though you'll see less growth than with common stocks. The real beauty of these stocks, however, is that, unlike common stocks, which may or may not increase in value, they offer two ways to make money: 1) through the potential increase in the stock's value and, 2) through divi-dends, providing consistent cash flow.

How they pay. Dividends are paid quarterly.

7. Blue-chip stocks

How they work. Blue chips are the stock issues that are more mature and have a solid history of generating re-turns. They also fare better in market slumps than smaller, less stable com-panies because they command a larger share of the market than their compe-titors. Corporate giants like McDonalds, AT&T, General Electric, Johnson & Johnson, Coca-Cola, Dow Chemical, Xerox and Bristol-Myers have become the backbone of the stock market, com-prising the Standard and Poor's 500 and the Dow Jones Industrial Average.

How they pay. Dividends are quarterly with growth potential.

8. Utility stocks

How they work. These have long been favorites of income investors be-cause they consistently pay higher, safer dividends than just about any other stock group. Why? Because no matter the state of the economy, people always need electricity and telephones. In fact, during the crash, no other stocks were as durable. In addition, as the pop-ulation grows coupled with the in-creased demand for consumer and business electronics (from Nintendo to fax machines), usage goes up, making these stocks even more profitable.

How they pay. Utility stocks pay quarterly, but a utility mutual fund (which has more growth potential) can pay monthly.

9. Mutual funds

How they work. Mutual funds give individual investors the opportunity to be in the stock market—but in the most diversified way. When you buy shares in a professionally managed fund, you're taking advantage of experts who are investing in a broad range of markets. In essence, they pool your money with thousands of other investors so they have enough clout to make the best possible deals. The typical fund will hold securities in dozens of different companies, with the investors as well as the management firm having a "mutual" interest in the overall performance of the fund.

How they pay. Mutual funds are liquid—you withdraw funds as needed. Dividends are paid monthly or quarterly. You can also arrange for systematic withdrawals, where the principal is reinvested each month, but you receive the earned interest on a monthly basis.

10. Government mutual funds

How they work. Fund managers invest in a portfolio of U.S. debt obligations with varying maturities, including T-bills, notes or bonds, Ginnie Maes, Fannie Maes (mortgage-backed securities, see #19 for further explanation), or even from the Federal Home Loan Corporation. If you're not comfortable investing in corporations, government mutual funds are a good alternative. They offer the underlying security of investing in the government, the funds are diversified, the minimum investment is $1,000 and the funds are liquid. Also, they've been great performers during the recession when interest rates have been at historic lows.

How they pay. Although these securities fluctuate in value, the principal on the underlying assets is guaranteed by the government. Monthly dividends

may also pay a capital gain. You can redeem all or part of your shares at any time.

11. Income mutual funds

How they work. Income mutual funds try to let you have your cake and eat it, too, by investing in established, but aggressive, companies that have a record of paying high cash dividends. Thus, you get growth (capital appreciation) *and* income. Portfolios usually include a mix of utility, high-tech and financial common stocks and bonds to assure stability of income payouts. Although yields are relatively high, share prices remain fairly stable. And because of their diversity, volatility is generally not a problem.

How they pay. Dividends are paid monthly or quarterly.

12. Corporate bonds, bond funds and bond trusts

How they work. Want to lend a company money in exchange for the corporation guaranteeing you'll get a return of your principal with locked-in interest? That's what corporate bonds are—investing in the debt obligation of public corporations in exchange for the return of your money plus a guaranteed interest rate. This is very different than buying stocks, which makes you an owner in the company and guarantees nothing insofar as rate of return. When you buy bonds, you invest in lots of $1,000 or $5,000. When the bonds mature, you get the face value (par value) back. In the meantime, interest payments have been coming every six months. Bond funds and bond trusts are ways to invest in a diversified portfolio of bonds and, at the same time, have total liquidity. As a new and favorable option, consider the international or global bond funds, which invest in both foreign currency, foreign government bonds, CDs and notes. This strategy takes advantage of the more favorable interest rates throughout the world, relative to the U.S. dollar.

How they pay. Bonds pay a set amount of interest every six months (bond funds pay monthly).

13. High-grade bonds

How they work. High-grade bonds are comparable to blue-chip stocks insofar as dependability and solid yields are concerned. Bonds are rated from AAA (the highest) to C (the lowest) by special bond-rating services such as Moody's and Standard & Poor's. Look for an AA ranking or better. High-grade corporate bonds often beat the yields on Treasury bonds with the same maturities and are considered safe and strong. At the same time, spread the maturity dates out to prevent a high-yield bond from being pulled away from you should rates drop before it matures.

How they pay. All bonds pay a set amount of interest every six months (bond funds pay monthly).

14. High-yield bonds (junk bonds)

How they work. High-yield bonds can be as tempting as Eve's apple, but just as dangerous. In today's market, who can resist a 12-percent return? Solo investors should. As with any high-as-the-sky yields, consider the source. These bonds invest in the debt obligations of companies with lower-rated, less-mature and/or financially troubled

companies that are also vulnerable to takeovers. They may also be trying to finance a rapid expansion. All of these are factors that could contribute to trouble spelled D-E-F-A-U-L-T. If you still can't resist, at least invest through mutual funds that have more diversity and liquidity. In some cases, the prudent use of these funds can strengthen the overall yield of your portfolio compared to the risk of going it alone.

How they pay. All bonds pay a set amount of interest every six months (bond funds pay monthly).

15. Municipal bonds

How they work. Municipal bonds invest in city, county or state debt obligations, which come about from making capital improvements, such as building new roads. A minimum investment is generally $5,000, or you can invest in a mutual fund's choice of muni bonds for as little as $500 to $1,000.

Muni's are very attractive investments for retirees because they are reasonably safe, they generally retain their value *and* the interest is exempt from federal income tax. Most are also exempt from state and local taxes if you live in the state of the issuer. In effect, they are as close to a tax shelter as you can get after tax reform. For example, if you're in a 28-percent tax bracket, a bond paying 6-percent interest could yield as much *after* taxes as a taxable bond paying 9 percent. Just be aware that while most muni bonds are exempt from taxes, it's a misconception that they all pay tax-free income. Some are subject to an *alternative minimum tax*, and, of course, all are subject to gains and losses. Please do your homework.

How they pay. Individual bonds always pay semi-annually. Unit trusts and funds can pay monthly or quarterly.

16. U.S. Treasury bonds and notes

How they work. These tax-exempt securities (state and local only) are considered to be at the top of the list of safe havens because of the unlikelihood that the government is going to default on its debts. Notes have a variety of maturities (2, 3, 5, 7 and 10 year). Bonds mature in 30 years. Both have par values of $1,000. There's a good resale market should you want to sell your 5- to 10-year notes prematurely.

How they pay. Because you make a much longer commitment than you do with T-bills, the yields on these securities are generally higher. Interest is paid semi-annually at a rate that is fixed at the time the securities are issued.

17. Short-term bond mutual funds, short-term government bond mutual funds

How they work. Portfolio managers invest in select government, municipal and corporate bonds. Unlike savings bonds, the yield fluctuates based on the rise and fall of interest rates. However, that means the potential yield may be greater because the funds hold both current bonds and notes, as well as those from past years, when the rates may have been higher.

How they pay. Generally, rates are comparable to short-term Treasuries or CDs. But, because they are short-term, there is less volatility, which minimizes your loss of value should interest rates

be climbing. Income is either monthly or quarterly and there's always the option to reinvest to buy more shares.

18. Zero coupon bonds

How they work. All bonds—municipal, government and corporate—can be offered as zero coupons. Basically, the dividends are stripped away until maturity (you don't get to collect every time you pass go). The big advantage is that you're buying the bond at a deep discount and getting the guaranteed return at maturity. This is ideal for investors who need a method of forced savings (you must reinvest the dividends) and who also have a specific dollar goal. For example, if you'll be needing $10,000 in a certain year, you can probably buy a zero coupon bond for $5,000 now and let it mature.

How they pay. Zero coupon bonds pay face value at maturity or can be sold before maturity at an appreciated value.

19. Ginnie Maes (mortgage-backed securities) and CMOs

How they work. Sounds like a new rock band, but *Ginnie Maes* are mortgage-backed securities issued and insured by the Government National Mortgage Association. Basically, banks sell their customers' home mortgages to either the government or other banks who then parcel them out to individual investors as 15- or 30-year bonds (maturities are modeled after home mortgages). Ginnie Mae holders receive a proportionate share of principal and interest paid by homeowners every month. Typically, the minimum investment is $25,000.

CMOs or Collateralized Mortgage Obligations, are Wall Street's version of the same game, but they've one-upped the government by "stepping" the maturities, which means they hold a variety of mortgage obligations, which are scheduled to come due at different times. This gives investors a better sense of when both principal and interest will be paid off and the bonds matured. Unfortunately, they're extremely complex and, now, with lower interest rates and so many homeowners refinancing or paying off mortgages early, it's even harder to anticipate what and when these investments will return.

How they pay. Count on monthly but taxable income, often 1 percent to 2 percent more than Treasury bonds. Basically as homeowners pay off their principal and interest every month, you get a piece of it. Of course, as the principal gets paid down, the interest income decreases proportionately.

20. Annuities

How they work. If you've ever been told by a doctor to come in monthly for treatments, you may begin to feel less like a patient and more like an annuity. Purchased through life insurance companies, annnuities guarantee income on a monthly basis. Or, similar to CDs, they allow you to invest for a period of time (one, three or five years) and withdraw interest after the term ends. With annuities, investors make deposits, agree to let the principal sit and let the money earn interest. Starting at a certain point and continuing for the rest of their lives, investors have the option to schedule withdrawals on a monthly basis. Contributions are not deductible, but annuity income is tax-

deferred until the interest is withdrawn. Unlike an IRA, there is no cap on what you can contribute each year. In addition, annuities can be used as an IRA investment. These are called qualified annuities.

How they pay. Unlike CDs, annuities give you the option to pull out the earned interest and/or principal for income on a monthly basis, so they work like pensions for the rest of your life.

21. RELPs (Real estate limited partnerships)

How they work. RELPs sell shares in real estate syndication offerings, which allows you to own a piece of major income-producing properties without the responsibilities of managing them. Further, as a "limited partner," your total liability is limited to no more than your initial investment. The real estate management company (the general partner) pools investors' money and buys, develops and renovates commercial properties (shopping centers, office buildings, condominiums and other income-producing real estate).

As a part owner, you can participate in three major benefits. The first is a tax advantage, which is important if you are still in a high tax bracket. The second is growth or appreciation and the third is income. Although the Tax Reform Act of 1986 declared RELPs as passive investments and altered the extent to which limited partners could deduct losses on rental properties, it is still possible to write off annual depreciation against other income. In addition, you can defer the gains as your shares appreciate in value during your holding period. However, the caveat is that the properties must have had time to rise in value. As with any real estate investment, you have to be in it for a minimum of seven years or longer.

How they pay. Payments are based upon real estate income and the sale of assets, which, in many cases, can be paid quarterly.

22. REITs (Real estate investment trusts)

How they work. When you buy shares in a REIT, in concept, you invest in a large real estate portfolio that holds an interest in a wide assortment of properties and mortgages. In reality, however, some of the most successful real estate trusts are the ones that specialize in a particular type of property, such as shopping centers. What's interesting is that, independent of how the trust is invested in real estate, the structure of the investment is more akin to a mutual fund. The shares that make up the trust are traded on the stock exchange or over-the-counter.

When shopping for a real estate trust, it's best to stick with a management company that has a solid history of real estate investments. Not only can you then track its success, but often its shares are very undervalued and can be sold for a handsome profit. It's best to stay away from blind pools, which don't invest until they've raised enough capital, as well as from any firm that hits you with up-front fees of 10 percent or more. Although REITs can be as volatile as the stock market, their liquidity, their diversity and tax benefits, depending on the type of trust, will presumably have capital appreciation or income potential. These are very important to a retiree's portfolio.

How they pay. You receive the income that the trust generates from rent payments and other means. Then when the trust sells off assets, you can expect dividends or greater earnings per share. The latter can result in commanding a higher share price in the REIT. There are several types you can look into. Property REITs own tangible property such as strip centers, office buildings, etc. These provide capital appreciation, but not necessarily income (dividends). For income, you should look into mortgage REITs, which use the funds in the trust to lend money. A hybrid REIT will both lend money and invest in property. Dividends, when distributed, pay quarterly.

23. Limited partnerships

How they work. After watching real estate companies raise capital by selling shares in their limited partnership programs, cable TV, film production, and oil and gas companies have followed suit. Investors who become part owners are lured by the prospect of potentially sizable profits. Their risk is limited to the amount of their initial investment. To buy in, investors purchase "units" ranging in price from $1,500 to $25,000 (the minimum investment is usually $5,000). But buying is the last decision limited partners get to make. When you buy in, you agree to let the management or general partner run the show. The appeal to small investors is that they can be an owner of a major asset—an oil well, a Hollywood motion picture, a cable television company, a shopping center, etc. For those in high tax brackets, limited partnerships are attractive because of the tax write-offs for depreciation. But the bottom line is, if the partnership works, it generates income and growth.

However, the downsides are many. Your money is not liquid, the laws have changed so now you can only deduct losses against passive income (rent), and the risks are steep. Estimates are that half the limited partnerships lose money. The problem is, which half?

How they pay. This long-term investment (8 to 12 years) doesn't see profits until the partnership is liquidated, if at all. But, because of the risks, returns can be double-digit. Oil and gas partnerships pay quarterly, with special tax credits tied to federal energy policies.

24. Equipment leasing

How they work. Another limited partnership arrangement, but one that shouldn't keep you up nights, is equipment leasing. With the advent of high technology, 80 percent of all businesses in this country have leased computer and other operational equipment, making it a $133 billion industry. Basically, leasing companies buy in-demand equipment and lease it to Fortune 500 firms and other emerging growth companies. Investors provide the capital to purchase new equipment, and get back their principal plus interest. Another benefit is the tax-deferral of a part of your distribution income, because of the pass-through of depreciation and interest expense (but don't confuse this with a tax shelter). The risks? Equipment could become obsolete and/or lessees might default on loans. Relative to other partnership programs, equipment leasing is safe and profitable.

How they pay. With a $5,000 minimum investment, there will be monthly or quarterly distributions, whatever has been dictated by the partnership.

25. Stock options, commodities

How they work. There are several types of options, but none are intended for the faint-of-heart. The two most common are called calls and puts. A *call* option is a contract to buy 100 shares of stock at a certain price within a certain period (generally three to nine months). A *put* option is the reverse. You sign a contract to sell 100 shares of stock at a certain price within an option period.

The lure of calls and puts is the sizeable profits you can make if you guess right that a particular stock is going to rise or fall in value during the option period. For example, if American Gadgets is selling at $50 a share, but you feel that in three months the price could jump to $90 because they're introducing a great new gadget, you can enter into a call option contract that permits you to buy the stock at $50 within that period. Your up-front cost to place a call option is generally 10 to 15 percent of the stock's value. Now, if the stock does go up to $90, you'll have made a tidy sum. However, if you were wrong and the stock plummeted to $35 a share, let your option to buy expire and all you've lost is your up-front fee.

How they pay. At the end of the option period, investors will either have a profit or a loss, based on the premium paid for the contract.

Now, let's compare the potential risks and rewards of these investments. The following chart presents investments by function served, starting from the most conservative to the most aggressive or unpredictable.

Investment Income Options For Retirees
(In Order Of Conservative To Aggressive)

Objective	Investment Income Options	Rewards and Risks
Emergency	Savings accounts, money markets	Short-term, interest bearing investments, totally liquid, stability of principal, ideal for emergencies. The risk or downside is the low, unpredictable interest rates. As for bank failures, only accounts with deposits over the maximum insurable by the federal government are potentially at risk.
Safety	Certificates of Deposit (CDs), U.S. Treasury bills, government securities (Treasury notes, bonds and government mutual funds), short term bond mutual funds, short term government bond mutual funds, Ginnie Maes, CMOs (Collateralized Mortgage Obligations), global or international bond funds	Income-producing investments with minimum volatility and risk of default, high safety rating, highly marketable for liquidation purposes. Risks are low rate of return, penalties for early withdrawals and fluctuation of principal on funds as well as some government securities prior to maturity. Global funds take advantage of favorable interest rates and currency fluctuations abroad.
Income	Corporate bonds, government bonds, preferred stock, high dividend paying stock, income mutual funds (primarily bonds), annuities, zero coupon bonds	Greater chance of producing income than with safety vehicles, but risk is proportionately higher due to unpredictable market fluctuations.
Tax-free income	Municipal bonds, unit trusts, municipal bond mutual funds	Income-producing investments not taxed by the federal government. Bonds issued in the state you reside are also free of state and local taxes. Interest rates of funds are not locked in and bond values will fluctuate. Look out for "early calls" when bond matures faster than expected due to falling interest rates and investor loses opportunity to hold on at the higher rates. There is also the possibility of defaults.

Retirement Ready or Not

Objective	Investment Income Options	Rewards and Risks
Growth and Income	Utilities (stocks with higher paying dividends), preferred stocks and bonds, growth and income mutual funds (stocks and bonds paying higher dividends)	The reward is investing in the potential for growth and income, and because the investments have both stocks and bonds, they offer a hedge against the normal fluctuations possibly resulting in higher rates of dividend income and growth. Risks are less volatile than the common market although there is fluctuation of principal and income. Still, there are no guarantees. Also new government regulations can affect returns (such as those regarding nuclear power plants, etc.).
Growth	Stocks, stock (equity) funds, growth mutual funds, global or international stock funds	Potential for substantial growth and appreciation through ownership interest in companies. The downsides are volatility of principal if only investing for short term. In the long term, the market generally beats inflation. Since tough times for individual companies or whole industries drop prices, and worth is unpredictable, it's best to go with funds and reduce your risk of making a bad choice. International and global stock funds are currently in favor because of rapid expansion and growth of companies that are investing in new technologies and industrialization overseas.
Real estate	Income properties, Real Estate Investment Trusts (REITs), Real Estate Limited Partnerships (RELPs)	Source of rental income and potential for long-term growth, Probable risks are lack or loss of tenants and declining market values and changes in interest rates could affect mortgage rates and return. Further, RELPs are not liquid and at certain times may not be marketable if you want to sell.
Specialty Markets	Oil and gas, equipment leasing, investments in partnerships and businesses	Investments in franchises, equipment leasing, cable TV, and other potentially profitable long-term income sources. Risks are lack of liquidity, ineffective management, and risks due to declining business conditions.
Speculation	Stock market options, commodities	Investor contracts to sell stock options or commodities on a certain date and bets on the spread (sell price vs. buy price) at the time of sale. The risks can be enormous and are best left to high rollers with money to burn.
Collectible/Hobbies	Art, antiques, gold, precious metals, stamps, coins, cards, etc.	Investment in marketable items that have potential for growth. There is generally not income to be had, only potential profits if items are sold.

Model portfolios

We've identified the most important principles of investing—diversification and risk tolerance, and we've reviewed the most popular, favorable investment products for building up retirement assets. As a next step, it's essential to address how to structure your portfolio. What is the point of investing if your choices aren't working in tandem to help you achieve your financial goals?

There have been many instances when new clients marched in to my office, presented their portfolios, and sat back waiting for the ooh's and aaah's. They're always convinced they've masterminded a brilliant strategy that is going to make them rich in retirement. More times than not, unfortunately, I have to tell them that not only is their rationale outdated, their investments are actually working at cross purposes.

For example, many people in their 50s and 60s are still of the mind that a portfolio heavily invested in CDs, municipal bonds and a smattering of stocks for good measure, is the most intelligent approach. They'll point out that the strategy offers diversity, safety and opportunities for growth. Technically they're correct.

However, considering the current state of the economy, the ever-increasing threat of higher taxes, the ongoing challenge of staying ahead of inflation and the difficulty most Americans are having with putting away for retirement, a portfolio comprised of only these investments is doomed to fail. It's like sending someone cross-country in a '57 Chevy.

That's why I've developed a variety of investment models that take all of these factors into consideration, as well as two other important matters: age (and subsequently the number of years until retirement) and investment personality (conservative or aggressive). Although the model portfolios are different insofar as structuring, their common bond is that they are built like the Egyptian pyramids.

Pyramid power

The image of the great pyramids has been likened to the ultimate towers of power. With an unwavering base, they are pillars of strength that can support the weight of whatever has been thrust upon them.

As a Certified Financial Planner, I have always believed that a model portfolio should also have the strength of a pyramid. It should be constructed in such a way that risks and rewards are completely balanced from top to bottom. The soundest, safest investments support the hierarchy while those that can potentially reap the greatest rewards, but also have the greatest risks, are positioned at the top.

To help people at different stages of their lives, the pyramid models at the end of this chapter are categorized by age range and preferred investment style—conservative or aggressive. Admittedly, both approaches can have negative connotations, which is not the intent. Rather, I want to differentiate between those who are looking for moderate growth with relatively stable asset value (conservative) as opposed to those who want maximum growth at the expense of greater volatility, but historically higher returns (aggressive).

On average, and there are no guarantees, a portfolio invested conservatively can generate an annual return of 11 percent; an aggressive portfolio, 14 percent.

But before you can determine which approach matches your investment philosophy, I urge you to consider your current and future needs rather than assume that what you've done in the past is still the best way to go.

For example, if you have always been conservative to a fault or have relied on a single, conservative investment because it is comfortable, you will be hindering your portfolio if you don't start to include the more volatile, but higher-yielding growth and income investments. In other words, when saving for retirement, it is actually risky to avoid risk.

This is your last time to stockpile money while you have the benefit of both annual raises *and* portfolio growth. Once you retire, you have only your investments to depend on for income.

Conversely, if your strategy has been to get rich quick through chasing hot stock tips and speculative investments, perhaps you should consider a more conservative approach—one that balances the risk with a safety net.

So as you review the model portfolios on pages 143 to 150, forget what you've done in the past. Now is the time to consider your current and future needs and circumstances, tax brackets, age and objectives.

NOTE: Specialty investments are those representing a particular segment of the economy, such as utilities, health care, pharmaceuticals, retail, banking, high-tech, etc. Specialties could also include limited partnerships in cable TV or equipment leasing, or any segment of the economy benefiting from unusual upswings.

Tax-free, tax-deferred or taxed to death

As you can see, the wide range of investment products available today allows people to maintain a diversified portfolio that can simultaneously meet different goals. But beyond that, the real trick is to make sure the tax bite isn't ravaging whatever financial gains you have made. You want to be focused on what you're *earning*, not what you're keeping! To overcome that concern, you need to understand the rules of tax-free and tax-deferred investing.

With tax-free vehicles, such as municipal bonds and tax-free mutual funds, the earned interest cannot ever be taxed. With tax-deferred products, such as IRAs, 401ks and tax-deferred annuities, the earned interest is not taxed until you make withdrawals, hopefully when you're in a lower tax bracket (in the past, that meant at retirement, but the latest round of tax proposals could unfortunately put retirees in higher-than-expected tax brackets).

As appealing as tax-free and tax-deferred investments sound, they're not for every investor. In fact, they might actually deliver a *lower* rate of return than a taxable investment—*if you don't do your homework.*

For example, the interest earned on tax-free investments is typically lower than on taxable investments. If you're in a 28-percent or higher tax bracket, however, it's possible that the tax savings will more than offset the lower yield. If you're not in a high tax bracket, it's possible to come out ahead—but not always. Let's say you're in a 15-percent bracket. With some tax-free products, not only will you *not* benefit, you'll be earning a lower yield than with a taxable investment.

That's why you can't consider tax-free investments until you know for certain what tax bracket you're in as well as the *taxable equivalent yield* of the investment you're considering. The first chart following will help you compare the *real* rate of return of tax-free and taxable investments for three different tax brackets. The following charts illustrate how the taxable equivalent yields makes it easier to decide which way to go.

Taxable Equivalent Yields																
IF YOUR NET TAXABLE INCOME IN 1993 IS		YOUR FEDERAL TAX BRACKET IS	*To match a tax free return of:*												
JOINT RETURN	SINGLE RETURN		2.00%	2.50%	3.00%	3.50%	4.00%	4.25%	4.50%	4.75%	5.00%	5.25%	5.50%	5.75%	6.00%
			You would have to earn this much:												
$0 – $36,900	$0 – $22,100	15%	2.3%	2.9%	3.5%	4.1%	4.7%	5.0%	5.2%	5.5%	5.8%	6.1%	6.4%	6.7%	7.0%
$36,901 – $89,150	$22,101 – $53,500	28%	2.7%	3.4%	4.1%	4.8%	5.5%	5.9%	6.3%	6.6%	6.9%	7.2%	7.6%	7.9%	8.3%
$89,151 – $140,000	$53,501 – $115,000	31%	2.9%	3.6%	4.3%	5.0%	5.8%	6.1%	6.5%	6.8%	7.2%	7.6%	7.9%	8.3%	8.7%
$140,001 – $250,000	$115,001 – $250,000	36%	3.1%	3.9%	4.6%	5.4%	6.2%	6.6%	7.0%	7.4%	7.8%	8.2%	8.5%	8.9%	9.3%
$250,001+	$250,001+	39.6%	3.3%	4.1%	4.9%	5.7%	6.6%	7.0%	7.4%	7.8%	8.2%	8.6%	9.1%	9.5%	9.9%

As you can see, often, the higher your federal tax bracket, the greater the value of tax-free investing. And, in most cases, the return is even better if you factor in the savings of state and local taxes (could range from 3 percent to 8 percent) on top of federal taxes. This is particularly true if you are in the 31-percent tax bracket.

As for tax-deferred investments, the key advantage is that you're not only deferring the tax on your principal, but on the growth as it is accruing. There are also favorable tax treatments as this money can be withdrawn with both principal and interest for the life of the investment. Here's an example of how tax-deferred growth accumulates.

Initial investment of $10,000 invested over 10 Years						
Federal tax bracket	Taxable 4% ROR	Tax Deferred 4% ROR	Taxable 6% ROR	Tax Deferred 6% ROR	Taxable 8% ROR	Tax Deferred 8% ROR
31%	$13,129	$14,802	$15,003	$17,908	$17,114	$21,589
28%	$13,283	$14,802	$15,264	$17,908	$17,507	$21,589
15%	$13,970	$14,802	$16,445	$17,908	$19,307	$21,589

NOTE: The tax-deferred growth figures *do not* reflect any income tax paid at distribution. As with any deferred investment, taxes are only paid on the amount withdrawn. To minimize the tax burden, investors should consider strategies that slowly draw the money out.

Initial investment of $10,000 invested over 20 Years						
Federal tax bracket	Taxable 4% ROR	Tax Deferred 4% ROR	Taxable 6% ROR	Tax Deferred 6% ROR	Taxable 8% ROR	Tax Deferred 8% ROR
31%	$17,238	$21,911	$22,509	$32,071	$29,288	$46,610
28%	$17,645	$21,911	$23,300	$32,071	$30,650	$46,610
15%	$19,517	$21,911	$27,043	$32,071	$37,276	$46,610

To show you how the numbers on a tax-deferred investment look after taxes, we'll take someone in a 28-percent tax bracket who invested $10,000 for 10 years, getting an 8-percent rate of return. At investment maturity, the investor withdrew all the money and paid taxes on it, leaving $18,344. Compare that to putting the money in a taxable investment—the investor would have gotten $17,507.

Because of the complexity of calculating real rates of return between taxable, tax-free and tax-deferred investments, it is best to follow the recommendations of your financial planner or advisor.

Good question!

Q. My brother-in-law referred me to an investment advisor, but I think I remember seeing his name in the paper relating to a big lawsuit. How can I check the guy out?
A. Excellent question, and one that's unfortunately not asked enough. The first step is to request the firm's Full Disclosure Document, which outlines its financial philosophy, types of clientele served, payment requirements, potential conflicts of interest and complete backgrounds of the firm's staff. By law, every firm that markets investment products must prepare this document annually. Secondly, confirm that the firm is registered with the SEC (Security and Exchange Commission) and that the firm's representatives are Registered Investment Advisors (stay away if they are not). Finally, if you want to find out if there is pending litigation against the firm, contact your state's security regulators. To get a phone number for the agency in your state that monitors disciplinary action, arbitration proceedings and other problems with investment advisors, call the North American Securities Administrators Association in Washington, D.C., at 202-737-0900.

Q. What should I look for in a money market account?
A. First, don't go crazy looking for the highest return. You shouldn't have so much invested that you feel obligated to watch the account like a hawk. Instead you should be comparing the required minimum deposits and balances, fees and service charges, methods for computing interest and range of services (and limits) such as check-writing and phone transfers. Some funds will only let you write checks for a minimum amount. Others will only allow you to write a certain number of checks in a month. These benefits can be more

important than getting an extra half-percent interest, particularly if you are an active customer. As an extra precaution, watch out for funds that have more than 100-day maturities and/or that show expenses in excess of 1 percent in the prospectus.

Q. How do tax-free money market funds work?
A. They are similar to taxable money market funds except the funds are invested in short-term municipal bonds and notes, which are tax-free. Tax-free money market funds offer lower yields, but it's still possible that after you calculate the taxable equivalent yield, you'll come out ahead.

Q. I'd like to invest in CDs, but I'm concerned about the penalties for early withdrawals. Is there any way to get around the penalties?
A. If there's any chance that you won't be able to let a CD mature, then buy several CDs comprised of small deposits instead of making a single large deposit. That way if you do withdraw early, the penalty may only be against one account. The bite won't hurt as bad as if it were against the entire investment.

Q. What is a stair-step or a yield spread?
A. This is a way to buy several small CDs at the same time, but buying them at different maturities—for example, with some six-month maturities and others at one-year terms. This is called *taking a stair-step*, or a *yield spread* with your maturities. The idea is to have different CDs coming due at different times so you've always got money to reinvest should market conditions change. That way, if you get locked into a low

yield and rates suddenly soar, only part of your investment will have to wait it out.

Q. I'd like to invest more of our portfolio in stocks, but want to reduce our risks. What's the best way?
A. The key to playing the stock market and still sleeping like a baby is to spread the risk. Again, it's the old story of diversification. The more stocks you can buy spanning different industries, the less vulnerable you are to the economic conditions that affect a particular business. The other key is to steer clear of the high rollers and head toward the conservative issues such as blue chips, high dividend stocks and utilities. That's why the best possible stocks are those that are already paying a decent dividend but also have growth potential. That way, there's dual opportunity: income plus growth.

Q. I've heard about dollar-cost averaging. How does it work?
A. Dollar-cost averaging is an excellent strategy when investing in stocks. Basically, you establish times to purchase shares at set intervals over a long period of time, regardless of what the market is doing. This way, you're taking advantage of the high-low fluctuations. Overall, this lowers your risk while allowing you to benefit from the most optimal trading periods.

Q. Which stocks have the greatest potential for income to offset inflation?
A. Ask your broker to search for issues that have paid dividends for at least 25 years, posted increases in seven out of the past 12 years and raised dividends

at least five of those years. That should lead you to stocks you can live with and love.

Q. What is an example of a high-dividend paying stock?
A. Utility stocks are an excellent example. They're terrific, no matter what the rest of the market is doing, because we can't exist without phones and electric services. The best way to buy is to select utilities that are geographically diverse (not all in the Southwest, for example). Then if there are any adverse climactic or business conditions in a region one year, your portfolio will be well-balanced.

Q. Is there any way to really know if you're picking a winning stock?
A. It certainly helps to be well-read on the company and the industry, but beyond that, there are no guarantees. That's why you can't go into the stock market betting on the success of one stock. The most intelligent way to be in the market is to spread the risk over many companies and industries, which is the reason that mutual funds are so effective.

Q. Why are mutual funds so advantageous to retirees?
A. How would you rather spend your retirement? Pouring drinks for friends or poring over the stock tables worrying that you're up two points here, down a point there, etc.? If you don't want the daily burden of monitoring your stock portfolio, but you want stocks for growth, then mutual funds are the ideal vehicle. In addition, one of the biggest benefits of investing in mutual funds is the reassurance that there are scores of seasoned pros keeping a constant watch

on market fluctuations, trends and other indicators. That's why it's safe to say there's a better chance for growth than if you were making all the decisions yourself, most likely in a vacuum and without the benefit of current research and data. At the same time, with so many investors in the fold, the blow is softened in the event the market sours.

Q. We're confused by all the different kinds of mutual funds. What's best for a retiree?
A. Today, it does seem that mutual funds are competing with Baskin-Robbins for variety. But in the long run, investors benefit from the amount of choices. For example, balanced funds invest in common stocks, and corporate bonds and are designed for investors who want income and appreciation with minimal risk. Aggressive-growth funds attempt to generate the maximum capital gains, but have virtually no interest in dividends because the objective is long-term growth, not income. The key is to understand the fund's overall strategy and to determine if it matches your investment objectives.

Q. How important is past performance in evaluating a mutual fund?
A. One of the best ways to evaluate a mutual fund is to consider its performance in both up and down markets, its one-, three-, five- and 10-year performance record and its rating by the respected services that track mutual funds. However, it is also important to know if the people who were responsible for the good track records are still managing the fund. Otherwise it could be a whole new ballgame, giving new meaning to the old saying, "What have you done for me lately?"

Q. How liquid are mutual funds?
A. You can redeem shares by picking up the phone and requesting a wire transfer or you can write a check from your account directly. Some funds allow you to set up a *systematic withdrawal plan* where you designate how much you'll receive from the fund every month.

Q. What are fund families?
A. It's when you own shares in a variety of funds managed by the same fund group. When market fluctuations occur, or when your needs change, you can switch funds from one account to another or into different funds that more closely match your investment goals at the time.

Q. What is an all-weather fund approach?
A. It is investing in a group of mutual funds that have a track record of weathering the storm in both up and down markets. However, because the funds are more resilient than others, they're not always the best performers in an up market. Still, after a down market, they're holding their own.

Q. If I purchased a bond several years after its issue at a different price and the yield is not locked in, is there any way to calculate the rate of return?
A. Ask your broker for the bond's yield to maturity (YTM), a chart that indicates precisely what your final return will be, regardless of when you bought and how much you paid.

Q. What are the downsides of investing in corporate bonds?
A. Technically, companies can default on the bonds—the big concern with junk bonds in the 1980s. In reality, if you invest in high-grade bonds, the risk is minimal. What can't be guaranteed, however, is the effect of fluctuating interest rates. When interest rates go up, you'll miss out on the "raise" unless you buy new bonds at the higher rate. Also, if you've got a locked-in rate of 8 percent and now the bonds are paying 10 percent, if you sell before the bond matures, you'll have to let it go at a discount. Of course, you could also get lucky and interest rates could drop so the bond is worth more and can be sold for over the par value.

Q. What are bond calls?
A. Bond calls are like when the cowboys rustle in the cattle earlier than expected. In other words, the bond issuers have the right to retire their bonds prior to the supposed maturity date, forcing investors to surrender them. This usually happens after a period of high interest rates. Once interest rates drop, it's better for the company to issue new bonds at the lower rate. However, the investor has rights. If a bond has a call feature, terms are stipulated so there are no surprises. You'll know when the bond can be called and what the call penalty will be. That means the bond issuer may have to pay a year's interest for disrupting your investment plan.

Q. What kind of municipal bonds are good for retirees?
A. The safest issues are the ones that are general obligation bonds, A-rated or better. These are the bonds that underwrite essential services and have the total and certain backing of the issuer. Bonds that are insured are also safe bets and are generally AAA-rated. Incidentally, 1992 was a record year for

muni bonds, with approximately $233 billion worth of bonds issued and purchased. That beats the 1985 record by about $30 billion. Low interest rates and President Clinton's election contributed to the renewed interest in these bonds.

Q. How do you buy muni bonds?
A. There are three ways: You can invest in an individual bond. Or you can invest through mutual funds. Finally, you can invest in a unit trust, which invests in a group of bonds that are professionally selected. One advantage of unit trusts or funds is that they can be purchased with insurance against default.

Q. Should I buy municipal bonds if I'm not sure I'll be able to hold on until they mature?
A. It is important to know that muni bonds are bought and sold on the open market and do fluctuate in value. Therefore, it's best to plan to hold on until the bonds mature. Otherwise you could end up selling when the market is experiencing some short-term losses. To reap the greatest return, you have to hang on for the full cycle or sell for a premium over market value. Or, create a yield spread similar to that used with CDs.

Q. Are Ginnie Maes still a good investment for retirees?
A. They used to be much more attractive when interest rates were high. But now that interest rates are at their lowest in years, homeowners have been running to the banks in droves to refinance and/or pay off their mortgages early. This has resulted in the Ginnie Mae bonds maturing too soon, forcing investors to take their money elsewhere or reinvest in Ginnie Maes offering a lower rate of return. However, the yield spread between mortgage rates and other investments can still be advantageous in a diversified portfolio constructed to generate income.

Q. What are the biggest differences between REITs and RELPs?
A. The up-front investment for a REIT, of $2,000 to $3,000, is less than you need for a RELP. Also with a REIT, your money is liquid because it's traded on the open market. In the past several years—with the recession, bank failures and a sluggish real estate market—RELPs have been out of favor. However, sometimes this type of environment represents the best opportunity for investors because they can buy in at lower-than-normal prices, with the potential for a strong turnaround in the future. Many REITs and real estate mutual funds have shown signs of strong recovery in the second half of 1992 and early 1993.

What I tell my clients

When is a good time to invest in stocks? *Pick a day.* Half the people who ask this question are convinced that there are certain times of year when everyone in the know secretly goes in and makes a killing. The other half thinks that whenever they invest, the market is automatically jinxed and prices will drop like the New Year's Eve ball in Times Square. Both are wrong. The only secret to succeeding in the stock market is getting in and staying in. Here's an informative chart from the University of Michigan illustrating the annual returns of those who came in and out of the market during a 1,276-day trading period compared to those who stayed in for the duration.

Period of Investment	S&P Annualized Return
Full 1,276 trading days	26.3%
Less the 10 biggest gain days	18.3%
Less the 20 biggest gain days	13.1%
Less the 30 biggest gain days	8.5%
Less the 40 biggest gain days	4.3%

Basically, this shows that because it is impossible to guess *when* the biggest trading gains will be made, you have to ride the short-term market fluctuations and be in for the long haul. Or as one client observed, "If you play the market only when the stocks are hot, you're already too late."

When it comes to your interest income, timing is everything. Over the years I have seen numerous instances of retirees withdrawing more interest income than they need to live on. Some fear that if they don't take the money, it will somehow dissipate. In other cases, people feel that living the good life means not worrying about every last dollar. Either way, they end up spending the money *and* paying higher taxes too boot, all of which erodes their retirement nest egg at a much faster pace than they realize.

When I see this, I recommend investing in annuities (variable or tax-deferred) because the internal growth in the annuity is not taxed until the income is withdrawn, thereby delaying income that could possibly push them into a higher tax bracket. For example, if you needed $30,000 to live on a year, but your investments were paying you $40,000 a year, you'd not only pay a higher rate of income tax, you'd also pay

taxes on Social Security benefits because you were over the $32,000 cap. Basically, the rule of thumb is take what you need to live a comfortable lifestyle and be cautious what you take over and above that.

Be leery of the OTOs (one time only). Nothing is more frustrating than thinking you've found the best way to evaluate mutual funds only to discover you don't have the whole story. For example, it's very common for a fund to claim to be number-one and have the numbers to back it up. This is impressive until you learn that it was only for a short time and that the long-term performance was nowhere near as promising. Conversely, sometimes the most favorable funds have down years because their investment style was temporarily overshadowed by a fund that featured flash-in-the-pan stocks.

When you compare the two funds, the one with the tried-and-true approach will have the best track record. Ditto for the funds that get beat up in a bear market or a crash. Their performance over the long haul is generally unparalleled. So the best way to see a mutual fund for what it is, is to find out which returns were a blip on the screen and which ones showed up consistently.

To load or not to load—*that* is the question. The eternal advice about getting what you pay for is very true when it comes to no-load mutual funds. Sure, you can save up to the 8.5 percent commission if you buy no-loads, but it means that your investment decisions are yours alone and that you'd better have the time and the skill to pick the winners. If you guess wrong, the sales commission you *didn't* pay is going to seem like a bargain by comparison. Something else to be aware of: A lot of funds don't charge an up-front commission, but get you in the end with either an annual marketing and distribution fee called a 12b-1 or a back-end commission when you sell. It's like watching an old gangster flick. "If you want out, you gotta pay us 5 percent." That's why it's often better to pay the commission up-front, get the best available selection and not have to worry that you didn't read between the lines.

FDIC-insured mutual funds? *NOT!* Today, it seems everyone is selling mutual funds, including the banks. At present, they market both funds they oversee directly as well as funds run by independent sources. Their appeal is that many customers assume that the funds are FDIC-insured or backed, just like bank CDs and money market accounts. But they're not, so let the buyer beware.

How to give yourself a raise after you retire. Annual pay raises are always cause for celebration and retirees often tell me how much they miss those pats on the back. What's worse, when there's no boss to hand out raises, retirees have to do the honors themselves—or inflation and taxes can put a crack in their nest egg on par with the San Andreas fault. In other words, once you're no longer working, the only way to get a raise is if your investments are growing at a rate that surpasses the inflation rate. But by how much? Ideally, you want your investments to yield at least 2 percent after taxes and inflation. For example, if inflation rose by 3 percent as in 1992, the real rate of return on your investments had to be 5.9 percent (15-percent tax bracket) or 6.9 percent (28-percent tax bracket).

The bottom line

From my many years of experience working with retirees, I know that their single biggest fear is running out of money. They are deeply concerned about illness, loss of dignity, loneliness, death and other emotionally charged issues, too. But this is nothing compared to the anxiety of becoming dependent on family, friends or the government for financial survival.

With the proper amount of planning, investing and budgeting, this fear can be eased. The key is knowing what are your potential sources of income and making certain that your money is safely invested in products that are primed for growth.

Ultimately, your only job in retirement should be to send your money out to work so you don't have to.

Model portfolio

Age: 40s-50s
Conservative

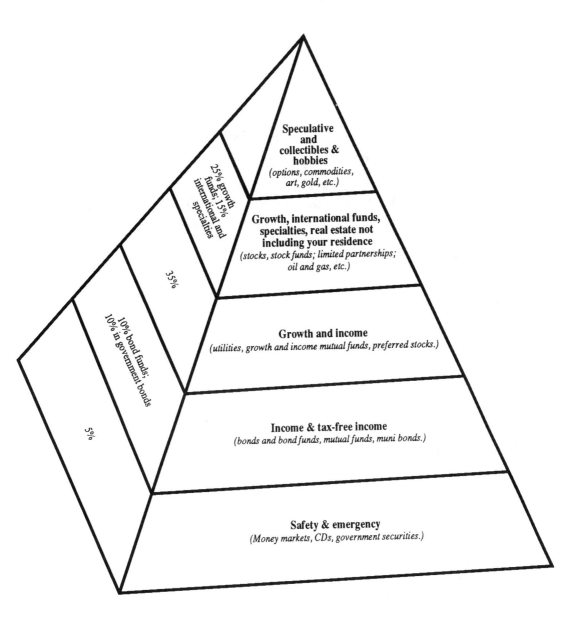

Speculative
and
collectibles &
hobbies
*(options, commodities,
art, gold, etc.)*

25% growth
funds; 15%
international and
specialties

**Growth, international funds,
specialties, real estate not
including your residence**
*(stocks, stock funds; limited partnerships;
oil and gas, etc.)*

35%

10% bond funds;
10% in government bonds

Growth and income
(utilities, growth and income mutual funds, preferred stocks.)

5%

Income & tax-free income
(bonds and bond funds, mutual funds, muni bonds.)

Safety & emergency
(Money markets, CDs, government securities.)

NOTE: Bonds can either be taxable or tax-free depending on your tax bracket.

Retirement Ready or Not

Model portfolio

Age: 40s-50s
Aggressive

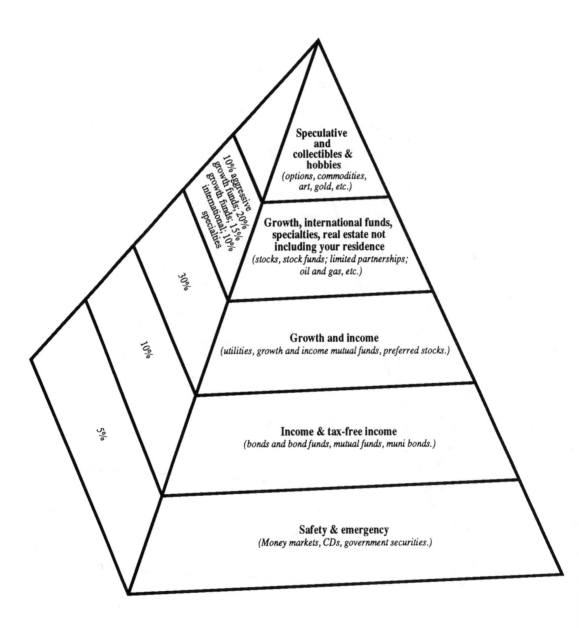

NOTE: Bonds can either be taxable or tax-free depending on your tax bracket.

Model portfolio

Age: 50s
Conservative

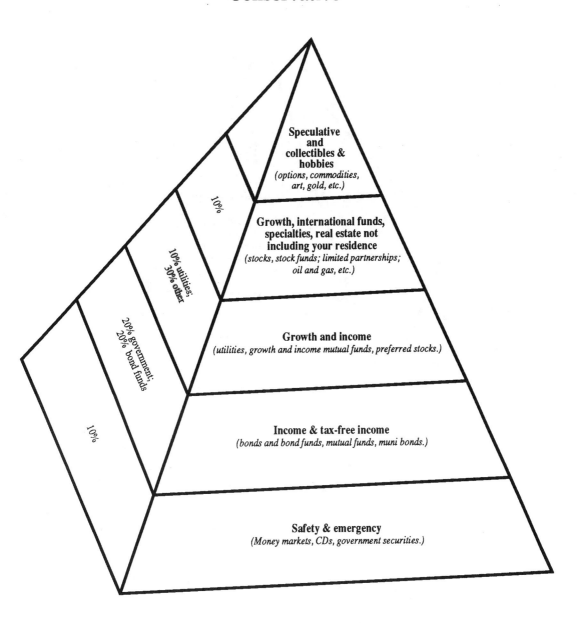

**Speculative
and
collectibles &
hobbies**
*(options, commodities,
art, gold, etc.)*

**Growth, international funds,
specialties, real estate not
including your residence**
*(stocks, stock funds; limited partnerships;
oil and gas, etc.)*

Growth and income
(utilities, growth and income mutual funds, preferred stocks.)

Income & tax-free income
(bonds and bond funds, mutual funds, muni bonds.)

Safety & emergency
(Money markets, CDs, government securities.)

10%

*10% utilities;
30% other*

*20% government;
20% bond funds*

10%

NOTE: Bonds can either be taxable or tax-free depending on your tax bracket.

Model portfolio

Age: 50s
Aggressive

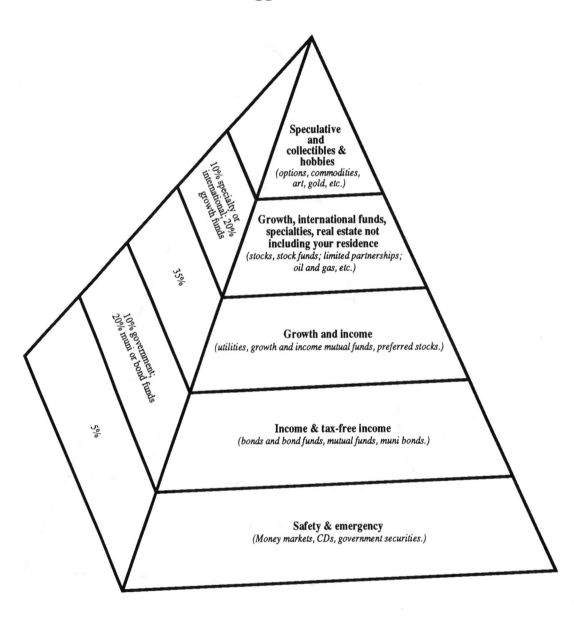

Speculative and collectibles & hobbies
(*options, commodities, art, gold, etc.*)

Growth, international funds, specialties, real estate not including your residence
(*stocks, stock funds; limited partnerships; oil and gas, etc.*)

Growth and income
(*utilities, growth and income mutual funds, preferred stocks.*)

Income & tax-free income
(*bonds and bond funds, mutual funds, muni bonds.*)

Safety & emergency
(*Money markets, CDs, government securities.*)

10% specialty or international; 20% growth funds

35%

10% government; 20% muni or bond funds

5%

NOTE: Bonds can either be taxable or tax-free depending on your tax bracket.

Model portfolio

Age: 60s
Conservative

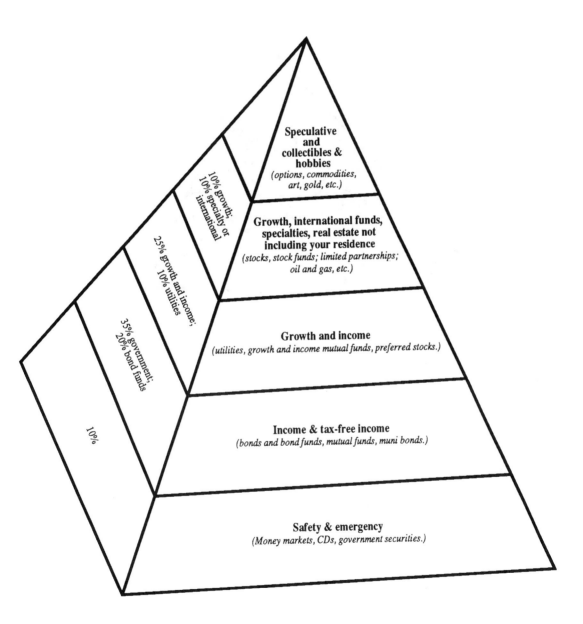

Speculative and collectibles & hobbies
(options, commodities, art, gold, etc.)

Growth, international funds, specialties, real estate not including your residence
(stocks, stock funds; limited partnerships; oil and gas, etc.)

Growth and income
(utilities, growth and income mutual funds, preferred stocks.)

Income & tax-free income
(bonds and bond funds, mutual funds, muni bonds.)

Safety & emergency
(Money markets, CDs, government securities.)

10% growth; 10% specialty or international

25% growth and income; 10% utilities

35% government; 20% bond funds

10%

NOTE: Bonds can either be taxable or tax-free depending on your tax bracket.

Retirement Ready or Not

Model portfolio

Age: 60s
Aggressive

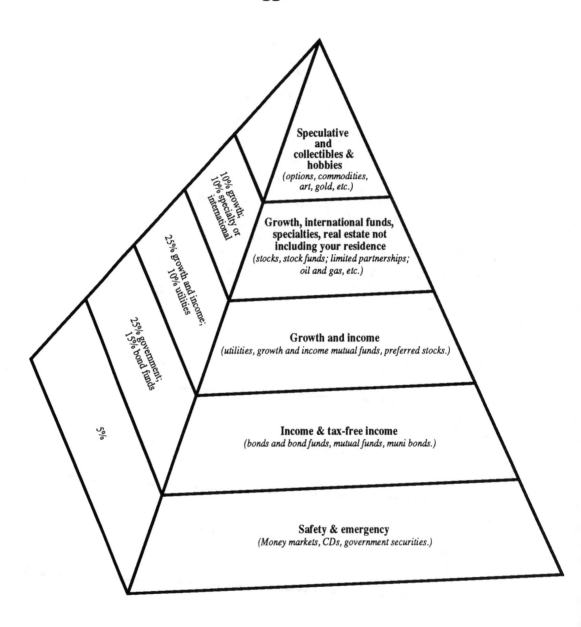

Speculative and collectibles & hobbies
(options, commodities, art, gold, etc.)

Growth, international funds, specialties, real estate not including your residence
(stocks, stock funds; limited partnerships; oil and gas, etc.)

Growth and income
(utilities, growth and income mutual funds, preferred stocks.)

Income & tax-free income
(bonds and bond funds, mutual funds, muni bonds.)

Safety & emergency
(Money markets, CDs, government securities.)

10% growth; 10% specialty or international

25% growth and income; 10% utilities

25% government; 15% bond funds

5%

NOTE: Bonds can either be taxable or tax-free depending on your tax bracket.

Model portfolio

Age: 70s
Conservative

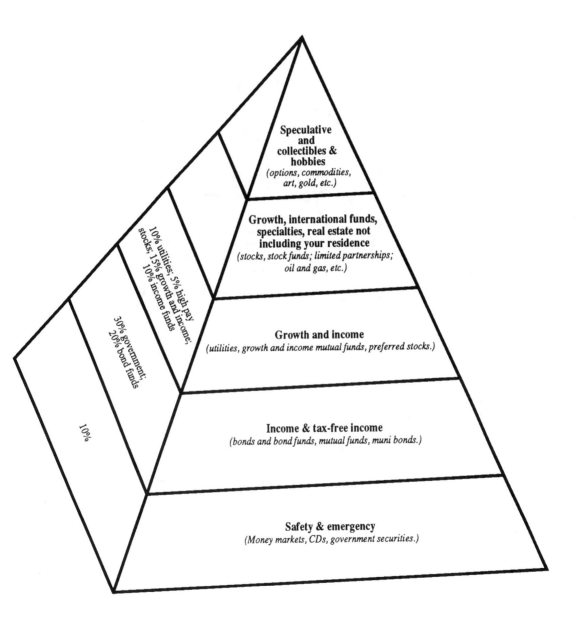

Speculative
and
collectibles &
hobbies
(options, commodities, art, gold, etc.)

Growth, international funds,
specialties, real estate not
including your residence
(stocks, stock funds; limited partnerships; oil and gas, etc.)

Growth and income
(utilities, growth and income mutual funds, preferred stocks.)

Income & tax-free income
(bonds and bond funds, mutual funds, muni bonds.)

Safety & emergency
(Money markets, CDs, government securities.)

10% utilities; 5% high pay stocks; 15% growth and income; 10% income funds

30% government; 20% bond funds

10%

NOTE: Bonds can either be taxable or tax-free depending on your tax bracket.

Retirement Ready or Not

Model portfolio

Age: 70s
Aggressive

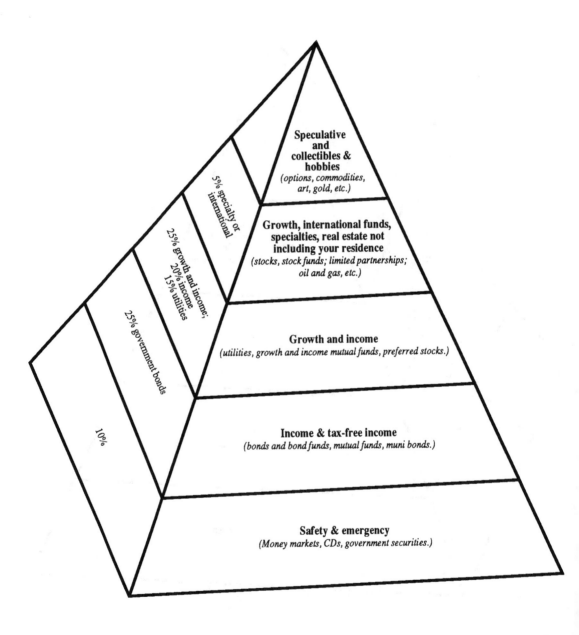

NOTE: Bonds can either be taxable or tax-free depending on your tax bracket.

6

Living on your assets: "Know when to hold, know when to fold"

Every time I see those diet ads with the "before" and "after" pictures, I think about some of my clients who have retired. It's not that they are fat. But they have compared their adjustment to retirement to trying to overcome a serious weight problem. It's a tough challenge, requiring courage, determination and the gift of time.

Take the case of Jack and Doreen. A year before they retired, they sounded like two kids in the back seat of the car. "Are we there yet," they constantly asked? They were so excited about retiring, it never dawned on them that there would be a downside.

"We had it all planned," recalled Doreen. "We were moving into a gorgeous development in Delray Beach, Florida, with close friends. The guys were old golfing buddies and Iris and I were an unbeatable doubles team. I guess we assumed we'd be so busy shopping, spending time at the club and getting settled, what could go wrong?"

Plenty! For one thing, Jack never expected that he would miss working. Nor did he anticipate how difficult it would be to manage their finances. "I thought everything was supposed to be simpler when we retired. But I never knew what checks were coming when, and everything cost so damn much. A week of eating out and entertaining doesn't come cheap." Not surprisingly, Jack became restless, irritable, and was often sidelined by lower back pain.

Doreen, on the other hand, was lonesome for her grandchildren, somewhat bored, but, worst of all, ready to send Jack packing. Close was nice, but who needed him to tag along to the supermarket or supervise meals? "I married you for better or for worse but not for lunch," she screamed.

Could this retirement be saved? Absolutely. All it needed was some fine-tuning, a little arguing and a lot of compromising. Today, Jack and Doreen have worked out a daily routine they both enjoy. Most days include the three "tions:" recreation (golf or tennis), socialization (evenings with friends) and education (every semester they enroll in interesting courses at a local college). And to keep the peace, the only time Jack can come within 10 feet of the kitchen is if *he's* doing the cooking.

As for managing their money, I offered them two simple ideas for keeping track of their income and expenses (you'll find them on pages 153 and 154). Once they felt as though they were in control again, things turned around. "The key," Jack told me, "is having enough money to live on, but not enough to worry about." Until you get comfortable with the amount of money coming in and the amount going out, you should expect a bumpy transition period.

You see, there are really two problems at the onset of retirement. The first is that it means the end of those reliable pay periods. Instead, your income will consist of "paychecks" from a variety of sources, which arrive at a variety of times. For example, Social Security usually arrives on the third of the month, but that may only be a small percentage of your monthly "salary."

You'll probably be counting more on your investment income. Unfortunately, there is no such thing as a pay day for stocks. When a dividend comes due, you get a check. Will it come in again next quarter? Who knows? As for pensions and IRA distributions, rental income, part-time work or consulting, etc., they can be expected with more regularity, but are not necessarily a guaranteed source of income as with Social Security or an annuity.

The second problem is that as soon as you retire, it's as if a buzzer sounds

and a game called, "How to live on your assets" begins. You've got to be resourceful and make all the right moves to preserve your nest egg, because there is no longer a way to replenish it, unless you go back to work. (For the record, 25 percent of all retirees do return to either a part-time or full-time job.)

These problems set off a whole chain reaction of both emotional and financial quandaries, the most common of which is becoming obsessed about expenses. Newly retired people often go into shock over the cost of everything from meat to mortgages. For instance, I'll get a call from a client who will scream, "Do you have idea what my water bill was last month? $83! Can you believe it?" Sure. But it so happens that they paid $83 before they retired, it just didn't hurt as much. What's happening is that when people don't know how much money they'll have to live on, they get nervous about being caught short. It's why one client proudly announced, "I know I'm doing good when the money and the month run out at the same time."

That's too much like Russian Roulette for most of us, which is why this chapter is so important. It offers a variety of ideas to help you live comfortably on your assets, right from the start of your retirement. First, I'll share my easy two-step plan, which will help you keep track of your income and expenses. Next, we'll examine and discuss an excellent strategy for living on your assets while they are still growing. Finally, we'll take a look at your potential tax burden, because nothing poses a greater threat to your continued financial well-being than your annual tax bills. There are many legal ways to play "keep away" before and after you retire.

How to keep track of your income at retirement

If you recall in the last chapter, we talked about creating an investment pyramid for your wealth-building years. The idea was to structure your portfolio so that the risks and rewards were completely balanced from top to bottom. The soundest, safest investments supported the base, while those that could potentially reap the greatest return, but also posed the highest risk, were positioned at the top.

Once you retire, whatever is in that portfolio is what you will have to learn to live on. So a logical question is, how do you know if you should liquidate certain investments so you have adequate income? As Kenny Rogers sings in one of my favorite songs, "You got to know when to hold 'em, know when to fold 'em." I believe the best way to determine what to keep and what to sell is to turn your investment pyramid upside-down. This automatically creates what I call a *funnel force*.

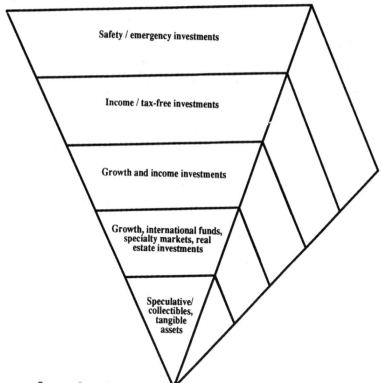

Safety / emergency investments

Income / tax-free investments

Growth and income investments

Growth, international funds, specialty markets, real estate investments

Speculative/ collectibles, tangible assets

As you can see from the diagram, with a funnel force, your riskiest investments are now at the bottom of the funnel and will be the first to be liquidated, if necessary. Your principal investments, those that are safest, are at the top and the ones that will be preserved the longest.

One reason it helps to think of your investments this way is that funnels allow you to control the flow of something. In this case, you'll be able to control the flow of funds by opening and closing the valve as needed. Ultimately you'll be able to regulate the rate at which your investments are sold off.

What happens to the funds that come through the funnel? They should all get poured into a *master account*, which will allow you to monitor all of your income in the most efficient manner possible.

Keep track of your income, expenses at retirement

The master account is a very simple idea, and one that helps you keep track of your income and expenses, regardless of how little or how much money comes in and out every month. To get started, you need to open up an interest-bearing checking account. Here is where you will

deposit every single check you receive, whether it's from Social Security, tenants, pensions, CDs, annuities or the state lottery.

Think of this account as the "Ellis Island" for your money. Nothing can get through the gates (dispersed) until it's been signed in and admitted through the system. After it sits in the master account, you can funnel money into a separate checking account that you use to pay bills, or you can dump the surplus into a savings account or when there's enough left over, to invest.

To illustrate how the master account works, the diagram below provides an example.

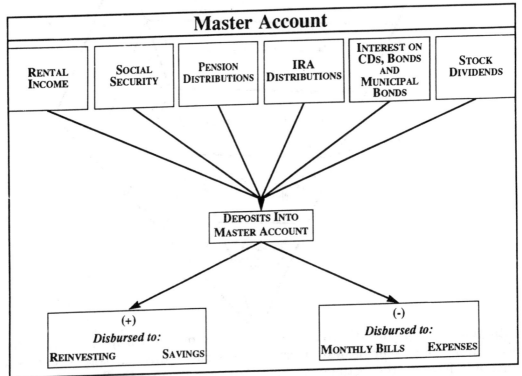

Master account

The master account assures that you will always know the total amount of income earned each month as well as

how much is available to pay expenses. In addition, because some deposits will be small, here is a way to pool your resources so that you always have a lump sum large enough to pay bills, invest or save. Otherwise, your income will be so scattered, it will result in mass confusion and the inability to take care of certain large obligations.

The other important benefit is that you'll receive a monthly statement that will offer you a painless reading of your financial well-being. I call this review the "One-Minute Check-Up on Your Financial Health." Basically, with all of your deposits and withdrawals listed in one place, you'll know immediately how much of a surplus you have, or, conversely, if your withdrawals are in excess of your deposits. In that case, it becomes your "damage control" statement—your warning to reexamine your budget and cut back to the bare necessities. At a minimum, you want to be at a break-even point each month.

The best investments that let you take a paycheck

As we've discussed, one of the hardest adjustments to make at retirement is living without a regular paycheck. For 40 years, you counted on bringing home a set amount every few weeks, and looked forward to annual raises. For many people, the sudden loss of a paycheck results in the sudden loss of confidence and self-esteem.

Fortunately, there is a way for retirees to replace their paychecks through mutual funds and IRAs. The first strategy is called systematic withdrawals, and it is the investment you set up with a mutual fund company to pay yourself. But this time, you are the boss. You can decide how much you want to earn, how often you want to be paid and the exact dates you want your shares redeemed and sent to you.

Systematic withdrawals from mutual funds

Here's how systematic withdrawals work. You make either a lump sum contribution into a mutual fund account (perhaps the rollover from your pension distribution), or open an account as many years in advance of retirement as possible. Either way, left untouched, the investment will grow at a steady rate. When ready to start withdrawing, you'll determine how much and how often you can afford to be paid, and the mutual fund will redeem the appropriate number of shares and pay you accordingly.

It's simple. And yet the real beauty of a mutual fund is not just the growth, but the ability to receive income every month without jeopardizing the current value *or* the appreciation of the account. The reason this plan is so effective for retirees is because regardless of what the market is doing, the dividends generally rise to the occasion. Furthermore, they pay out in today's dollars, which helps combat inflation, and they are a steady, predictable source of income. Even better, you'll be amazed when you see what kind of income!

Let's say you made a lump-sum investment of $100,000 in a conservative, balanced mutual fund in December 1982. Starting in December 1983, you withdrew $12,000 a year ($1,000 a month). By December 1992, you would have withdrawn a total of $120,000 ($20,000 more than you invested) and even with that, your share values would still be worth $119,417 and growing! And you never invested another dime. You simply reinvested the income and the capital gains of the original contribution, which yielded an annualized rate of return of 13.8 percent (an annualized rate takes the total increase in value and divides by the number of years invested).

NOTE: The rate of return is a net figure, reflecting the mutual fund's expenses and sales costs. Here's how it looked on a year-to-year basis.

Even the most sophisticated investors get giddy with excitement when they receive their account statements. They can't believe that one investment can grow at such a rapid rate even while they're withdrawing money.

Balanced mutual fund
Set up for systematic withdrawals

1. Original investment: $100,000
2. Annualized rate of return: 13.8%
3. Load fee (expenses/sales costs) on $100,000: 5.75%
4. Income and capital gains reinvested
5. Starting shares-12/83: 9,444. Shares as of 12/92: 8,729
6. Effect of income taxes not reflected

Date	Withdrawal	Amount reinvested (Income/cap gains)	Market value of account
12/83	$12,000	$10,626	$ 97,848
12/84	$12,000	$10,855	$ 98,648
12/85	$12,000	$15,180	$112,382
12/86	$12,000	$13,809	$116,913
12/87	$12,000	$14,040	$106,546
12/88	$12,000	$ 7,648	$109,766
12/89	$12,000	$11,518	$121,868
12/90	$12,000	$ 8,707	$105,947
12/91	$12,000	$ 8,294	$117,928
12/92	$12,000	$ 9,137	$119,417
TOTAL	**$120,000**	**$109,815**	**$119,417**

Mind you, this particular example reflects the performance of a conservative fund. Investors who were in many of the aggressive growth funds benefited from much higher rates of return, ranging from accounts valued at $140,000 to $200,000 over the same 10-year period. However, when selecting a fund, you first have to determine your risk tolerance. If being in an aggressive fund would make your blood pressure rise, then it's not worth it.

But regardless of which type of fund you choose, the most important thing to consider is that, either way, mutual funds outperform just about every other investment for growth and income. For example, if you compared the return of Treasury bonds or notes to mutual funds over this same 10-year period, the difference is astounding. Let's take a look at the chart on the next page.

10- Year Performance		
	Balanced mutual fund (Conservative)	Treasury bond or note
Original investment	$100,000	$100,000
Annualized return	13.8%	7.8%
10% annual withdrawal	$12,000	$7,800
Total withdrawal after 10 years	$120,000	$78,000
Value of account after 10 years	$119,417	$100,000
Total gain (total with. + value of account	$239,417	$178,000
Difference in value	**$61,147**	

I know you'll agree this is a pretty remarkable difference for the same $100,000 investment. Again, the exciting thing about systematic withdrawals is that over time, because of the historically high rate of return, investors have been able to withdraw a fixed amount every year without affecting the principal. And even when the number of shares has declined since the withdrawals began, because of the natural market fluctuations, the dollar value of the account more than holds its own because of the high rate of return. This is one investment that promises safety, income and growth. It's the ultimate win-win situation for retirees.

Dollar-cost averaging

Another way to establish a systematic withdrawal program is to invest in a mutual fund on a regular basis *prior* to retirement. This allows you to take advantage of the natural market fluctuations over a longer period of time, thereby purchasing a greater number of shares when the prices are low, and fewer shares when the prices are high. This means that the *average* cost per share will be lower than the actual value of the shares. Now while dollar-cost averaging does not guarantee profits, it certainly does increase the odds in your favor for higher returns because there are more years for the fund to perform.

Here is an example of how an account looked as $1,000 contributions were being made every month over a 10-year period *prior* to retirement. The chart that follows shows what happened to the same account once withdrawals started *after* retirement.

After investing a total of $120,000 over 10 years, the mutual fund account now had a value of $149,241—almost a $30,000 gain. Then starting in 1980, the investor started taking systematic withdrawals so he'd receive an annual paycheck of 10 percent of each year's ending balance. And even though he no longer made any contributions to the account after 1979, the portfolio continued to grow. By 1991, he had received paychecks totaling $313,312—all from an original $120,000 investment.

Pre-retirement savings		
Date	Cumulative Investment	Total Value
12/31/70	$12,000	$12,178
12/31/71	$24,000	$25,973
12/31/72	$36,000	$41,454
12/31/73	$48,000	$41,824
12/31/74	$60,000	$36,971
12/31/75	$72,000	$59,719
12/31/76	$84,000	$82,546
12/31/77	$96,000	$87,943
12/31/78	$108,000	$103,944
12/31/79	$120,000	$149,241

Again, the reason a mutual fund set up for systematic withdrawals is such a remarkable investment strategy for retirees is that it gives them the opportunity to make an investment of a certain amount—$120,000 in this example—receive a paycheck that should provide for a raise every year to fight increased taxes and inflation (this investor got a raise from $14,924 a year to $30,155 a year in just 10 years)—and still leave you with an investment that is continuing to grow and provide income.

The only downside is that the capital gains on the growth are taxable. But, remember, our priority was to devise a way to replace your paycheck, and to give you the added security of consistent pay periods.

Drawing down on your IRA account to get a paycheck

To avoid paying taxes on an investment while it is in its growing stages, the best strategy for retirees is to put money into an IRA account (discussed in detail in Chapter 4). But most of the questions I get about IRAs, understandably, are about withdrawing the funds at retirement without letting taxes dilute the value.

Of all the investments people make, the ones they seem most anxious to tap into at retirement are their IRAs. Perhaps because they've watched the accounts grow for so long, or maybe because they've been "forbidden fruit" all these years, they feel they should be able to tap into these funds. The problem is, your IRA is one investment

Systematic withdrawals at retirement		
Date	Annual withdrawal	Year-end value of account (Avg. annual return of 17.32%)
12/31/80	$14,924	$186,152
12/31/81	$18,615	$178,590
12/31/82	$17,859	$219,560
12/31/83	$21,956	$263,597
12/31/84	$26,360	$257,953
12/31/85	$25,795	$308,085
12/31/86	$30,809	$328,953
12/31/87	$32,895	$291,345
12/31/88	$29,135	$298,333
12/31/89	$29,833	$349,757
12/31/90	$34,976	$301,550
12/31/91	$30,155	$364,165
TOTALS	$313,312	$364,165

that gets an opportunity to grow at a substantial rate, without being impeded by taxes. When properly invested, it offers a solid hedge against inflation. Therefore, it is the one investment that is most advantageous to postpone withdrawing from until absolutely necessary. I urge my clients to resist the temptation and let the money sit as long as possible, or until the mandatory age 70½.

The exception to this is if you are in a low (15 percent) tax bracket. In this case, the reverse strategy is better. You should start to draw down on the account starting any time after age 59½ (the first age you can withdraw without paying a 10-percent penalty over and above the income tax). However, we're still not talking about touching the principal—only the dividends. The longer you postpone your withdrawals, the greater the risk that your tax rate will increase over time. In addition, when you are already in a low tax bracket, you don't want to accumulate so much income that it not only raises your bracket, but triggers a tax on your Social Security benefits.

Now if you find that you do need your IRA income prior to age 70½, and you are in a high tax bracket, remember that there is no minimum requirement for withdrawals—you can take what you need. Ideally, you never want to withdraw any more than the income being earned on the assets in a given year. Again, the reason you are in an IRA is for the potential growth without the taxes, and the more you withdraw, the more you dilute the benefits of the IRA.

When the tax man cometh

Any retiree will tell you it is a big weight off your shoulders to finally get a handle on how much money you have coming in every month from Social Security, investments, pension distributions, etc. Even if the amount is less than expected, it is still better *knowing* than being in limbo. Unfortunately, determining your annual earnings is only half the battle. The other great mystery that needs to be solved is, "What will I owe in taxes?"

I believe that most Americans are honest taxpayers who would rather give than deceive. But I also know that in the U.S., the four most dreaded words in the English language are "Congress is in session." That's because every time they meet, the end result seems to be a tax hike on something. Gasoline. Cigarettes. Diamonds. You name it.

It's no better at the state and city level. These taxes have gone up 6.84 percent a year for the past 10 (1982-1992), rising 11 percent faster than federal taxes. All told, according to the Tax Foundation, a Washington, D.C.-based research group, today the average household is forking over 40 percent of its income to pay the feds, state and city.

It's enough to make anyone scream, but the ones who would be most justified in leading a revolt are older Americans. As of this writing, the Clinton administration is going to attempt to raise $275 billion over the next five years to reduce the budget deficit. Supposedly, the lion's share will come out of the wealthy man's pocket (the balance from a transportation fuel tax). But everyone knows that the most vulnerable group is the retired middle class. For the most part, they don't have enough assets to

shelter their income, they have great difficulty reentering the job market if they need to increase their earnings, and, at the same time, Congress is eliminating exemptions and deductions faster than you can say, "It's the economy, stupid." In addition, declining interest rates, CDs and other poor performing investments are eroding their nest eggs faster than a speeding bullet. In the last three years alone, retirees investing in CDs have taken a 70-percent cut in pay!

But the problem is further exacerbated by the fact that the latest round of tax proposals has a gun pointed at Medicare and Social Security. Both the Senate and the House bills want to remove the limit on the $135,000 of annual income subject to the Medicare tax. And both want retired couples with incomes exceeding the $32,000 to $40,000 range to pay taxes on up to 85 percent of their benefits (as opposed to the 50-percent maximum they currently pay). That's hardly a tax on the rich! (Income is defined as a combination of adjustable gross income, tax-exempt interest and half of Social Security benefits.)

What is a retiree's best defense when the tax man cometh? Being prepared for the knock at the door! If you've implemented the right strategies in advance, you can send the tax man away—fed, but not stuffed! Let's first take a look at the current federal tax rates, effective in 1993, and then we'll look at some ideas to reduce your tax burden.

To project your federal taxes, the chart following offers a guideline based on taxable income (after deductions and exemptions). Look in Column 1 for the amount closest to your taxable income without exceeding it. Then determine if you will be filing a separate, joint or single return. The tax column indicates the base amount, the adjacent column indicates the rate at which you'll be taxed on the excess.

Col. 1 Taxable Income	Separate returns		Joint returns		Single Returns	
	Tax on Col. 1 $	Tax rate on excess %	Tax on Col. 1 $	Tax rate on excess %	Tax on Col. 1 $	Tax rate on excess %
0	0	15	0	15	0	15
3,750	563	15	563	15	563	15
11,250	1,686	15	1,688	15	1,688	15
18,450	2,768	28	2,768	15	2,768	15
22,100	3,790	28	3,316	15	3,316	28
29,600	5,890	28	4,441	15	5,416	28
36,900	7,934	28	5,536	28	7,460	28
44,575	10,083	31	7,685	28	9,609	28
53,500	12,850	31	10,184	28	12,108	31
76,400	19,949	31	16,596	28	19,207	31
89,150	23,902	31	20,166	31	23,160	31

To better understand this chart, follow this example. The Millers filed a joint return, with a taxable income of $60,000 (after deductions and exemptions). According to the chart, taxes on the first $53,500 were $10,184. The excess of $6,500 ($60,000 minus $53,500 equals $6,500) would then be taxed at a rate of 28 percent, which equals $1,820. The final federal tax bill would come to a total of $12,004 ($10,184 plus $1,820 equals $12,004).

How to reduce your federal tax bill

Here are five of the most effective planning strategies to keep your federal taxes as low as they can go when you retire.

1. Do your taxes twice a year. The government only requires that you do your taxes once a year, but that's for *their* benefit, not yours. I have always urged my clients to prepare a mock return every fall to determine what tax bracket they will be in that year. This gives them enough time to make some mid-course corrections, if necessary. For instance, you and your tax preparer or financial planner can determine if it would be smart to sell off an investment that would result in a tax gain in a year in which you anticipate you'll be in a lower tax bracket (often the first year after you retire).

Or, you may determine that you need to take a loss from your portfolio so you have added deductions. Or perhaps it would make sense to defer income into the following year, accelerate deductions (make more charitable contributions), or bunch up medical expenses so that they qualify in excess of the nondeductible limits. All of these tactics will reduce your overall tax obligation. But if you wait until January to size up your tax bill, it's already too late.

NOTE: Preparing a mock return is actually an effective strategy for any taxpayer—retired or not.

2. Filing errors that cost you time and money. You know how athletes always complain that they miss the easy shots? The same is true for tax filers. According to the IRS, people don't make mistakes on the complex sections, they make simple math errors. Or they use the wrong tax-rate tables. Or they don't sign the pages or forms properly. Or they fail to correct the pre-addressed labels—all of which will seriously delay the processing. To avoid these problems, prepare the return but don't mail it. Review it again in a few days when you're fresh, and it's very likely you will discover errors. That second look can save you plenty of time and money.

3. Adjusted gross income (AGI) is where it all starts. You can't change what you earn after you've earned it, but you can take steps to reduce your bottom line (remember, the amount of allowable exemptions and deductions is determined by the AGI). For example, if you and/or your spouse are working but not participating in a qualified retirement plan, each of you can fully deduct an IRA contribution of up to $2,000 a year. Even if you are in a qualified plan, if your AGI is under $40,000 (married filing jointly) or under $25,000 (single), you can get a full deduction on the annual $2,000 contribution. If you are self-employed and missed out on contributing to a business retirement plan by December 31, you have until April 15 to set up a simplified employee pension

(SEP). The limit on the annual contribution is 15 percent of your income, up to $30,000 and its totally tax-exempt. Work with your financial planner or tax preparer to find other opportunities to reduce your AGI.

4. Try on a different filing status. If you file a joint return out of habit, you may be missing out on personal exemptions and deductions you'd be entitled to if you filed separately. For instance, if you or your spouse had a year with a lot of medical and/or miscellaneous expenses, it might be detrimental to file jointly. The only way to really know if you should change your filing status is to calculate your tax return both ways. Another thing—this exer-cise works best when the deductible expenses were paid by the spouse with the lower of the two earnings.

5. It's a family affair. Today, many people who are supporting someone outside the immediate family are overlooking a potentially big exemption. If you and other members of your family are each contributing 10 percent or more to a dependent's support (an elderly parent, a grandchild, sibling, etc.) you may be entitled to claim an exemption by filing Form 2120, the "Multiple Support Agreement." Each year you have to alternate who gets the exemption. Divorced and separated parents also have potential tax credits. Discuss these with your financial planner or tax preparer.

Projecting your state income tax bill

In terms of state taxes, the one positive aspect is that theoretically you've got 50 choices. If you are so inclined, you can move to where you can take advantage of lower rates. Not that I would ever recommend moving away for this reason alone. But if you are considering a relocation, it's helpful to know which states are tax-friendlier than others.

For example, the states that require no income tax are Alaska, Florida, Nevada, New Hampshire, South Dakota, Tennessee, Texas, Washington and Wyoming.

States allowing deductions of part or all of federal income tax include Alabama, Iowa, Louisiana, Missouri, Montana, North Dakota, Oklahoma, Oregon and Utah.

And states allowing deductions of some or all of Social Security contributions from state income tax are: Alabama, Massachusetts and Missouri.

States allowing exemption of Social Security benefits from state income tax: Alabama, Arizona, California, Delaware, Georgia, Hawaii, Idaho, Illinois, Indiana, Kentucky, Louisiana, Maine, Maryland, Massachusetts, Michigan, Mississippi, New Jersey, New York, North Carolina, Ohio, Oklahoma, Ore-

gon, Pennsylvania, South Carolina and Utah, and the District of Columbia.

Finally, there are 34 states in which the standard deduction might be more advantageous, even if your federal return is itemized. If you itemize, you must add back to your taxable income the state taxes you write off your federal taxes.

Other tax breaks retirees should inquire about in their state include state, federal or private pension exemptions, elderly income credits, death taxes and medical deductions. (Alabama, New Jersey, Wisconsin, North Dakota and Oregon offer varying exemptions over and above what is allowable on your federal return.)

As for comparing tax burdens across the U.S., the following chart ranks the states from lowest to highest taxes (includes state income tax, sales tax, property tax and death taxes) as of 1993. Those states with an asterisk (*) are predicted to see tax increases of some sort by the end of 1994, according to *Money* magazine and Ernst and Young, the international accounting and management consulting firm.

States ranked in order of tax burden (from lowest to highest)

1. Alabama	14. Mississippi	27. Arkansas	40. Vermont
2. Wyoming	15. New Mexico	28. Illinois	41. Hawaii
3. Nevada	16. West Virginia	29. Virginia	42. Minnesota
4. Florida	17. Missouri	30. North Carolina	43. Rhode Island
5. Tennessee	18. South Carolina	31. Colorado	44. Connecticut
6. South Dakota	19. Arizona	32. Georgia	45. Oregon
7. New Hampshire	20. Indiana	33. New Jersey	46. Maryland
8. Texas	21. Kentucky	34. Michigan	47. Maine
9. Washington	22. Montana	35. California	48. Massachusetts
10. North Dakota	23. Oklahoma	36. Idaho	49. Wisconsin
11. Delaware	24. Kansas	37. Nebraska	50. District of
12. Alabama	25. Pennsylvania	38. Ohio	Columbia
13. Louisiana	26. Iowa	39. Utah	51. New York

Good question!

Q. How can we increase our income yearly to keep up with inflation?

A. The only way to give yourself an annual "pay raise" is to make certain that around 10 percent to 25 percent of your portfolio is invested in growth funds that are projected to outpace annual inflation rates (discussed in detail in Chapter 5). Those funds, including dividends and interest should be continuously reinvested, particularly during the first 10 years of retirement, so that your retirement nest egg has the opportunity to steadily build up without interruption of withdrawals, taxes and penalties. Generally, the best avenue for this strategy is through your IRAs. As for the balance of your investments, if properly invested, you should be able to live off the interest and dividends.

Q. Is there any way to predict the next year's inflation rate?

A. To try to project how much more money you'll need each year, I suggest that you review your monthly expenses at the end of each year and multiply that times the current rate of inflation (this year it was 3 percent). So for example, if you spend $3,000 a month now, next year you'd likely spend $3,090 a month just to have the same purchasing power ($3,000 X 1.03 = $3,090). What's most important is not that you correctly guess the inflation jump every year, but that you anticipate and plan for living-cost increases—period. You might as well prepare yourself for them.

Q. Should I be afraid of using up my principal?

A. Given our longer life expectancies today, it is ideal to hold off on tapping into your principal investments for the first 10 to 15 years of retirement. In other words, at half time (around age 70), it should be fine to start drawing income from them. If you cannot hold out that long, refer to the chart on page 31 (Chapter 1) that shows how long your money will last based on the rate of withdrawals and the interest earned.

Q. How much should we set aside for emergencies?

A. Ideally you want to have enough money to cover three to four months of expenses. Quick access is top priority here, earned interest is secondary.

Q. How often do I need to check on how my portfolio is performing?

A. For many people, the tendency at the beginning of retirement is to watch their money like a hawk. They read the stock page daily and call their broker the minute prices fall. But eventually they gain confidence and remember that fluctuations are normal. Ideally, at the beginning, you can review your portfolio's performance monthly to see that, at a minimum, it is maintaining its value. You also want to be certain that the amount you are withdrawing is at least equal to the dividends you are earning. Once you are comfortable living on your income, quarterly reviews should be sufficient unless you start hearing about major fluctuations in the market. Obviously, your goal is to be in the highest returning investments. However, just because you monitor doesn't mean that you automatically make changes.

Q. So how are you supposed to know when it's time for a change?

A. If you and your financial advisor have determined that a particular investment no longer has the potential to meet your expectations, it is appropriate to choose a different one. Other instances where a change is warranted? When an investment is going to substantially decrease the dividend amount, when interest rates become less attractive than another fund or bond, if you change tax brackets, or if you require a major purchase (a home or car). It may also be necessary to make changes when you lose your spouse. Because this generally results in a loss of income (Social Security and pension benefits, salary or wages, etc.), you may need to move more of your assets into income-producing investments.

Q. I'm a year from retiring and know my last year of income will be high. My company owes me back pay from unused sick and vacation days. Is there anything I can do to reduce my taxes before I retire?

A. If you are anticipating large, lump sum payments when you retire, reflecting final commissions, bonuses, back pay, etc., the first thing you should do is ask your employer if they would be willing to spread these payments out over two years so you could potentially reduce your tax liability. Another option if you are anticipating a higher-than-normal income your last year is to increase your tax deductions before you retire by increasing your 401k contribution. Excess income can also be put into long-term deferral vehicles such as tax-deferred annuities and nondeductible IRAs. It could also be helpful to look into investments that create a one-time tax deduction or credit, such as an oil and gas program or a senior subsidized housing investment.

Q. I'm set up with a company pension and in a solid mutual fund for income when I retire. But I'm still not sure it's enough. Are there any other investment products I should look at?

A. Because interest rates have plummeted while tax rates continue to climb, we're seeing a record number of investors buying variable-rate annuities (VRA) for the excellent rate of return and the tax-deferred growth. When compared to a mutual fund, for example, the return can be quite impressive. Let's say you invested $50,000 into both a mutual fund and a VRA, both of which grew by 10 percent a year. After 15 years, the annuity would be worth $208,863. The mutual fund would be worth $136,031 after taxes (in a 31-percent tax bracket). Granted, you'd have to pay taxes on the growth portion of the annuity when taking withdrawals, but not on the portion that was a return of the capital. Investing in this type of annuity is most beneficial after you have made maximum contributions into 401ks and other vehicles that use pre-tax dollars.

What I tell my clients

Mutual funds are not set in cement. Many people are under the impression that the decision to invest in a mutual fund is an irrevocable one. They assume this because the only way the money can grow to such an extent is if it is left alone. This part is true, but it doesn't mean that if the fund is not performing to expectations that you can't sell it off and choose a different fund. When comparing funds, what you are betting on is the fund's track record over a five-year to 10-year period. The real confidence-booster is when an equity fund has performed well in good economic times and bad, even if that meant an occasional downturn.

Not locked in. Another misco-ception about systematic withdrawals from mutual funds is that if you start out by withdrawing a certain percentage every year, you can't alter the percentage. Not true. Let's say the fund showed unusually high profits over a two-year period. If you needed the income, then by all means you should take advantage of the "pay raise" and increase your withdrawals. Obviously you should consult with your planner or broker first.

Don't pay the tax man unless you've asked for his ID. Every year there are reports of taxpayers who are taken to the cleaners by crooks posing as tax collectors. The most vulnerable are the elderly, particularly singles and widowers/widows. According to the IRS, impostors come to the door demanding checks for back taxes and threaten to arrest the person if they don't pay on the spot. Or they insist on getting Social Security or credit-card numbers, which they can then easily use to request replacement cards. So, if you get a knock on the door from someone who says he's with the IRS, ask to see a photo ID (all IRS employees have them). Then verify the address of the local IRS office by looking in the phone book or calling 1-800-829-1040. If you think the "agent" is a fraud, call the IRS inspector at 1-800-366-4484. And *never* write a check to an IRS employee, or even the "IRS." All checks should be made payable to the Internal Revenue Service to hinder someone's ability to change the payee's name or to cash the check.

Beware of the "source" tax. Just because you retire to another state doesn't mean your tax obligations to your home state retire. Twelve states now impose a source tax on income from retirement plans when retirees move out of state. They justify this by claiming that you received tax deductions and deferrals for pension, IRAs and business retirement plan contributions when you lived and worked in the state. Now they want a share of the money they never got to tax. Look out for this if you leave Arkansas, California, Idaho, Iowa, Kansas, Maryland, Massachusetts, Oregon, New York, Utah, Vermont and Virginia.

Will the real zip code please stand up? If you choose to maintain two residences when you retire, it is possible to reduce your taxes by claiming that your principal residence is in the lower tax state. However, you should never take this action without consulting with your planner or tax preparer because there are numerous factors that determine the feasibility of this strategy.

For starters, residency is defined by most states as the place you live for six or more months of the year. And don't think you can gloss over this matter with the IRS by waving a voter or car registration at them. To cut down on the number of residents who are claiming their primary residence is Florida or another low- to no-income tax state, many have reciprocal agreements to tap into each other's data. Furthermore, the IRS no longer hesitates to challenge residency claims, so you better be able to back up your claim. Conversely, if you are few years away from age 55 and the ability to sell your house by taking the $125,000 capital gains exclusion, it may be better to maintain your primary residence in the higher-taxed state. At some point, however, you ideally want your primary residence to be in the low- to no-tax state to reduce your tax liability.

Living on your assets

If you think it's going to be difficult making do on your fixed income, you aren't alone. Even the Sultan of Brunei, the richest man in the world, is having a tough time because of the world economy. Here's a guy who's worth an estimated $37 billion dollars, and he's got the same problem as you and I. He invested in real estate and oil and he's struggling to keep pace with inflation.

Last year, his net worth, and that of the world's 101 richest families, only increased by an average of 2.27 percent. Some things you can't control.

But with the proper amount of planning, investing and monitoring, you can control your future security. You can be financially independent at retirement. This means you have to know the size of your retirement nest egg before you retire, you have put the money in safe places where it can grow and provide income, you have to know your tax bracket before the year ends so you have a chance to reduce your tax liability, and you have to keep monitoring your income and expenses closely so that you are living within your means.

7

Real estate decisions made *real* easy

Life is funny. Many of us spend the better part of our lives trying to amass our fortunes and build our empires. When we arrive at the door of success, we buy the biggest, most expensive house we can afford. Then one day, we realize we're at the age where it's time to simplify things. Time to get out from the rambling, four-bedroom, two-and-a-half bath, heat monger that every year needs re-*something* (painting, caulking, you name it). Alas, we no longer want the burden of maintaining the very castle we worked so hard to build.

Does that mean the pursuit was all a waste of time? Not a chance! When you combine the appreciation in value over the years with the significant tax deductions you got, your "castle" may well have been one of the smartest investments you ever made. According to the Census Bureau, most Americans can attribute 32 percent of their entire net worth to their principal residence.

That's why the real beauty of your home was never in the European-styled kitchens or Jacuzzi tubs—it was in the equity!

The purpose of this chapter is to help you understand the different ways to take advantage of the equity in your home when you retire, given that it could possibly be your single largest asset. We'll also address other critical real estate decisions, such as whether to rent your home instead of sell it, whether to buy another home or rent one and, if you do decide to buy, whether to pay cash for a house or take a mortgage (and which kind). The financial implications of all these decisions will not only have a tremendous bearing on your retirement nest egg, but on your sanity as well.

How much equity do you have?

Before you can determine the best strategy for retiring on the house, it is essential to know how much equity you've built up over the years. Many people are embarrassed to admit that they don't know how to calculate their equity. Basically, equity is the difference between the balance of your mortgage and the house's current appraised value.

For example, if you sell your house for $167,000, and you still owe $27,000 on the mortgage, your equity would be $140,000. In other words, subtract what you owe from what you own.

Interestingly, people who bought their homes in the 1950s and '60s could never have predicted that values would appreciate as they did. In many areas of the country (with the exception of parts of California and Texas), houses are worth at least five to 10 times their original price. So, if you've paid off the mortgage by the time you retire, or still have a small mortgage but with substantial equity, you own a virtual "cash cow!" Equally important, this equity position gives you a variety of options in terms of how and even *where* you live when you retire.

Since the 1980s, one of the most significant trends among retirees has been to sell their home and buy one that is less expensive, perhaps in another part of the country where overall living costs are also lower. Realtors often refer to these people as "equity immigrants." Thanks to their equity build-up, they are in an enviable position to simultaneously relocate, retire and reinvest in another property. The process is called *trading down*.

How to trade down, but really trade up

By definition, when you trade down, you sell a larger, more expensive home and trade it in for a less expensive residence. That sets off a whole chain reaction of financial benefits: lower property taxes, reduced insurance and maintenance costs and overall cutbacks in overhead (utilities, supplies, furnishings, etc.). The icing on the cake is, then, being able to use the equity or profits from the sale to invest for retirement income and/or to buy another principal residence.

That's why trading down is one of the most effective retirement strategies available today. In one shot, you can generate income, reduce your cost of living, preserve the value of your estate and maintain an acceptable—if not *improved*—standard of living.

How do you set the wheels in motion? The first step is to turn 55. That's when the IRS has a very nice tax credit waiting for you.

The capital gains exclusion: A present from the IRS

For some, 55 is a much-dreaded birthday. But, cheer up! Uncle Sam has a gift for you. It's called the *capital gains exclusion* and it's a once-in-a-lifetime opportunity to sell your house without paying any taxes on the first $125,000 of profit.

Here's how it works.

If either you and/or your spouse have reached the age of 55 *before* you sell your house, you are eligible to exclude up to $125,000 in capital gains at tax time, even if you choose *not* to reinvest in another residence.

There are several other provisions to be aware of:

1. The capital gains exclusion is elective, but it is available only once in a lifetime.

2. In order to take advantage of this tax break, your property must have been owned *and* used by you (or your deceased spouse) as your principal residence for at least three out of the five years preceding the sale. For example, if you'd been renting out your house for the past three years so you could enjoy your vacation home year-round, you should delay the sale of the house until you are able to come back and meet this minimum residency requirement.

   NOTE: It is not necessary for the periods of "ownership" and "use" to coincide.

3. If the taxable gain is less than $125,000, the tax exclusion is still permissible but it means not taking advantage of the break to its fullest extent. And once you've used this exemption, it's gone forever. If your taxable gain was only $75,000, the remaining balance of $50,000 could never be applied to another house sale. It's a one-time-only deal.

4. If you are a widow or widower over age 55 who is considering marriage, you and your intended should both sell your own homes before the wedding. That way, you can each take advantage of the tax break. Once you are husband and wife, only one of your homes can be sold with the tax exclusion privilege.

   NOTE: If either one of you have already taken the tax exclusion during a previous marriage, you are both disqualified from the tax break if you ever sell the home once remarried.

5. If you are a professional who used part of your home as an office, only that portion of the house that was used as your primary residence would qualify for the capital gains exclusion. In other words, if you lived in half of the house and used the other half as an office, only 50 percent of the profits of the house could be earmarked for the $125,000 tax exclusion.

The whole rationale for this capital gains break is to give retiring taxpayers the opportunity to reduce their living expenses and their tax burden at the same time. In effect, the government is providing an incentive for seniors to *sell* their primary residence, *avoid* taxes on the first $125,000 of profit, *defer the taxes* on any excess profit by buying a smaller, less expensive home, and then *reinvest the $125,000* so it provides additional income during retirement years.

The strategy is even more appealing if you relocate to another part of the country where home prices are lower than where you now live. By virtue of this, homeowners often end up trading down price wise, not quality wise.

For instance, today it would be possible to sell your 35-year-old three-bedroom, split-level on Long Island for $200,000 and buy a comparably sized home for $100,000-plus in Florida, Texas, the Carolinas, the Southwest, the Northwest and the Midwest. Since the house would presumably be younger because there has been so much growth and new construction, it's more likely to be loaded with desirable features and amenities, it's bound to need considerably less maintenance, and it may very well offer lower utility costs if the climate is milder. More luxury, more facilities, more services for less maintenance costs, less taxes, less expenses! Wouldn't you call that trading *up*?

When you move to a part of the country where you need less to live on, you're also in a good position to invest a greater portion of your profits in your retirement nest egg. If properly invested in tax-free or tax-deferred funds, you would then have the ability to increase your retirement income without the growth being eroded by taxes.

Now, while I realize that there are many people approaching retirement that wouldn't ever dream of moving away from family and friends, I can tell you that this is a growing trend today. And it's not just to live more cheaply.

Every year, I meet with more New Yorkers, for example, who are planning to leave the area because of the cold climate, high crime, runaway property taxes, and because they want access to a wider variety of leisure activities year-round. Ironically, they're also moving because the family and friends they wanted to stay close to moved to Florida or other states! So, *never* say never!

Here are examples of how trading *down* can work for you.

Example 1: Trading down with the capital gains exclusion. In 1968, the DeMarcos bought their four-bedroom split-level for $50,000. In 1993, they sold it for $285,000. Since Ginny served as her own real estate broker, she didn't have to pay a commission. And since they had paid off their 20-year mortgage on Ed's 55th birthday, they enjoyed their profits, free and clear of debt. That was gratifying—until they considered the tax implications. They had $235,000 in appreciated value. Fortunately, Ed was now 57, so they were able to take the entire $125,000 capital gains exclusion. That left them with a $160,000 gain to roll over.

Their next step was to purchase a brand-new three-bedroom condo on a Boca Raton golf course. The price was $175,000 and they decided to pay cash, which left them with no taxable gain.

Finally, they had to make a decision as to what to do with their remaining sale proceeds after purchasing the condo. They had a balance of $110,000 to invest and opted for tax-free municipal bonds. At 5½-percent interest, that yielded $6,050 a year, tax-free.

Here is how the numbers looked:

$285,000	Sale proceeds of home up north
$125,000	Capital gains exclusion
$160,000	Taxable profits
$175,000	Florida condo
$0	Taxable gain
$285,000	Sale proceeds
$175,000	Florida condo
$110,000	Net proceeds
$110,000	Balance to invest
$110,000	Invested in municipal bonds @ 5½% yield
$6,050.00	Annual tax-free yield

NOTE: In other instances, a real estate commission, closing costs, state and federal income taxes and attorney's fees could add to the cost of the transaction and would need to be included in the calculation for the gain or loss on the sale of a home.

Example 2: Trading down *without* the capital gains exclusion. The Esterhauses did it a little differently. They sold their three-bedroom house in Reston, Va., for $250,000. They were pleased, since they'd only paid $140,000 and spent $60,000 in improvements over the eight years they lived there. When they sold, they paid off their $20,000 mortgage, plus closing costs, the attorney and the broker's commission (another $20,000). That left them with net proceeds of $210,000, a taxable profit of $30,000 and a difficult decision to make. They weren't sure whether it would be better to use the $125,000 tax credit, which would eliminate the $30,000 taxable gain, but fully exhaust the credit and waste a $95,000 exclusion difference. Or, perhaps they should preserve the once-in-a-lifetime credit and pay the capital gains tax (state and federal), which would be an estimated $10,000. Because they knew they were going to buy another property, they decided to postpone the use of the tax credit until such time when they sold the next home—hoping that their taxable gain would be higher.

Within the year, they moved to Myrtle Beach, S.C., and bought a three-bedroom condominium in a new retirement community for $150,000. They could have paid cash, but opted instead to put $100,000 down on the property and finance a $50,000 mortgage. With a portion of the remaining proceeds (approximately $50,000), they decided to invest $50,000 in a quick-print franchise. They invested $50,000 in mutual funds, which would be available to pay down the mortgage. In the meantime, their money was earning interest.

Here is how the numbers looked:

Net	$250,000	Sale price of house
Proceeds	$20,000	Balance of mortgage
	$20,000	Real estate commission, closing costs
	$10,000	Capital gains tax (state and federal)
	$200,000	Net proceeds

Where the money went: 1) purchased $150,000 condo; 2) $100,000 down payment on condo (took $50,000 mortgage; 3) $50,000 mutual funds; 4) $50,000 quick print franchise.

Capital gains	$140,000	Original purchase price of Virginia home
liability	$60,000	Improvements
	$20,000	Real estate commission and closing costs
	$220,000	Cost basis
	$250,000	Sale proceeds
	$220,000	Cost basis
	$30,000	Taxable profits subject to capital gains

Example 3: Taking the capital gains exclusion without buying another home. David and Maryann Greene bought their home in 1961 for $28,000 and paid off the mortgage in 1991. Over the years, they made substantial improvements to the house, adding a two-car garage, expanding the kitchen, and building a sunroom with a deck. All told, they spent about $82,000, which gave them a cost basis of $110,000. Because of all the extras, their home sold quickly for $190,000. After paying the realtor's commission ($11,000) and closing costs ($1,000), they showed a profit of $68,000. Then they applied the capital gains exclusion to wipe out the taxable profits, even though their sale didn't produce as much as the $125,000 capital gains exclusion.

Unlike our first two examples, however, the Greene's did not roll over their $178,000 tax-free proceeds into a new home. Instead, they decided they no longer wanted the obligation of owning a home and, instead, rented a beautiful new condo in Las Vegas. It freed up their money to travel while allowing their financial planner to invest the lion's share in their retirement portfolio. They invested $150,000 in a combination of utilities, government funds, bonds and blue-chip stocks—earning an average of 7.5 percent and generating an annual return of $11,250 which they now use to pay their rent.

Here is how the numbers looked:

$28,000	Original purchase price of home
$82,000	Improvements
$12,000	Real estate commission, closing costs
$122,000	Cost basis
$190,000	Sale proceeds
$122,000	Cost basis
$68,000	Taxable profits subject to capital gains, but applied to the $125,000 capital gains exclusion, eliminating gains tax
$190,000	Sale proceeds
$12,000	Commission and closing costs
$178,000	Net proceeds to invest
$150,000	Invested in their portfolio
@7½%	
$11,250	Annual return
$28,000	Earmarked for new home furnishings, travel and other expenses

Although your retirement scenario will no doubt have a different set of facts and figures, trading down can potentially result in a similar financial success story. The key is to be realistic about what you can sell your house for as well as what it is going to cost to replace it with a home that is acceptable to you. In addition, you absolutely want to have a strategy in place for how the profits from the sale are going to be invested. Sit down with a financial planner who can help you generate the greatest amount of income, while allowing the smallest tax bite.

How to trade down without selling the house right away

In spite of how advantageous the $125,000 capital gains exclusion can be, you may be in a situation where it is *more* advantageous to *temporarily delay* the sale of your home.

Let's say that you want to move, are willing to sell, but are concerned that with today's lethargic real estate market, the bids you get will be lower than you expected or needed to buy another suitable home.

It's a fact that in real estate, the name of the game is *timing*. So it's fair to assume that at some point the market will pick up. But when? The key questions to pose to local realtors are, "If we hold on for another year or two, are we likely to see greater profits than if we sell now?" And, "Will those profits be enough to offset any increases in maintenance costs and property taxes that have occurred during this period?"

If the answers are "yes," it may be worth it to sit tight. If the response is "no" or "it's hard to say," it may be an indication that the market hasn't bottomed-out yet and it would be wise to sell now and take what you can get. Keep in mind that real estate markets follow the law of supply and demand. In many areas of the country, demand is down and prices have fallen, so the delay may not be to your advantage.

As one trusted realtor friend has reminded me over the years, "The housing market may be soft, but it can always get softer."

Another possible reason to delay the sale of your home is if you are the least bit hesitant about becoming a permanent resident somewhere else. Not everyone is able to adjust to a new community. Some think it's worth all the money in the world to know that they have an escape valve if they change their minds and want to return home. It also gives them time to investigate and shop around.

Here's another consideration for delaying the sale of your home: if you or your spouse are within two years of age 55 and could benefit from taking capital gains exclusion at this time. This is especially true if your profits would be equal to or would exceed the $125,000 tax credit.

What to do if you can't sell, but still want to trade down

Most people don't get to retirement age without discovering how very complicated life can get. This is especially true of retirees who are anxious to move into a smaller, less expensive home, but for one of the reasons just mentioned, aren't ready or simply can't sell their home. Does that mean they're stuck? Not necessarily.

If you find yourself in this situation, one possibility is to consider renting your home as an interim step.

Now I know there are going to be people who would rather lose money than have strangers take over their closets. On the other hand, with the help of a reputable realtor, I do see more and more people taking advantage of this option, and it works out fine. In numerous instances, the renters eventually buy the house and everyone is a winner.

This discussion is fresh in my mind because I just got off the phone with clients who bought a condominium in Sunrise, Fla., a few years ago. Because they were so enthusiastic about relocating and so sure they'd never move back, they sold their home on Long Island. What they didn't anticipate was that they'd hate Florida summers and that Jack would miss working a few days a week in his business in Manhattan.

So for the past three summers, they've been coming back to New York and renting an apartment in their old neighborhood. And, every year, the price for returning goes up. They're disheartened. They'd like to buy a condominium in their old neighborhood, but the prices are prohibitive. They considered taking equity out of their Florida home as a way to raise cash, but their current appraisal was too low. And without a substantial amount for a down payment, taking a new mortgage would be unaffordable. They are in quite a bind, but, unfortunately, not an unusual one.

That's why, in spite of your thinking at the moment, I tell my clients that it doesn't hurt to step back and ask themselves, "If for nothing more than peace of mind, what do we have to lose by renting the house out for a year?"

In order to determine if renting is a viable option from a *financial* standpoint, ask yourself these questions:

1. Is your home located in a community in which the demand for housing proven to be greater than the supply?

2. Is your home located in an area near universities or companies that continually hire or transfer employees?

3. Do you have considerable equity in your home?

If you answered "yes" to these three questions, renting could make a lot of sense. Here is how it would work:

Let's say your home is worth $175,000 and you owe $40,000 on the mortgage. If you rented the house, your monthly mortgage payments could be covered by the tenant. For the next year or two, the house, which would then be considered a real estate investment, would continue to escalate in value (by how much is very much dependent on where you live, but could be as much as another $10,000 to $20,000).

Obviously, this strategy was more of a sure thing in the '80s. In the '90s it's more of a risk. However, if it works, it gives you the means to take the equity out of the house so you can invest in a business, make a down payment on another house or simply reinvest. Potentially, that would allow you to have more than one investment increasing in value: your old home, your new home, a business, and/or investments.

This scenario, however, works best when your home is situated in a desirable neighborhood, where there is a continued demand for housing and when you have built up enough equity in the house to remove a sizable sum. Finally, you must be able to charge adequate rent in order to at least break even on the expenses. If average rental prices in your area won't allow you to cover your mortgage, utilities and maintenance, then it probably *is* wise to sell.

To help you look at the bottom line of selling as compared to renting, work with a trusted realtor and try to project the following figures. Sometimes, the numbers speak for themselves.

If you rent your home

Income

Monthly rental $_____ X 11 = $_____
(Use 11 months to allow for tenant changes)

Expenses

Mortgage payments $_____
Property taxes   _____
Repairs and maintenance   _____
Liability insurance   _____
Management/collection fees _____
Other costs   _____

TOTAL COSTS $_____

If you sell your home

Income

Estimated sale price $_____

Expenses

Real estate commission $_____
Spruce ups & repairs $_____
Mortgage balance $_____
Attorney's fees $_____
Potential taxes $_____
Miscellaneous costs $_____

TOTAL COSTS $_____

Net benefits

Rental income minus expenses $_____
Selling price minus expenses $_____
Income on Sale Proceeds
if invested at _____% $_____

Regardless of how the numbers look, however, it's vitally important to consider some unexpected problems that could alter even the most positive-looking figures.

For example, what would happen if your home were vacant for several months because your tenant was suddenly transferred? You'd still have all the expenses of the house, but without the income. What if the house required a major repair, such as a new roof? The expense could feasibly wipe out your profits for the year. Yes there would be tax advantages to offset the losses, and your home could have continued to escalate in value, but that wouldn't be of much solace if you were counting on a monthly income.

Another subject for discussion is how you feel about being a landlord. Some people are just not cut out to deal with the two T's, toilets and tenants, no matter how profitable the set-up. You and your spouse need to iron it all out—decide who will take responsibility for the accounting, maintenance and repairs, emergencies, etc.—before you rent the house.

Finally, if you convert your home to a rental property, there will be certain tax breaks you won't be able to take full advantage of should you sell at a later time. This may be offset by the fact that, in the meantime, you will have been able to deduct management fees, property taxes, and other expenses on your income tax. And although depreciation is also deductible, it must be added back to your tax basis at the point that you do sell the house.

NOTE: If you rent your home for *more* than three years, the IRS assumes this house is no longer your principal residence. It is a rental property, and, therefore, not eligible for the $125,000 capital gains exclusion when you sell.

Renting your home out while buying another

Should you decide that it makes sense to rent your home, but you still want to buy another one, you might be wondering how you could afford to do this. Many people assume that without the proceeds from the sale of their home, they won't be able to purchase a new house or condo.

It is possible, if you consider either refinancing your mortgage or taking out a home equity loan. If you did, you wouldn't be alone. Last year, Americans went back to the banks and renegotiated an estimated $3.5 million in home loans, no doubt to get reacquainted with the 8-percent interest rates they hadn't seen in 20 years.

Basically, if you refinance, you are using the increased value of your home to apply for a larger mortgage. In other words, if your home is currently valued at $150,000, and you only owe $50,000, you could refinance and take out up to 80 percent of the house's value—in this case, an additional $70,000. That would give you the needed money to buy another house. Then you could rent your home and use the rental income to pay back the higher mortgage. With this new mortgage, you'd receive a lump sum and immediately begin paying interest on the total amount owed.

If you take a home equity loan, again, you are borrowing against your property's appreciation. But this time, you're take an additional loan out on top of your current mortgage commitment and/or the difference between the house's current value and the existing mortgage.

Unlike refinancing, you don't surrender the first mortgage. Typically, you can borrow up to 80 percent of your equity. This gives you a ready amount of cash, as much as you like at a time, up to the limit of the loan. In other words, home equity loans are like buying a line of credit. You can borrow from it at any time and then pay interest on only what you borrow.

The other major difference between refinancing and home equity loans, is that the interest on home equity loans is almost never fixed, but rather adjustable. Again, that means that at some point during the life of the loan, you could be faced with higher monthly payments.

Now although both of these tactics obligate you to higher monthly payments (or, in the case of home equity loans, two payments instead of one), you might feel that these advantages are worth the added expense:

- You'll still own your home in case you want to come back
- Even if you don't live there, your home may have continued to appreciate in value
- In the meantime, you'll have had the necessary cash to buy another place or to put down a decent down payment.

When shopping for financing, start with the bank that is holding your current mortgage. It's possible that they will waive certain fees, or offer you an "insider" deal because they would love to renegotiate an old mortgage or to simply increase the loan to a good customer.

In addition, before you get locked into a home equity loan or a second mortgage, I must caution you about two things: Either of these commitments will obligate you to increase your monthly expenses—there'll be another bill on the pile at a time when it's better to reduce your overhead. Secondly, if you have recently become unemployed or are concerned about your credit history, it's possible the banks won't approve your application. It's best to consult with a banker you have a relationship with to determine the best strategy.

How to sell the house quickly when the time is right

At the point that you are ready to sell your home, here are a number of recommendations to sell quickly and at the best possible price, even if the market is as soft as a baby's bottom:

Price your home fairly. Everything about your home is tied to 1,001 fond recollections—of first steps, Thanksgiving dinners, slumber parties, weddings, etc. Memories are wonderful, but they add nothing to the value of your house on the open market. When you're deciding on an asking price, leave your emotions out of it and concentrate on the reality of what the market will bear. Homes that are priced appropriately are always the first to be sold in either an up *or* down market.

Choose an aggressive broker. Sounds easy, you say. They're all barracudas. Perhaps, but not all of them have the savvy to market a house during a soft period. Look for one who will go right to the multiple listings service, will pursue more unusual ways of finding buyers, such as relocation services and companies that are transferring employees, and will commit to a solid advertising effort for you. If you find such a broker, don't haggle over the 6-percent to 8-percent commission. If the market is flat and the broker finds a qualified buyer who can meet your price, he or she certainly deserves compensation.

Be a "lender" to the "buyer." If the real estate market is soft and/or very competitive when you put your house up, one resourceful strategy is to offer seller financing. Home buyers, particularly first-timers, are known to pay top dollar for a house if financing is part of the package. The risks are minimal, since you'll insist on a substantial, 20-percent down payment to protect your principal. In addition, you'll still own the property. In the unlikely event that the buyers default on the loan, you'll still have a property that may have continued to appreciate in value. Further, the interest you require should, at a minimum, be equal to what you could earn on other investments, But, ideally, you should get a higher rate as a premium for providing the loan.

Don't forget the home improvements. As we've already discussed, a home that gives the appearance of being well-cared-for is the one that people want to own. So fix up, touch up, get rid of, repair, renovate—whatever it takes, within reason, to make your home the kind of place a new family will want to start making memories in.

Be ready with the facts. Compile answers to the most-asked questions, such as the room dimensions, the square footage of the property, heating systems (water, kitchen and house), average monthly utility costs, boundaries of the property, distances between the house and shopping, schools, houses of worship, recreation facilities (preferably in minutes, not miles). You should also prepare a list of recent home improvements and their costs, a list of household appliances that are still under warranty, and the results of any recent termite or other inspections. Ask yourself what else you would want to know if you were buying the house, and be prepared with the answers.

Relocating: Rent or buy?

Retirees who are planning a relocation have another important decision to make. And that is, should they rent or buy a place in their new home town? I have worked with many people who would never consider renting for a number of reasons. Some feel there is a stigma attached to renting. Others want to avoid the hassle of moving a second time when they buy, and everybody questions the wisdom of renting when interest rates are at the lowest point in 20 years. All of these concerns are understandable, and yet there are some very logical reasons to rent. Consider these advantages:

- You'll have a great deal of leeway when it comes to how you allocate the profits from the sale of your house. Perhaps you can invest in a business and/or investments that are more likely to exceed the return of the appreciation on the house.

- If the move doesn't work out, you won't be stuck with a house or condo you can't sell. Please don't gloss over this under the guise that it could never happen to you. My phone rings every day because someone is calling from somewhere to say that they're in this exact bind. It is not unusual for newcomers to settle in a new area, only to discover months later that they would have been happier in another development, another town or in another state altogether. As a renter, you won't have to be concerned if the real estate market has gone soft or if you'll be able to get your money out of the house. You just wait for the lease to expire or somehow maneuver your way out of it. In either case, it will be a lot easier to make a move.

- By renting, you'll have the luxury of up to two years to buy or build a home to your liking. You won't have to settle or compromise because the clock is ticking and you have to be out of your house in two months. The IRS gives you 24 months to roll over the profits from the sale of your house. Take advantage.

- Finally, on a month-to-month basis, renting is cheaper than owning. There are no property taxes, no homeowner's insurance (although you should still purchase renter's insurance), no maintenance and repair costs. It's a hassle-free existence. If you're unhappy, you complain to the landlord. If there are problems that can't be resolved, you move!

Of course, for every advantage, there is a disadvantage—and renting is no exception. It is true that when you rent,

there are no financial rewards. You'll have no tax deductions, no hedge against inflation, and less control over rising rental costs. In addition, in some parts of the country, rental inventory is at a premium. Not only will there be a better selection of new homes and re-sales than rental properties, when you compare costs, it might be more advantageous from a financial position to buy.

In spite of all of this, I still contend that renting for six months to a year is the ideal strategy for newcomers. There is no better way to get a feel for an area—the neighborhoods, the outlying communities, the local builders, etc.—than when you already live there. Ask anyone who's actually gone through the relocation process and they'll tell you in no uncertain terms that their perspective was entirely different as a resident than as a visitor. It's that very perspective that will help you make the right decision—to stay or to go.

Should you pay cash or get a mortgage?

One of the last decisions to make when you retire and buy or build a home is whether to pay cash or take a mortgage. As with any other important decision, there are pros and cons to each. To decide which is the right strategy for you, ask yourself these questions:

- Are you still in a high tax bracket and in need of deductions?

- Are you willing to carry a long-term liability again? Sometimes, the best part of retirement is being free of major financial responsibilities.

- Will you have a predictable cash flow at retirement?

If you answered "yes" to these questions, it doesn't appear that a mortgage commitment would be a problem. On the other hand, there may be other considerations. Answering "yes" to these next questions points to the advantages of paying cash.

- Do you need to stay liquid in order to meet personal financial obligations, such as college tuition, health care costs, business commitments? If so, a mortgage will tie up your cash in a non-income producing asset until such time when there's considerable equity again.
- Do you anticipate having any difficulty getting a mortgage because of recent problems in your financial or employment history?
- If you or your spouse die, will it be a problem keeping up with mortgage payments? Paying cash guarantees the house is yours free and clear.
- With today's lower interest rates, is it possible that your diversified portfolio can earn a rate after taxes that exceeds the cost of a mortgage? If so, it may pay to keep your cash invested in the portfolio.

Getting through the mortgage maze

If you decide that financing your next house is in your best interest, the next question is—which kind of mortgage? Unfortunately, mortgage shopping is like a free-for-all today, with banks hawking their weekly specials like supermarkets. One-year adjustables with no income checks. Convertibles, 15-year, 30-year, no-points mortgages. Which one is right for you?

Overall, it is best to avoid *variable-rate mortgages*. The last thing retirees on fixed incomes need is to worry that at any time there could be a sudden increase in monthly payment. It's bad enough that property taxes will invariably climb, so you want at least one constant, which is what a fixed mortgage offers.

But beyond that, most people run into trouble when they ignore the fine print in mortgage advertisements. I'm here to tell you that even if you have to invest in a new pair of reading glasses so you can see all the information in minuscule type, read it! Otherwise you won't have the slightest clue what you're really going to pay until after you've agreed to pay it.

You see, most consumers compare lenders by their advertised interest rates. But that's only half the story. There's a little asterisk at the bottom of most ads that indicates the APR, or Annual Percentage Rate. The APR equals the advertised interest rate plus all the extras: points, service charges, origination fees, mortgage insurance and other charges. Similar to unit prices you see on supermarket shelves, the APR is the best piece of information for comparison shopping.

For the purpose of determining which is better—a higher interest rate with lower points, or a lower interest rate with higher points—refer to this helpful chart. It provides a comparison by showing the effective interest rates of various mortgage obligations. This comprises the cost of paying principal and interest only, not actual loan costs as is shown in the APR.

By reading down the interest rate column, and then across the points column under the proper loan term, you can determine which combination of interest rate and points may cost less over the entire term of the loan. This value is called the effective interest rate, which is a more accurate reflection of what you'll be paying than the APR.

Interest Rate %	15 Year Term Number of Points:				30 Year Term Number of Points			
	1	2	3	4	1	2	3	4
7.00	7.16	7.33	7.49	7.66	7.10	7.20	7.30	7.41
7.25	7.41	7.58	7.75	7.92	7.35	7.45	7.56	7.67
7.50	7.66	7.83	8.00	8.17	7.60	7.71	7.81	7.92
7.75	7.92	8.08	8.25	8.43	7.85	7.96	8.07	8.18
8.00	8.17	8.34	8.51	8.68	8.11	8.21	8.32	8.44
8.25	8.42	8.59	8.76	8.94	8.36	8.47	8.58	8.69
8.50	8.67	8.84	9.02	9.19	8.61	8.72	8.83	8.95
8.75	8.92	9.09	9.27	9.45	8.86	8.97	9.09	9.21
9.00	9.17	9.35	9.52	9.70	9.11	9.23	9.34	9.46
9.25	9.42	9.60	9.78	9.96	9.36	9.48	9.60	9.72
9.50	9.67	9.85	10.03	10.21	9.62	9.73	9.85	9.98
9.75	9.93	10.10	10.29	10.47	9.87	9.99	10.11	10.23

The rule of thumb? If you plan to live in the house for more than five years, it can save you money to go with the deal offering a lower rate of interest, but higher points (the points are a one-time, up-front fee; the benefits of a lower interest rate are felt every month). If you know you'll be selling within two to five years, it may be advisable to take the deal with lower points and slightly higher interest rates. Why pay a steep fee for the short-term use of the bank's money?

As for the mortgage options, here is a rundown of the conventional and even unconventional choices.

1. Fixed-rate mortgages. These are the granddaddy's of the mortgage market—the conventional 15- or 30-year loans that remain constant insofar as interest rates and monthly payments are concerned. If you're paying $1,250 a month in principal and interest in 1989, you'll be paying the same $1,250 a month in 1999, and so on.

2. Adjustable-rate mortgages (ARMs). Compared to fixed rates, ARMs are still considered the new kids in town, brought in by the banks as a way to prevent the severe losses they took when they were lending money at 6 percent to 8 percent while paying 11 percent to 13 percent on CDs and money market accounts.

With ARMs, the interest rate you pay and, therefore, the monthly payment you make, is adjusted at regular intervals based on a fluctuating index.

For example, a one-year ARM index might be tied to the price of one-year U.S. Treasury securities, or Ginnie Maes. If the index moves up, so does the interest you pay. If it goes down, you pay less—for that period only.

This is not to say that, if interest rates go up by 5 percent, you'll suffer accordingly. In order to insure consumer acceptance, adjustable mortgages do have caps on the interest rates. There are usually two caps built in. The first is on the amount that can be adjusted annually; the second is the total adjustment that can be made over the life of the loan.

A typical cap is 2 percent a year, with a 6-percent life cap. This means that interest rates can move either up or down by 2 points from the index in the contract year, and no more than 6 points up or down through the span of the loan.

If you take out a one-year ARM, your loan payments will fluctuate on the anniversary of the loan each year. Three-year ARMs adjust every three years at the anniversary of the loan, and so on. Some ARMs adjust every six months, others at five-year intervals. Read the fine print.

The major selling point of ARM loans is that their initial interest rates are 1 percent to 3 percent below typical fixed-rate loans.

3. The convertible ARM. Given the potential downsides of ARMs to those who *do* intend to stay in a home for the long haul, lenders have devised a less risky strategy for getting the best of both adjustables and fixed-rate mortgages. It's called Convertible Adjustable Rate Mortgages, and, just as the name indicates, it allows borrowers to take advantage of lower interest rates at the start of the loan and then have the option to convert to a fixed-rate mortgage, usually between the 13th and 60th month.

The option costs the borrower approximately 1 percent of the loan plus a few hundred dollars in administrative fees for converting. The decision to go to a fixed rate is at the discretion of the borrower, not the lender. And 1 percent is a small price to pay for getting in and staying in the real estate market, where the potential for appreciation is greater than most other types of investments.

4. Reverse mortgages. In the past few years, another strategy for tapping into the equity of your home has begun to catch on. The concept is called home equity conversions (HECs), or reverse mortgages. The idea behind them is to help "house-rich" seniors who want to stay in their homes, but are too "cash-poor" to do so.

Reverse mortgages allow homeowners to sell off the equity in their homes to the bank in exchange for being able to continue living in the house and receiving monthly checks from the bank. At the end of the term (three to 12 years), the bank will sell the house and keep the profits.

The majority of plans I've seen require that one of the spouses be at least 62 and that the mortgage be paid off already.

There are numerous variances in this strategy. But if your intent is to sell your house and use the profits to live on when you relocate, then none of them will be any help to you.

Also, keep in mind that the ability to borrow against your home in exchange for monthly payments to you is not yet allowable in every state. You'll have to check with the banks in your area to find out what type of reverse mortgages are available, if any.

5. Sale leasebacks. Sale leasebacks can be the ideal set-up for seniors who want to continue living in their home but who can longer afford—or who no longer want—the obligations of ownership. It's also a way to help your adult children get their first mortgage.

A retired homeowner can transfer the ownership of his or her home to a family member (an adult child who can afford to buy it), but continue living in the house and paying rent every month. In exchange, the child gives the parent a down payment at the sale, and continues to make monthly payments until the mortgage debt is repaid. In the meantime, the child pays taxes, insurance and maintenance. Now although the child won't be living in the house, he or she will have a solid real estate investment and will benefit from the annual tax deductions as well. In addition, the "buyer" can negotiate a more favorable sale price because he or she is enabling the senior to live in the home at a reduced rent (or none at all), while avoiding real estate commissions.

6. Gift annuity plans. This plan is exactly as it sounds. Give a gift, get a gift back: an annual annuity payment. This is an interesting strategy if you are a retired homeowner who is still in a high tax bracket and who has no heirs. You make the ultimate charitable contribution: you donate your house to a legitimate charitable organization. In exchange for this donation, you'll get a substantial annual tax deduction and an annual annuity payment until your death. The payments you receive will be smaller than if you'd gone for a reverse mortgage, but the difference is you'll still be receiving payments after you've moved out. If you do opt to stay in the house, you'll pay the taxes, insurance and maintenance.

Colleges and hospitals are often interested in this arrangement.

Before you sign on the dotted line...

Reverse mortgages and the variations thereof may be a lifesaver for some people. But even when that's true, you have to proceed with extreme caution. If you end up with a costly payment schedule with high interest rates, you could be in a worse situation than the one you were trying to avoid in the first place. In other words, you might end up having to sell the house in order to repay the loan at a time when you most need the house and the money.

The best way to proceed is to discuss your current and future needs with family members and see if there is an arrangement that benefits all involved.

Equally important, don't sign anything until your lawyer has reviewed the papers. These new loan commitments are extremely complex, and in many cases, untested. The opinion of a trusted attorney could save your whole family a fortune.

For additional information, send a stamped, self-addressed 8½-by-11 envelope (for a 47-page booklet) along with your request for bulletin #D12874, "Home-Made Money: Consumer's Guide to Home Equity Conversion" to: AARP Fulfillment, 601 E Street, N.W., Washington, DC 20049. The first copy is free.

Good question!

Q. I'm recently divorced and got the house as part of the property settlement. I'm only 53, so I can't take the $125,000 capital gains exclusion yet, but I really can't afford to stay in the house for another three years. I'd like to sell it now and buy a more affordable condo. How can I work it so I don't get killed with taxes?

A. The best strategy would be to convert your home to a rental property until you turn 55. At the same time, you can borrow from the equity in the house so that you can make a down payment on a smaller residence.

Q. What if I sell my house before I turn 55?

A. As I've indicated, the $125,000 exclusion at age 55 is a once-in-a-lifetime opportunity. If you sell your home before turning 55, you'll lose the exclusion. But you can always buy and sell another principal residence after age 55 and take the tax exclusion at that time. Just be aware that by postponing this tax credit, you are delaying unlocking the equity in your home on a tax-free basis.

Q. What if I buy a home for equal value? Can I postpone the $125,000 tax credit?

A. Of course you could buy a home of equal or greater value so that the purchase qualifies as your principal residence within the required 24-month period. By doing so, you could defer paying taxes on the profits by taking advantage of the 1034 rollover provision in the IRS code. However, buying an equally or more expensive home really defeats the purpose of trying to reduce living expenses and tax burdens at retirement.

Q. When we sell our house, can we deduct our fix-up costs to reduce the profits that are subject to the capital gains tax?

A. Yes, provided the home improvements are done within 90 days prior to your buyer signing the contract. Deductions are allowed for cosmetic work that make your home more salable, such as painting and repairs. Don't forget that selling expenses (marketing, broker's commissions, etc.) can also be deducted. When you subtract both home improvement costs and selling expenses, that is your adjusted sales price. To determine the amount that is subject to capital gains taxes, follow this example:

$150,000	Sale price
-10,500	Broker's commission (7%)
-7,500	Fix up costs
$132,000	Adjusted sale price
-$89,500	Purchase price of replacement home
$42,500	Profits subject to tax (unless you are 55 and eligible for the capital gains exclusion)

Q. How can the banks get away with promoting what looks like bargain-basement interest rates when they're not the total cost?

A. The banks are very clever in claiming that these additional charges aren't interest payments per say. They are added expenses for the privilege of using the lender's money. They can call them whatever they like, but those fees are a very large part of the cost of borrowing money. And every month when you pay the APR, you'll be reminded of just how much.

Q. What should we know about points?

A. The dreaded "P" word for mortgage shoppers is points—the prepayment of interest that buyers pay at the closing. Each point you pay is equivalent to 1 percent of the loan. Thus, if you're borrowing $100,000 and are being charged 2 points by the lender, you will pay an additional $2,000 just for the privilege of doing business with the bank. Remember that this charge is separate from the down payment and other closing costs.

Q. We're in our early 60s and plan to finance our next house. We don't expect the banks to give us a 30-year mortgage, but what we want to know is this: Are our monthly payments going to double if we apply for a 15-year loan?

A. The biggest difference between a 30-year and 15-year commitment is that with the shorter-term loan, you'll pay a quarter to a half-percent less in interest rates while saving 15 years of interest payments. Think of it as 180 big checks you won't have to write! The interesting thing about 15-year mortgages is that most people assume that the monthly payments will be twice as high as a monthly payment on a 30-year loan. Surprisingly, it doesn't work that way. Payments on a 15-year loan are usually only 10 percent to 20 percent higher. So on that same $50,000 loan, your payments would be another $463.51 a month (at 7½ percent), compared to the 30-year loan, which would run $358.21

a month (7 3/4 percent). The difference is $105.30 a month. But again, the 15-year mortgage has 180 less payments.

Q. Can we deduct the interest on our home equity loan?

A. As of 1987, Congress passed laws that stated unless you were borrowing to buy, build or improve a home, home equity loans were considered home equity debt, which limited their deductibility. Given the immense popularity of these loans due to low interest rates, the restrictions over the amount of interest you can deduct have been eased a bit. Basically, the loan is fully deductible up to $100,000. If the loan exceeds $100,000 and is less than the homeowner's equity and improvements, no further interest deductions are allowed.

Q. I understand how mortgages work, but I'm not sure I know what to ask when shopping for a home equity loan. What do you suggest?

A. There are dozens of deals around, and they may all look and sound the same—until you investigate further. Bur since we're talking about putting your home up as collateral, you want to be sure you know precisely the terms of the agreement. Here is a list of questions to ask each prospective lender:

1. What does it cost to apply for the loan, and is the fee refundable if I change my mind or don't qualify?

2. How long will it take the bank to approve the loan? (One month should be enough time.)

3. What are the minimum and maximum allowable loans? (Determine in advance how much you'll need for your move to Florida.)

4. If I'm borrowing let's say $50,000, what are the terms? What will be the monthly payments and for how many months? Is there a large balloon payment at the end of the loan?

5. Is there a penalty for prepayment? Is there an annual maintenance fee, even if I owe nothing on the loan?

6. Which index is my variable interest rate tied to? How often will rates change, and, therefore, how often will increased costs be passed along to me?

7. What is the annual ceiling or cap on the interest rates?

8. What portion of each payment will be tax-deductible?

9. Adding up the monthly payments along with the upfront fees, how does the total compare with the amount I'd pay if I took out a second mortgage or used some other sort of financing arrangement?

10. Finally, what are the closing costs? How many points will I be paying for the privilege of using this bank's money?

Remember that in today's competitive home financing market, there are plenty of fish in the sea. If you're dissatisfied with the deal at one place, keep shopping.

Q. What would happen if we defaulted on the home equity loan?
A. Just as you would with a primary mortgage, you'd face foreclosure or be forced to sell the home. No if's, and's, or but's about it.

Q. When is it advantageous to consider an adjustable rate mortgage?
A. Lower interest rates and lower monthly payments make ARMs ideal for people who are certain they'll sell the house within five years of buying or who are in the process of selling off other real estate and will be able to use the proceeds from the sale to pay off this new mortgage early. Just remember that the advantage of ARMs means betting that interest rates will stay low. Nobody has that guarantee in writing!

Q. What should we know about adjustables?
A. First of all, people are sometimes so pleased about paying less up-front that they neglect to consider what happens when interest rates do go up—and they most certainly will at some point in the life cycle of the loan. Secondly, banks use different market indexes to determine rate fluctuation. For example, some banks interest rates are tied to T-bills, Treasury securities, Fannie Maes, etc. (it just has to be a public index that the lender doesn't control). Thus, when comparison-shopping, the comparison is only relevant to the APR at the moment. In other words, on the loan's anniversary, if you didn't go with the bank whose mortgages were tied to the six-month T-bill and its interest rates are now lowest, you'll pay more than those who chose the bank tied to one-year T-bills. From year to year, it's a horse race, but that's the name of the game.

Q. What else should we compare when looking at adjustables?
A. Compare the bank's margins over index. Many people aren't aware that lenders adjust their rates not only

against a financial index, but against a separate "profit" margin. This margin is extra interest charged by the lenders to cover their administrative expenses. An example of this is a loan that starts out at 7 percent. At adjustment time, the lender's index might be at 6 percent. But an added 2.5 percent for "margins" could be tacked on, making your new interest rate 8.5 percent. What this means is that even if interest rates did not fluctuate by 2.5 percent by the anniversary date, you'll pay an increased amount anyway (or whatever the maximum cap is in your contract). You can count on an annual cap of 2 percent, which in this case would have resulted in an interest rate of 8 percent.

Q. What is negative amortization?
A. Negative amortization is the bank's revenge for not making enough money. Some ARMs contracts allow that when your total monthly payment is insufficient to cover the amount of interest due because the bank is limited to a 2-percent cap per year, the bank can just make up the difference at the end of the loan. It's possible that your last payment could represent the entire difference between what you paid and what the bank had to pay for the money. That could be a whopper. Lenders argue that negative amortization keeps the customer's monthly payments lower and more stable. This is true, but be aware that it increases your overall indebtedness. Make sure you understand how your bank handles this situation before you sign on the dotted line.

What I tell my clients

When a mortgage broker holds the key. With such a tremendous range of options, it is not surprising that some people are more than delighted to let a mortgage broker call the shots. The question is, is using a broker the right decision? Unfortunately there is no easy answer. It really depends on the particular broker, his or her reputation and staying power in the business, and the relationships he or she has with the local lenders.

If you apply for a mortgage at the bank where you are currently a depositor, it's possible to get an "insider discount," which could be better than the deal a broker gets for you. On the other hand, working with a professional who knows the intricacies of this complex financing could well work to your advantage. Nothing can compare with previous experience with various lenders, knowledge of mortgage trends, and skill at handling complex problems such as needing a bridge loan or trying to overcome a questionable credit history. A broker may be familiar with banks that are going to be accommodating.

But there is a possible catch. If the broker does a considerable amount of business with only certain banks, you need to question whether that relationship benefits the broker more than you. You just have to do your homework. If you can find a broker who's been referred by family or friends and you think they can arrange for better financing than you could on your own, it could be a smart move.

Do it yourself, with a little help. Another option if you'd like to do the shopping yourself, but with some impressive weaponry in hand, is purchasing the *Homebuyer's Mortgage Kit* from a New Jersey-based firm, HSH Associates. It is the nation's largest publisher of mortgage information. For a nominal $20 fee, you'll receive a host of user-friendly tips on negotiating the best deal for yourself, along with updated comparisons of interest rates, terms, down payments, points, lender margins, indexes, application fees, number of days the bank will lock in quoted rates and much more information—on the major lenders all over the country. Call 800-873-2837 or 201-838-3330 (New Jersey residents). For more information. Or write to HSH Associates, 1200 Route 23, Butler, NJ 07405.

Get it in writing. After you've gone through the trouble of negotiating a satisfactory mortgage commitment, the most important step is getting everything confirmed in a letter: interest rates, points, the length of time they'll lock in the offer, etc. Also, you want to know what will happen if the lending rates go down by the time you're ready to close. Finally, make sure that letter is signed by a bank officer.

Finding a fabulous place to retire. Finally, one of the most difficult decisions retirees have to make today is whether to relocate. We've discussed the numerous reasons it can be advantageous from a financial perspective, but what about all the personal issues that would come up? How could you ever leave your children and grandchildren? What if you still want to work or own a business? What if you don't know anyone living in the cities that appeal to you? And, most important, how would

you even begin to get started on a search for the ideal place? I grappled with these and many other tough questions when I recently co-authored the book, *50 Fabulous Places to Retire in America* (Career Press, $14.95). We not only identified some of the most wonderful places for active retirees to settle, but we spent the first part of the book telling you how to arrive at your decisions and how to save time and money in the process. There are helpful chapters on how to pick out the ideal retirement destination, how to prepare financially for a relocation, and even how to keep moving costs down. Then we go on to describe 50 fabulous places in great detail, providing easy-to-read information on real estate buys, taxes and living costs, recreation and culture, climate, crime, health care and many other essential criteria. If you are seriously considering a relocation when you retire, I know you'll find this book extremely useful. It's in all the major bookstores, or you can order a copy by calling the publisher at 1-800-955-7373.

In these uncertain economic times, the ability to trade down and/or relocate at retirement and to have a whole host of mortgage options have truly been lifesavers for millions of retirees who would otherwise not have known where to turn for income and security. And isn't it wonderful that, in the end, the home they cherished and enjoyed all those years actually had a slush fund growing in the backyard the whole time?

8

Early retirement:
Ready or not

It seems you can't pick up a news-paper or magazine today without reading about early retirement. Understandably, for millions of Americans who are overworked and underpaid, telling the boss you are retiring to Tahiti would be a dream-come-true (especially if the *boss* is older)! Short of winning the Powerball lottery, early retirement is the ultimate beat-the-system fantasy. And yet, ironically, in today's economy, you have to be careful what you wish for. Checking out of the rat race prematurely is wonderful, unless it is because your company has terminated you. Or because your health is preventing you from working at the same pace—or at all. And then there are those for whom the early retirement issue is a complete puzzle, now that their employer has presented them with a once-in-a-lifetime offer. Should they take the money and run? Or stick around and take their chances?

If you are in the throes of an early retirement decision, whether planned or forced, this chapter will help you better understand your choices, so you can make the best possible moves.

Are you being forced to retire?

Consider the "fiftysomething" crowd, many of whom are in the fight of their lives! In one corner of the ring stands the former heavyweight champ, the giant corporation. In the opposing corner is the older American worker, a mere featherweight in the scheme of things. The corporation, once a proud contender, hasn't had the strength to withstand the vicious left-and-right hooks—foreign competition and incalculable debts. To stop the bleeding, it retaliates with massive layoffs. The challenger ducks, just hoping to stay in the ring long enough to reach retirement age.

Unfortunately, since 1990, close to a quarter of a million older workers haven't ducked fast enough! According to the Department of Labor's Bureau of Labor Statistics, more than 2,600 U.S.-based companies instituted substantial layoffs, severing ties with 586,690 workers. Of those, 12.2 percent, were between the ages of 55 and 64. Currently, the unemployment rate for this group is an astounding 5.5 percent, compared to a rate of 3 percent in 1990. And it has also been projected that an additional 85,000 older employees could be terminated by year's end.

While there is never a good time to be out of work, the 50- or 60-year-old who loses his or her job in the middle of a recession is more likely to experience a forced retirement! Evidence of this comes from recent Labor Department estimates that 66 percent of all pink slips issued between 1990 and 1992 are expected to be permanent. Certainly, this affects people of any age, but the older generation has the *greatest* risk of not being rehired.

Even in the best of times, given a choice between bringing in a junior employee or an older, experienced one, companies will invariably give the job to the "kid." The younger the worker, the lower the salary, the less costly the benefits and the less likely he or she will be to stick around to tap into those coveted pension funds. But during uncertain economic times, carrying employees to the ends of their careers has become too heavy a burden for many financially strapped firms.

It's the very reason corporations, school districts and manufacturers that are *not* laying off, are dangling lucrative early retirement offers in front of long-time employees ("Take all the time you need to decide, just get back to us in 10 days"). It's also why older employees

who suddenly face unexpected personal circumstances, such as needing time off to care for an elderly parent, are genuinely concerned that if they miss work, they'll be out a job.

What is so bad about retiring early? Nothing, if you are financially prepared. But as we've discussed, an estimated 90 percent of all Americans are not financially prepared for retirement by age 65. A *forced* retirement five to 10 years before then is the ultimate knockout! After paying off mortgages, investing in the children's education and juggling financial obligations, older workers find that the final years of a career are generally the most critical. It is most often the last, best hope to *save* for retirement. To make matters worse, it also usually deprives people of earnings that would have been at the highest level of their careers. Taking away this opportunity to "stash the cash" is the cruelest punishment of all.

What to do if you are forced to retire

I remember a few years ago when a friend of the family was terminated from his management job at a national optical chain. After months of rumors and ominous memos circulating through the office, the chain was in fact bought out by a large conglomerate and several hundred employees were let go. Although he had been expecting this, and actually felt relief that the limbo dance was over, he had a nagging suspicion that he was in for a rough time. Companies weren't rolling down the red carpet for high-paid professionals in their late 50s. And yet he really wasn't prepared to retire either. Both from an emotional and a financial point of view, he wanted a few years to get ready. After a year of interviews, consulting, and facing the prospect he might never work again, he got a call to come back to work for the company that had let him go. He said it made him feel like the accident victim who fully recovered and got a new lease on life. From now on, he would take nothing for granted.

His experience, and that of dozens of clients who have been similarly shell-shocked by the loss of a job has given me some important insights on how to cope with being forced to retire—even temporarily. It's a big debate as to which is worse—the psychological or financial impact. But both have to be dealt with. So whether you knew it was coming or were completely startled by the pink slip, here are my recommendations for pulling yourself through the crises:

1. Be like a TV and network. While it is understandable that someone would feel shame and embarrassment about losing a job, in today's economy, millions of hard-working and talented people have been let go. This has nothing to do with skills or competence. So let the word out about your availability. As they say, "telephone, telegraph and tell your mother!" The point is, the more people who are aware of your circumstances, the more likely you are to have someone give you contact names that could land job interviews. One of the regrets I heard people express was that they let their pride get in the way of asking colleagues, friends and family for assistance. They later realized this was the time they needed their help most.

2. Have a funeral and bury the loss. The traditional mourning period and burial rituals observed throughout the world when a loved one dies are perhaps some of the smartest customs we humans ever established. It allows the survivors to express their deepest sadness, be surrounded by family and friends, face the reality of the death by watching the burial and then gradually learn to accept the loss and get back to living. Psychologically speaking, it could be very helpful to go through a similar process, even if the loss is a job rather than a person. Acknowledge, mourn, accept and move on so you don't waste precious time (months and even years) being consumed with anger and anxiety. Too often, we see people so shattered by the experience, they are unable to be objective about their circumstances or to have enough self-confidence to turn things around. Perhaps, then, the best way to survive the ordeal is to allow a "mourning" period and then force yourself to get on with it.

3. Turn lemons into lemonade. When I've talked to clients who are dismayed at losing their jobs, invariably I discover that they were unhappy anyway. Perhaps they were bored or stifled after many years of performing the same tasks. Or maybe the politics were so unbearable they dreaded going in altogether. Whatever the cause of dissatisfaction, the feelings are somehow forgotten if they are let go. All the person can think about is that they were jilted. But I think it is important to look objectively at the job to determine if you are actually better off without it. Things do have a tendency to work out for the best. Maybe this is the push you needed to pursue something of great interest, something you have always wanted to do. In effect, it is more helpful to focus on what you have to gain than what you have lost.

4. Thinking on your feet. Sometimes, the worst part of being out of work is that you end up spending too much time at home. And, suddenly, that home you loved feels like a prison. The phone doesn't ring when you want it to (or when it does, it's not for you), you confirm that daytime television is the worst dreck in the world, and you always feel you're in the way of your kids and spouse. Even the cleaning lady makes you feel like you are a nuisance. No wonder people get depressed and revert to overeating, smoking, drinking, etc. To avoid these temptations, use some of your free time to walk, jog, play tennis, work out—anything that will help you clean out the cobwebs. It is also common knowledge that some of our best brainstorms occur when we're working out (it's all that oxygen to the brain). I guarantee you that continuous physical activity will help you cope and think more clearly than if you spend the day moping. Besides, when you do get a job, the last thing you'll want is to be 15 pounds overweight when you start.

5. The haves and the have nots. The other crisis unemployed people have to deal with is feeling sorry for themselves and comparing their lives to those who are seemingly much better off. Here you are, just trying to make it through the month and your best friend is getting ready to take her family on a ski vacation, etc. After a while the tendency is to avoid contact with the enemy (translate: anyone who has a job). You avoid social engagements, family parties and, more important, doing the things you really enjoy out of fear that you will

feel humiliated when you meet your contemporaries. But all this does is alienate the people who care most about you and leave you starved for contact. The idea is to keep moving, stay involved and maintain a positive attitude.

6. Make a decision. People who have been fired often talk about feeling a complete loss of control. And while it is true that being let go was clearly not your decision, that doesn't mean you aren't free to pursue choices you do have control over. Decide to go back to school, learn new skills, or to interview with your former company's biggest competitor. Maybe you'll decide to do consulting work or open a business. It almost doesn't matter what you decide—just that you are determined to do something and that whatever it is, it was *your* decision!

7. Nobody can force you to retire. The ultimate decision you can make is deciding to retire—or not. And don't, for one second, think it is something in which you have no choice. No one can tell you that you are too old or out of touch to be marketable. So consider your options. If you can afford to retire and you had planned to do so in a short time, it may be OK that your timetable was pushed up. If you absolutely want to go back to work, then pursue it with a vengeance. Either way, it is your call!

Keep your financial house from being a house of cards

As if it isn't bad enough not having a place to go when you are out of work, what's worse is the likelihood of being home to greet the mailman, who may greet you with bills, bills and more bills. The question is, what can you do to keep your financial affairs in order when you are temporarily out of work or retiring earlier than expected?

Incidentally, these tough questions have to be addressed whether you've been fired or were forced to resign because of a health problem. An estimated 30 percent of all early retirees stopped working because of a medical condition, disability or accident.

In either case, there are numerous steps you can take, on an as-needed basis, to stay in control of your money. Often, your biggest decision is not *what* to do, but *when* to do it. If you are out of work for six months with no prospects on the horizon, do you sell off your investments and cash in your IRA? If you are out of work for a year, do you put the house on the market?

These are some of the difficult choices you will have to make, but this doesn't mean you have to make these decisions in a vacuum. The ability to preserve your assets may be one of the most important steps you take, so it will be vital to get the guidance and expertise of a financial planner, accountant or investment advisor. A financial professional has the experience and will be up to date on the laws so he or she can make the best possible recommendations for you.

In the meantime, there are many common-sense strategies you can use to keep your finances in check when you have been fired and are unable to find a new job right away. Ironically, they are identical to the concepts we have already discussed in each of the previous chapters. The difference is, now they must go from the "good idea" file to the "must-do" file.

To help you reevaluate the most appropriate money-saving, money-preserving, and money-making ideas from *Retirement Ready or Not*, here is a list of the recommended strategies that will be most helpful while you are out of work or getting a head start on your retirement.

In addition to all of the strategies we have already covered, here are some other money-saving suggestions for your consideration.

1. Don't pay a premium unnecessarily. Why pay premiums for a disability policy when you don't have a salary that can be replaced if you become disabled? As for life insurance, if your home is paid off and your children grown, you may want to consider reducing your coverage since your financial obligations have changed. The savings could be substantial enough to be redirected to pay for health insurance, long-term care, a Medicare supplement, etc. A word of caution—by no means should you cancel all of your life insurance. You've probably paid premiums your whole adult life—why leave your survivor without death benefits when they are closer than ever in age to receive them? Furthermore, life insurance benefits may still be needed to pay for funeral expenses, estate and income taxes, and other debts.

2. Aggressive investing will help, not hurt. Although the tendency, when you are out of work, is to minimize your investment risks because you are afraid to jeopardize the few things that are secure, it may actually be more effective to take a more aggressive position with your investments. This way, you'll have a better shot at making up for the loss of a paycheck. Naturally, you want to work with a financial planner or advisor to determine the best strategy for you.

3. Think small. Trading down the house is not something to jump into, but may be advisable after a year or two out of work. Even if you are not yet 55 and can't take the capital gains exclusion, just moving into a smaller home where your overall living expenses, property taxes and maintenance will be less. could be a tremendous help. However, I would not recommend selling a home in favor of renting one, if you can help it. Even though real estate is not the inflation hedge it once was, the tax deductions and equity build-up are still mighty valuable assets.

4. You have the right to remain intelligent. It may seem too great a luxury to spend money on a lawyer, accountant, financial planner, etc., but what you don't know *can* hurt you. You may be entitled to much more than you are receiving, either in terms of your pension, medical and other benefits. But how will you know that unless you consult with the experts? A financial planner can guide you through reinvestment decisions to maximize your return while minimizing your tax burden.

5. Don't stop thinking about tomorrow. It's understandable when you are in the middle of a crisis to just concentrate on getting through today. But just because your plans for the future have been sidetracked doesn't mean the future isn't coming any sooner. When you make financial decisions during this period, as difficult as it may be, try not to short-change the next 20 to 30 years of your life because of this setback. In other words, do everything possible to hold onto your retirement nest egg. Hopefully, you will soon be back on your feet. But if, in the meantime, you have started to deplete your long-term investments, you may never again have the opportunity to save at the rate you had to this point.

Evaluating an early retirement offer

Somewhere in between being forced out of a job and voluntarily retiring young is a predicament referred to as the early retirement offer. This is the bait a company dangles in front of older employees to get them to quit sooner than later. And, unless the national economy gets rolling again and fast, benefits and human resources experts are predicting that the early retirement offer will become as commonplace as coffee breaks. Once an unthinkable gesture, today more and more companies consider these "employee buyouts" as important to their bottom line as any other cost-saving or austerity program. Here's why companies look so favorably at them (and why they probably are here to stay):

- If a company needs to cut its payroll and benefit costs, it's much better for its image to extend peace offerings rather than announce massive layoffs.
- Since pension funds have been put aside over the years, the money to pay retirees is often available for distribution. It's not as if the company has to sell more "squidgets" to raise the money.
- With Wall Street and stockholders breathing down their necks, many companies today adhere to the philosophy that you do what's good for the short-term. So reducing the number of high-paid employees and replacing them with younger, lower-paid (albeit less-experienced) personnel is one way to squeeze more profits out of revenues. For example, if a company can get rid of a dozen people earning $50,000 and who might otherwise work for another 10 to 20 years, and replace them with people earning half that, that will make a huge impression on the bottom line.

But what about *your* bottom line? If you are presented with an early retirement offer, how can you know if it is advantageous to you? Nobody wants to wake up five years later kicking themselves for taking the offer or walking away from it, either. The key to evaluating an early retirement offer is to simply estimate the financial impact of staying compared to going.

Let's say you are a 62-year-old earning $70,000. After paying income taxes, Social Security and Medicare taxes, and work-related expenses, your net take-home is around $40,000. Then let's say your company offers you early retirement. The package starts off with a bonus offer of $30,000 ($10,000 for each of three years retiring before age 65), which is added to your $20,000-a-year pension (approximately 30 percent of your average salary for the past three years). Other income sources include $10,000 a year from your IRA, $9,400 in Social Security benefits and $2,000 a year from a 401k plan. After $15,000 in income taxes, plus $5,000 for medical insurance, which would no longer be covered by the employer, your net take-away pay would be approximately $31,000. That's a difference of $9,000 a year less. But if you divided that amount by the number of hours you'd be working per year (comes to about 2,000 hours), your total profits for staying would only be $4.50 an hour ($9,000 for

2,000 hours). Would that be worth it? Probably not.

But then there may be other factors that more definitively tip the scales one way or the other. You need to consult with a financial planner, lawyer, or other expert to determine the following:

- What is the after-tax value of the "sweeteners" the company is offering to get you to say yes? Although it would unlikely compensate you dollar-for-dollar for the loss of salary and benefits if you continued working, would you at least be satisfied with the sweeteners?

- What would be the tax implication of receiving a sizeable bonus for taking an early retirement over and above your salary, vacation pay, final commissions, Christmas bonus, etc?

- If you are shy the years of service required for full vesting, is the company waiving the requirement or "bonusing" you the years so you get 100 percent of the proceeds you are entitled to?

- If the annual pension benefit is based on average salary over the past three years and you agree to leave three years early, is the company offering you enough of a bonus or additional benefits to compensate for the raises you'll miss out on because you've left? This is important, because the incremental increase in salary over this period might have boosted your annual benefits by thousands of dollars.

- If you retire early, would you have to tap into your IRA, mutual funds, etc., right away, or could you delay withdrawals until normal retirement age? If not, what are the financial implications of drawing down on this money earlier than expected?

- If you retire at age 62, would you need to apply for Social Security benefits right away, or could you hold off until age 65? Remember, if you start receiving benefits between the ages of 62 and 65, henceforth, your benefit checks will be smaller than if you had waited to start collecting at age 65.

  NOTE: Refer to the chart on Page 52 in Chapter 2 (Social Security) to determine your estimated monthly benefits if you retire early.

- Who will pay for medical coverage? If the company is not going to pick up the expense, what will your out-of-pocket costs be to continue the same coverage?

- On a personal note, what are your current financial obligations? Do you still have several more years of paying for college? Are you supporting a parent? Are you up to your eyeballs in debt? If you couldn't possibly function on less income, that may be your answer.

These are just some of the questions you'll want answered before you decide to grab the carrot being dangled in front of you. But again, never underestimate the importance of the number-one personal question: "Do you really *want* to retire?" Not everyone does. Since 1977, for example, the Grumman Corporation on Long Island has made four different early retirement offers. The affirmative response from eligible employees has ranged from 17 percent to 51 percent. In the last offer made to 6,000 employees, only one-third have said yes. What will happen to those who stay on? Unless you've got a crystal ball, it's hard to say. However, it shouldn't surprise you that many older employees who pass up these offers walk on eggshells. They are concerned that they may not ever be offered as sweet a deal again or that their jobs will eventually be phased out anyway.

There is something else. You can add and subtract all day long, but that won't change the fact that the only choice many companies are giving employees is 1) take it or 2) leave it.

That's why you have to view the early retirement offer as a whole-life proposition. You can't just consider the money, just as you can't only consider your emotional needs and desires. You have to look at the whole picture, along with the advice of a knowledgeable benefits person, and, hopefully, see your way to a rightful conclusion.

Early retirement by choice

And then there are those for whom early retirement is a dream-come-true. Whether they had the benefit of favorable circumstances or just the foresight to save enough money, every year, more and more people are getting a head start on the good life. According to the Social Security Administration, over 50 percent of men who are age 65 today, have already been retired for at least three years. But that's nothing compared to the increasing numbers of Americans who are plunging into the retirement pool in their 50s and even 40s. While this doesn't mean they are guaranteed

satisfaction or their money back, they are to be commended for seeing to it that their fantasy became a reality.

If you are one who is committed to checking out of the work force before they hand you a gold watch, more power to you. Early retirement could well be the best gift you ever gave yourself, if you plan carefully. Retirement has very little to do with age. It has to do with how many years it will take you to accumulate enough assets so that your money can go to work for you, instead of you for it.

Before we get into the financial implications of an early retirement, it is important to step back for a moment and to consider the emotional impact of this decision. I am no psychologist, but from my experience working with clients who retired early, I've been reminded that, as with every other stage of life, all the money in the world will not buy happiness.

Take the case of my clients, Greg and Paula. They came into my office 10 years ago and told me that they would do whatever it took to retire in their mid-50s. That gave them approximately eight years to save aggressively. Not independently wealthy by any means, they told me about their three-step plan. They would sell their large four-bedroom home and move into a smaller one in a less-affluent area so their property taxes, mortgage and housing costs would be cut by one-third. Next, they would develop a monthly budget and stick to it—even if it meant cutting back on expensive ski vacations and Greg's fetish for antique cars. Finally, they intended to save and invest every dollar that didn't go to pay expenses so that both their retirement funds and college funds for their daughters would flourish.

I was quite impressed by how much thought they'd put into their goals, and quite naturally assumed they were this committed because of a deep desire to do something lofty or exotic with their retirement. Perhaps they wanted to open a sailing school in the Caribbean or work with handicapped children. Imagine my surprise when I asked them about their plans after retirement and they just looked at each other. Paula blurted out, "We're not sure what we want to do. We just know we don't want to be working."

You don't have to be an expert to see that these well-intentioned people were on a collision course. Only in rare exceptions are people content to spend 30 or 40 years aimlessly going about their lives. The rest of us, and particularly those who believe in sacrificing today for a brighter tomorrow, are not the types who could enjoy whiling away the dog days of retirement.

So I urged them think about a variety of activities, hobbies and projects they would consider pursuing. Or to think about new careers that would be so much fun, it wouldn't feel like work. Or to decide if they would be happy owning a small business. Or devoting their days to some type of volunteer capacity. It really didn't matter what they decided—only that they made a decision. Because the only thing more pathetic than a bored teenager is a bored retiree.

The lesson, of course, is that a successful retirement depends as much on planning for your *time* as for your money. If you can't think of at least 10 things you want to do with your freedom, perhaps you shouldn't rush into it. There is no shame in the fact that not everyone is cut out for the leisure life!

Matching luggage, but not matching retirement plans

In another case, my clients Shelly and Vincent were at odds about their retirement plans. Vince had a sizable pension and profit-sharing settlement from his law firm that he was eligible to take at age 55. He was ready, willing and able to retire, especially since their second home on Hilton Head Island was almost complete. Shelly, on the other hand, had just started her career a few years earlier and was now a successful realtor. She loved her work and was equally pleased when the investments she'd made with her commissions grew to be substantial. "Like hell I'm going to retire now!" she told me. "I'm having the time of my life." To which Vince responded, "I just can't warm up to the idea that I'd be out golfing every day while my wife was putting in long hours at the office. What is the point of retiring early if the two of us can't enjoy it together?"

The issue of a dual retirement is a very common dilemma today, in light of the vast numbers of homemakers who didn't start working until their children were grown. She's in the prime of her career while her husband is winding down. What should they do?

As with most other major decisions you've made along the way, the answer is in the compromise. In many cases, I recommend to my clients that they establish a period of time over which they will both ease into retirement. This can be preferable to flicking a switch and changing your lives overnight. If you agree to a weaning process, you can gradually cut back on your hours at work as well as leisurely turn over your accounts or train replacements. This will generally make the transition period go more smoothly, without the usual boredom or loss of self-esteem that is often associated with crash landing on "Planet Retirement."

The acid test: Are you really ready to retire?

At the point that one or both of you have made the decision to retire, invariably the soul-searching begins. Are you really ready for this? On the other hand, how do you know if you are ready for something you have never done before? (If this sounds like a familiar quandary, it's because you may have asked yourself the same thing when you were contemplating marriage for the first time.) And yet, it is very important to be sure you are emotionally and financially prepared to downshift into retirement after 60 or so years of being in high gear.

Over the years, I've had many clients call me with cold feet a few months before they were scheduled to retire. When that happens, I suggest that they practice retiring before they take the plunge. Do a dress rehearsal.

The way this works is you try to simulate a schedule that would most closely match how you would spend your days. For example, one weekend you could pretend that it was really two weekdays instead. If you were retired, what time would you get up and how would you fill your day? With hobbies, volunteer work, a golf or tennis game, a consulting job? In addition, you'd rehearse your budget to find out how much money it took to get through the day doing the things you enjoyed.

After a few days of "rehearsals," most people report back that it was an enlightening and motivating experience.

For example, my clients Craig and Beverly used a week's vacation time six months before retiring to play the role of the retired couple. Beverly called a few days later to say she felt like the lady in "Diary of a Mad Housewife." "This isn't going so great," she said. "We've kept busy with activities, but it's like being on vacation. You feel guilty if you're not on the go all the time. Also, most of our friends still work, so we spend a lot of time with each other, which we're not used to. Our daughter asked me to baby-sit so she could go to a matinee in the city, which I sort of resented. But the worst part was being home to answer the 150 calls from phone solicitors. This isn't what I expected."

Craig had concerns, too. "In one week, we spent over $300 eating out, going to the movies, renting a fishing boat, going to the museums in the city and buying a new tennis racquet for Beverly. If we did that every week, we'd be in big trouble."

Fortunately for this couple, and others who do a run-through, there is still time to think through the problems and try to resolve them before the real starting gun sounds. You can try to create a more realistic budget and a more realistic schedule, based on your retirement experiment. You can have a better sense of what is considered an essential expense and what is a frill. You can determine if you enjoyed the free time and lack of responsibility or if you'd be much happier with a routine.

In spite of the possible trepidations or obstacles, if having personal freedom and the ability to make real choices would be an absolute dream for you and/or your spouse, what can you do to insure that an early retirement is a viable option when you are ready? There are dozens of savings and investment strategies, but they all boil down to this: You have to start saving as early as possible and you can't let up until you see the whites of your boss's eyes—from your rear view mirror!

What's age got to do with it?

It has been said that youth is wasted on the young. But the one thing a 20- or 30-year-old most definitely has over his or her parents is the gift of time. This is especially true when it comes to saving for retirement. Because of the opportunities for compounding both principal and interest, which can accrue at an almost dizzying pace if properly invested, the younger the investor, the more dramatic the bottom line.

Take a look at the example on the next page, which shows what happened to two different investors—one who started saving for retirement at age 35, the other at age 45. Both earned 10 percent annual interest on their respective mutual fund investments.

As you can see, in spite of the fact that the 45-year-old invested triple the amount invested by the 35-year-old, he never made up for the 10-year savings delay. In spite of spending $100,000 more, the 45-year-old's earnings were close to $170,000 less than those of the 35-year-old, a differential of approximately 30 percent.

The lesson is quite sobering and very real. For every year you fail to put away the maximum allowable and/or affordable, you will be forced to put away a higher amount for an ultimately smaller return. That's why the price of procrastinating is simply too high.

When all is said and done, who gets to retire early?

I wish I could tell you that there was a magic formula for guaranteeing an early retirement, but there is no replacement for hard work, systematic savings, aggressive investing and, yes, some good luck along the way. (If not for luck, how else could you attribute success to people you don't like?) When the race to retire approaches the finish line, the people who are invariably there first match one of the following profiles:

1. Those who methodically put away 20 percent of their earnings every year for at least 15 years and who did not live beyond their means during this period. If they were part of a two-income household with two pensions and/or other retirement plans, that probably cemented the deal.

2. High-level executives or successful entrepreneurs who accumulated significant wealth throughout their careers.

3. People who received sizable inheritances.

4. Serious investors who, as a result of wise and sometimes lucky choices, made a killing in real estate and/or the stock market.

5. Lottery winners.

Since the vast majority of us are not likely to fit in categories of 2, 3, 4 or 5, that leaves 1. The one that depends not on luck and circumstances, but on having a steady and deliberate savings program. It's a harder road, but still more

Retirement savings starting at age 35 vs. age 45

| Age | Investor: Age 35 | | Investor: Age 45 | |
	Invested	Accumulated Value	Invested	Accumulated Value
35	$5,000	$ 5,524	0	
36	$5,000	$ 11,626	0	
37	$5,000	$ 18,366	0	
38	$5,000	$ 25,813	0	
39	$5,000	$ 34,040	0	
40	$5,000	$ 43,128	0	
41	$5,000	$ 53,168	0	
42	$5,000	$ 64,258	0	
43	$5,000	$ 76,511	0	
44	$5,000	$ 90,046	0	
45		$ 99,476	$7,500	$ 8,285
46		$109,981	$7,500	$ 17,438
47		$121,398	$7,500	$ 25,549
48		$134,111	$7,500	$ 38,719
49		$148,154	$7,500	$ 51,059
50		$163,667	$7,500	$ 64,691
51		$180,806	$7,500	$ 79,751
52		$199,736	$7,500	$ 96,387
53		$220,653	$7,500	$114,765
54		$243,759	$7,500	$135,068
55		$269,284	$7,500	$157,496
56		$297,481	$7,500	$182,274
57		$328,631		$209,645
58		$363,043		$239,883
59		$401,059		$273,827
60		$443,055		$310,190
61		$489,448		$350,956
62		$540,700		$395,991
63		$597,318		$445,742
64		$659,865		$500,702
65		$728,962		$561,417

TOTAL INVESTMENT: $ 50,000
TOTAL RETURN: $728,962

TOTAL INVESTMENT: $157,500
TOTAL RETURN: $561,417

than possible. Here are the keys to unlocking the dream:

- Take maximum advantage of company-sponsored savings plans, particularly the ones that offer matching funds and tax-deferred growth.

- If you are a professional, freelancer or business owner, establish the proper retirement plan(s) and contribute the absolute maximum every year.

- Set up a payroll deduction program where a set amount is taken from your paycheck and invested in a savings or retirement plan before your paycheck hits your desk.

- Unless there is an extreme emergency, don't touch the money. Once you start withdrawing the money and accepting the penalties and taxes as the price of owning a safety net, say good-bye to your nest egg. Even if you pay back the money you borrowed, it is hard to break the habit of tapping into a growing resource. As with cigarettes, the best way to stop is never to start.

- Live within your means. Live within your means. Live within your means.

The bottom line is that in most instances, to make early retirement happen, there has to be more than wishful thinking. You must be 100-percent committed to the cause and be willing to sacrifice.

Good question!

Q. What is a retirement window?
A. It is the amount of time a company gives employees to decide to take or leave its early retirement offer. The average company gives employees a 30-day window of opportunity, but others are pushing for answers in as little as 10 to 14 days.

Q. How much does age have a bearing on whether the early retirement offer is good or not?
A. A lot. The problem with early retirement offers is that the younger the employee, the more likely he or she will come out on the short end of the stick, no matter how many sweeteners are in the deal. For example, a person who retires at age 55 not only loses potential salary increases over the next 10 years, but, subsequently, loses the raise in pension benefits as well. According to the actuarial tables, a 55-year-old is only likely to receive 25 percent of what a 65-year-old would get. That's why the older you are, the more meaningful the offer.

Q. My company is offering lifetime medical coverage as part of my early retirement offer. I figured that could save me about $4,500 a year. The problem is, the reason they're making the offer to 2,000 employees is because they're in trouble. How do I know they'll meet this commitment down the road?
A. If the company gives itself the option to reduce or terminate medical benefits for retirees, you are out of luck. Even if that option isn't in the contract, but the company goes bankrupt or is bought out, you still have no guarantee of holding on to that benefit. The only realistic

way to weigh the value of this coverage is to say that it will be great for every year you have it, which might not be for long. The number of companies with 200 or more employees paying the medical benefits of retirees is now down to 41 percent (KPMG/Peat Marwick).

Q. I turn 62 in December and thought that would be the perfect time to retire. But the company's fiscal year begins in June. Does that have any bearing on when I leave?

A. It certainly could. It's possible that if you stayed the extra six months, you'd earn a credit for another full year of service for the purpose of calculating your benefits.

Q. I plan to take my company's early retirement offer. Does that disqualify me from applying for unemployment benefits?

A. I have urged several clients to go down and apply for unemployment after they've accepted early retirement offers and they discovered they were entitled to benefits. I've heard of other instances of people being turned down. It seems to depend on how the agreement is worded and also the specific terms of the agreement. It certainly wouldn't hurt to apply at the local unemployment office.

Q. Because of a recent heart condition, my doctor has advised me to retire or work from home. I am only 57. I have a small disability policy, but do you think I may be eligible for any other benefits?

A. Possibly. It all depends on the nature of the disability. But it won't hurt to check out the following: Contact Social Security and find out if you are eligible for disability benefits. If you have a company pension, find out whether your disability qualifies you for early withdrawals from your retirement benefits. Also, check your life insurance policies to determine if you can stop paying premiums because you are disabled.

Q. I've read a lot of magazine articles recently about early retirement and they make it sound so exciting. But what are the pitfalls?

A. The most obvious potential drawback of retiring early is boredom. Not everyone is a hobbyist or has ambitions to travel, start a business, etc. Often the lack of routine and long days to fill become a nemesis rather than a joy. From the financial end, the two biggest headaches are inflation and medical coverage. The younger you are when you retire, the more important it is to insure that your investments are outpacing inflation so that you can maintain the status quo every year. For example, since interest rates have dropped, it has taken the wind right out of the sails (and sales) of CDs and other so-called "thoroughbred" investments. This has resulted in tens of thousands of retirees scrambling for cover and trying to make ends meet because they can no longer live off the interest. As for health care costs, the further away you are from being eligible for Medicare, the more years you'll have to pay your own medical benefits. Not only will that represent a major and growing expense every year, if you don't have good coverage, it will take away a big piece of your nest egg. In the end, you can't seriously consider an early retirement unless you have anticipated and planned for all the cost-of-living increases.

Q. Next year I'll be 47 and plan to retire after 25 years with the local police force. I have a good pension, but I want to know, if I take another job that has a pension plan, would I still be able to participate?
A. The more pensions, the merrier. In fact, it is quite common for young retirees to start second careers, many of which allow them to participate in second pensions. However, if you take a job that doesn't offer a pension, remember that just because you are receiving pension benefits already, this would not prevent you from contributing to an IRA or other type of retirement fund.

What I tell my clients

Did you hear the one about the guy who semi-retired? He drove half way to work and then went home! I know it's a joke, but there's actually a bright idea behind the punchline. Over the years, I've discovered how beneficial it can be for people to ease into retirement by working part-time. Certainly you can try to cut back your hours, but if your employer balks at the idea, propose an arrangement that would benefit both you and the company. Offer to fill in during its busy season, or when other employees go on vacation, maternity leave, disability, etc. This is an excellent way to work part-time, while staying in touch with people you enjoy *and* earning extra income.

How about switching hats? Here's an idea from all the young, enterprising hotshots who have chosen to be independent contractors rather than employees. All over the country, companies who needed to cut payroll and benefits costs have been retaining the services of former employees. Although the person may essentially be performing the same duties, the company has contracted the former employee for those services, instead of hiring him or her as a full-time worker. This is an excellent strategy for an older worker who wants to slow down but doesn't want to be confined to the 9-to-5 grind. It's also a way to focus on the areas of your business that you find most challenging and gratifying. Before you propose the idea, sit down and put together a written plan that outlines the services you'd provide, the hours or days you would work and what your rates would be. If you strike out with your boss, present the proposal to your human resources department or to the head of the company. There may be other needs in the company, for which you would be the perfect person to turn to.

Let's see a show of hands for all those who want to take early retirement. With all the corporate downsizing and work force reductions going on today, it is no longer unthinkable to volunteer for early retirement. In fact, if you sense that there are going to be major layoffs in your division or company in the near future, it may be wise to play offense instead of defense. Present the company with an offer they can't refuse. Tell them you don't really want to leave, but given the high cost of holding on to senior staff, perhaps it would be helpful if they let you retire early (assure them you have no plans to join a competitor). What is your price? Perhaps a few extra years of service added to your pension, a fatter severance package than normal, guaranteed health benefits—whatever you've been advised is reasonable by a lawyer, financial planner or other severance expert. If you don't jump before the pink slips or early retirement offers are announced, it is probably too late to negotiate. Also, if your plan fails, be prepared for possible consequences. You could be passed over for a promotion down the road if the company doesn't think you are committed to staying.

Don't forget to write. To former employers, that is, if you have pension benefits coming due from them. Sometimes people get so caught up in the blizzard of paperwork with their current company, they forget to notify former employers of their intentions to retire. It is best to start corresponding with these other companies about six months in advance.

If you can't get a job, *buy* a job. In many parts of the country where the shrinking job market makes it difficult to find good employment opportunities, sometimes a logical solution is to buy a job by starting or buying a business. For funding or to make a down payment, you may be able to use the proceeds from your severance package, tap into your home equity, apply for a business loan from the bank, and/or find investors. Mind you, this approach is not for everyone and it does require a tremendous amount of research and hard work. The hours may be long and, in this day and age of specialists, may be difficult for those who suddenly have to be a jack-of-all-trades. On the other hand, the potential for profits, the opportunity to be the boss, and the job security may be the best reasons to give the idea consideration.

In July 1993, IBM announced that it was eliminating 35,000 jobs and offering another 25,000 employees early retirement (this was in addition to the 25,000 employees who had already agreed to take early leave). It would be hard to imagine a corporate employee anywhere who didn't pause at this news or wonder, if the giant has become a shrinking violet. Is anyone safe?

Unfortunately, American workers have fast become accustomed to headlines such as this and are resigned to the fact that job security is a contradiction in terms.

In light of all the short-term thinking that has resulted in putting so many people out of work, the only prudent course is to do as the girl scouts do, and be prepared. Treat every paycheck as though it were your last, take nothing for granted and stash the cash to the best of your ability. Then, if the other shoe drops, or you decide you want out, you'll be in the enviable position of landing on your feet while others are going into a tailspin. They used to call this attitude PMA, for "positive mental attitude." Now it stands for "protect my assets."

You do what ya gotta do!

Retirement Ready or Not

Your pre-retirement checklist

When the countdown to retirement does begin, refer to the list below to make sure you've covered all the important bases in terms of financial preparation. Place a big "X" by all those that require *immediate* attention.

_____ Do you know the size of your retirement nest egg?

_____ Have you contacted your employer(s) regarding the amount vested in your pension plan(s)? Have you decided how the funds will be disbursed?

_____ Have you contacted Social Security to determine your estimated retirement benefits? Have you informed them that you are ready to receive benefits?

_____ Are you making arrangements to move some of your liquid and equity assets into income-producing vehicles?

_____ Are you aware of the most current tax laws and how they will affect your retirement income?

_____ Have you estimated your living expenses after retirement?

_____ Are you aware of how much it costs you to live now?

_____ Are you cutting back on your living expenses now so that you don't carry unnecessary debts into retirement?

_____ If you plan to work after retirement, are you aware of the income limitations established by Social Security (this is for people who plan to collect benefits *and* work)?

_____ Will your mortgage be paid off when you retire?

_____ Have you reviewed your insurance policies to determine which policies can be restructured or canceled?

_____ Do you have a will and an understanding of the laws pertaining to inheritances, taxes and probate?

_____ Does your spouse, children, relatives or close friend know where important records are kept?

_____ Do you know where you want to live after retirement?

_____ Have you discussed your retirement needs with a Certified Financial Planner?

9

Retirement Jeopardy

Let's see how well you've paid attention. By playing this little game, you'll discover just how high your retirement planning IQ is.

Object of the game: To answer as many questions correctly so that you can build as much as a $1 million dollar retirement nest egg.

How to play the game: Start by selecting a subject you are most knowledgeable about (Social Security, real estate, etc.). Then try to correctly answer each of the questions under that subject. The questions are presented in order of difficulty (although some are total giveaways because we all deserve a break occasionally). The more challenging the question, the more money the correct answer is worth. After you have completed the first subject, move on to the others.

Each subject is worth $125,000. If you answer all 80 questions correctly (eight subjects, 10 questions each), you'll have amassed $1 million! To check your answers and your score, turn to page 228. (If you want to refer to the chapters for answers, it's fine with me. The truth is, in this game, it is more important that you *learn* than earn.)

How to win the game: Anyone who accumulates enough money to retire comfortably is a winner. But for argument's sake, here is how to evaluate your score.

$0 - $250,000. Your nest egg may not even be large enough to keep a chicken in style. Return to the beginning at once and review the chapters again.

$250,000 - $500,000. You're getting the hang of retirement planning. You understand savings and investment strategies, but may still be far from putting words into action. Make retirement a top priority now.

$500,000 - $750,000. Congratulations! You probably have a good head start on saving for your retirement because you're putting money away at a reasonable pace. You may be falling down in your investment selections. Meet with a financial planner and determine which vehicles will help you accelerate the growth of your nest egg.

$750,000 - $1,000,000. You either have a photographic memory or started the game with lots of financial savvy. Either way, you'll be able to call the shots as to when you can retire. You should be able to live the rest of your life with financial security. Enjoy, enjoy.

Getting financially prepared for retirement
(Chapter 1)

True or false (worth $2,500 each)

1. ____ The average 50-year-old man today is expected to live for another 25 years.
2. ____ The average retiree has a minimal tax burden because he or she doesn't earn a salary any more.

Multiple Choice (worth $7,500 each)

3. ____ To establish your personal net worth, you just:

A. Add up your annual earnings and subtract your annual expenses.
B. Make a list of your assets and add up their worth.
C. Add up all your assets (savings, investments, insurance, etc.) and subtract your liabilities (bills, loans and debts).
D. Project your earnings over your lifetime based on your current income.

4. ____ If you are spending this percentage of your income to pay off loans and bills, you may be in over your head, or worse, unable to have money left over at the end of the month to save.

A. 5%
B. 10%
C. 15% - 20%
D. 20% - 30%

Matching (worth $10,000 each)

5. Match up the amount you would need to save every month in order to save up $250,000, with the correct number of years it would take you to accumulate that amount.

# of Years to Retirement	Monthly Savings Needed to Reach $250,000
5	$168
10	$3,402
20	$424
30	$1,367

6. Match the following terms with the correct definitions.

Cash reserve assets	A. Vested pensions, 401k plans, IRAs, employee stock options
Equity assets	B. Clothing, furniture, cars, jewelry
Retirement assets	C. Checking, savings, money market accounts, CDs
Personal property	D. Stocks, bonds, mutual funds, T-bills, annuities

7. If your retirement nest egg is currently valued at $100,000, match the amount of annual income these assets would pay you at age 65, if you are currently this age:

Annual Income from $100,000	Current Age
$19,827	60
$12,982	40
$30,283	55
$70,638	50

Fill in the correct answers (worth $25,000 each)

8. To save money, the best thing to do with your paycheck is _____

_____

_____

_____

_____

_____

9. What percentage of your current income will you need to live on when you retire?

_____

10. If you are living on a fixed income of $3,000 today, and the inflation rate continues at 4 percent a year, how much money will you need to live on in 15 years to have the same purchasing power? _____

_____

Social Security: Things your mother never taught you
(Chapter 2)

True or false (worth $2,500 each)

11. _____ If the working spouse hasn't yet retired, the nonworking spouse is not yet entitled to receive benefits.
12. _____ If you have not earned 40 work credits or "quarters of coverage," you can still apply for your own benefits, you'll just get less money.

Multiple Choice (worth $7,500 each)

13. _____ How much you will receive in benefits depends on:

A. The age you retire
B. If you were either an average or maximum contributor
C. If one or both spouses worked
D. All of the above

14. _____ The maximum amount of earnings the government taxes for Social Security today is:

A. $57,600
B. $40,500
C. $135,500
D. $75,200

Matching (worth $10,000 each)

15. Match the following terms on the left to the correct definitions to the right.

Fully insured worker   A. Age 65

Delayed retirement credit   B. An individual who has earned 40 work credits or quarters of coverage

Normal retirement age

Personal Earnings and Benefits Statement   C. Earnings records kept by Social Security for the purposing of determining eligibility for benefits

D. A percent increase in benefits for every year you hold off on requesting benefits until age 70

16. Match the percentage of benefits workers are entitled to, depending on the age they retire.

% of Benefits Entitled to	Age Worker Retires
100%	63
80%	65
93%	62
87%	64

17. Match the percentage of benefits workers' spouses are entitled to, depending on the age the worker retires.

% of Benefits Spouse Entitled to	Age Worker Retires
50.0%	64
45.0%	62
41.7%	63
37.5%	65

Fill in the correct answers (worth $25,000 each)

18. If you were born between 1943 and 1954, the normal retirement age established by Social Security will then be _____.

19. Countable income is:
    A. Adjusted gross income before Social Security benefits
    B. Tax-exempt interest income
    C. _____

20. The current ceiling on earned income if you are between ages 62 and 65 and receiving Social Security benefits is $_____.

Examining your medical insurance needs
(Chapter 3)

True or false (worth $2,500 each)

21. ____ The cost of health care is rising annually at more than twice the rate of inflation.

22. ____ Because of the COBRA law, companies are required to allow former employees to continue individual coverage at the company's group rates for up to 18 months.

Multiple Choice (worth $7,500 each)

23. ____ A Health Maintenance Organization (HMO) is:

A. A neighborhood clinic where you can get information on nutrition
B. What you join if you want low out-of-pocket medical care and services provided by physicians under contract to the facility
C. Is a good way to supplement your medical plan at work
D. An organization for seniors who want to stay in shape

24. ____ The important advantages of a Medigap policy is that coverage includes:

A. Dental, occupational therapy and psychotherapy
B. 100 percent of medical care and services not covered by Medicare
C. Deductibles, co-payments, and the difference between actual charges and Medicare's reasonable charges
D. None of the above

Matching (worth $10,000 each)

25. Match the following terms with the correct definitions.

Long-term care

A. Federal health insurance program subsidizing health care coverage for citizens 65 and older, regardless of income and assets

Medicare

B. Federal medical assistance program paying for health care for low-income individuals, the blind and disabled

Medigap   C. A policy that covers nursing home costs or facilities
                                 that provide varying levels of care for those who are
                                 not ill but unable to care for themselves

Medicaid   D. Medicare supplemental policies

26. Match the type of policy with its appropriate benefits.

Catastrophic policy   A. Health care coverage you can buy directly from
                                         an insurance company without an agent

Hospital/medical/surgical policy   B. A high deductible, low-premium policy that
                                         provides hospitalization and medical coverage
                                         in the event the policyholder suffers a major
                                         illness or accident

Major medical policy   C. A private insurance policy for those not eligible
                                         for Medicare that covers hospital room and
                                         board, hospital services and supplies, doctors
                                         visits and surgical procedures

Mail-order health care policy   D. A private insurance policy for those not eligible
                                         for Medicare that covers doctor's visits, lab
                                         tests, x-rays, and possibly prescriptions and
                                         private duty nurses

27. Match up the correct benefits that are covered under either Medicare Part A
(hospital insurance) or Medicare Part B (medical insurance).

Under Medicare Part A   A. Physician's services, inpatient medical services
Under Medicare Part B   B. Skilled home health care
                                 C. Post-hospital skilled nursing care
                                 D. Semi-private room and board

Fill in the correct answers (worth $25,000 each)

28. Other than insuring that a spouse or child will not have to bear the burden of
paying for a loved one's long-term care, the other major advantage of buying a
long-term care policy is: _____

_____

29. If you continue working after age 65, can your employer terminate your health
care coverage because you are now eligible for Medicare?_____

30. If you retire at age 65 and enroll in Medicare, does your younger spouse become
eligible for your Medicare benefits as well?_____

What your retirement plans are really worth
(Chapter 4)

True or false (worth $2,500 each)

31. ____   Most workers are covered by employer-sponsored pension plans.
32. ____   A profit-sharing plan allows the company and employee to share
revenues during a good year by paying out bonuses at year-end.

Multiple Choice (worth $7,500 each)

33. ____   A 401k is an employer-sponsored retirement plan that:

A. Gives employees the opportunity to reduce their current tax bill for
every year because the contribution comes from pre-tax income
B. Requires a contribution from the employer
C. Pays a fixed amount to the employee at retirement
D. Does not limit the contributions of the employee

34. ____   IRA plans are fully deductible up to $2,000 a year of earned income if:

A. Any contribution is made in the tax year of the deposit
B. You and your spouse are not actively participating in a company
sponsored pension plan, or are covered in such a plan but do not
have joint earnings over $40,000
C. You contribute the maximum amount of $2,000
D. IRA plans are no longer tax deductible

Matching (worth $10,000 each)

35. Match the following terms with the correct definitions.

IRA   A. Personal pensions, with contributions from after-tax earnings

ESOP   B. Pensions for self-employed people or private practitioners who want
to contribute up to 30 percent of their net business income

401k   C. Stock ownership plans for employees who want to invest in the
growth of their companies as a way to save for retirement

SEP   D. Self-directed retirement plan that is funded by employee with
possible matching funds from the employer

36. Match the following terms with the correct definitions.

Joint and survivor options   A. The option to take the maximum monthly amount from your pension annuity because payment will end upon your death

Maximum pension benefit   B. Pension annuities that pay a certain amount each month for 10 years, regardless if you died within that period

10-year certain   C. An option for the annuity to revert to the higher benefit amount if the pensioner's beneficiary dies first

Pop-up feature   D. One of four basic options that establishes the amount of the annuity's monthly payout if the beneficiary survives the pension owner

37.   Match the following terms with the correct definitions.

IRA rollover   A. The option to roll over proceeds from one company-sponsored pension into another

Portability   B. The 20 percent of your pension distribution the IRS holds on account until you file your taxes

Withholding tax   C. When you elect to take your pension distribution in both the form of an annuity and a lump sum

Partial distribution   D. The option to roll over proceeds from a company sponsored pension into a personal IRA account

Fill in the correct answers (worth $25,000 each)

38. One of the key advantages of an IRA rollover is the ability to _____ taxes on the lump sum distribution.

39. To further reduce the withdrawal amount of your IRA at age 70½, you should name a _____ as your beneficiary.

40. To tap into your IRA account before 59½ without paying a 10-percent penalty, you must agree to receive a specified amount per month, for no less than _____ months.

Investing for income

(Chapter 5)

True or false (worth $2,500 each)

41. ____ Pensions, annuities and investments will represent more than 50 percent of your retirement income.

42. ____ Over the past 20 years, bank CDs have proven to be the best investments for beating inflation.

Multiple Choice (worth $7,500 each)

43. ____ When managing your retirement portfolio, the best strategy is to:

A. Buy the highest-yielding investments on an annual basis
B. Sell your lowest-paying stocks each year and hold on to only those that showed the strongest gains
C. Design a diversified portfolio based on your risk tolerance and potential income requirements
D. Take your pension annuity choice and let your employer guarantee you a monthly income

44. ____ Municipal bonds are popular income investments for retirees because:

A. They are backed by state and local government
B. They pay a fixed coupon rate for a predictable time period
C. They offer tax-free interest income from federal and, in some cases, state income tax
D. All of the above

Matching (worth $10,000 each)

45. Match the following investments to their respective tax status.

Annuities	A. Tax-free
Municipal bonds	B. Tax-deferred
REITs	C. Taxable
Income mutual funds	D. Tax-advantaged

46. Match the following terms with the correct definitions.

Preferred stocks

A. A way to invest in stocks in the most diversified way by pooling your dollars with other investors so there is enough money to invest in the securities of dozens of different companies

Government mutual funds

B. Bonds that invest in the debt obligations of lower-rated, less mature companies in exchange for a potentially high rate of return

High-yield bonds

C. Investing in a portfolio of U.S. debt obligations with varying maturities, such as T-bills and Ginnie Maes

Mutual funds

D. A hybrid offering the safety of bonds because it pays fixed dividends, but has the potential growth and appreciation of stocks

47. Match the investment options with the proper investment objective.

Growth and income   A. Muni bonds, muni bond mutual funds
Tax-free income   B. CDs, T-bills, government securities
Safety   C. Stocks, stock funds, mutual funds
Growth   D. Utilities, preferred stocks and bonds

Fill in the correct answers (worth $25,000 each)

48. Between 1925 and 1991, what investment outperformed CDs, T-bills and treasury bonds? _____

49. One of the important advantages of a retirement annuity is that you can choose to have it pay you income for either a *period certain* or _____

50. In your investment pyramid, which type of investment should be positioned at the base for safety purposes? _____

Living on your assets
(Chapter 6)

True or false (worth $2,500 each)

51. ____   A funnel force is an instrument you use to shove all of your bills in so
            when they come out the other end, there's enough money to pay them.
52. ____   A master account is an interest-bearing account where you can
            deposit all of your checks when you retire so that you can closely
            monitor your income before disbursing the funds to pay bills or invest.

Multiple Choice (worth $7,500 each)

53. ____   The biggest advantage of setting up a systematic withdrawal account
            with a mutual fund company is:

    A. You can predetermine how much income you'll need and how often
       you'll receive checks
    B. You can get income every month without jeopardizing the current
       value or the appreciation of the account
    C. The account will generally pay dividends, regardless of what is
       happening in the stock market
    D. All of the above

54. ____   To reduce your federal tax bill, you should:

    A. Do your taxes twice a year, double-check your return for errors and
       possibly change your filing status
    B. Voluntarily take a cut in pay
    C. Move to a state that doesn't impose income tax
    D. Switch tax preparers to see if the new person can find "lost"
       deductions

Matching (worth $10,000 each)

55. Match the following terms with the correct definitions.

Adjusted gross income (AGI)   A. Calculates your total investment return by
                               looking at the increase in value and dividing
                               that by the number of years invested

Dollar cost averaging   B. Your annual taxable earnings after allowable
                               exemptions and deductions

Annualized rate of return

C. The special exemption you can claim if more than one family member is supporting a dependent

Multiple support agreement

D. Purchasing more mutual fund shares when prices are low, which will bring down the average price per share but not the actual value of the share

56. Place the investments in their correct order in the funnel force, starting from top to bottom. (HINT: the safest investments are at the top.)

A. Growth and income investments

B. Speculative investments, collectibles, tangible assets

C. Safety and emergency investments

D. Income and tax-free investments

E. Growth, international funds, specialty markets

57. Match the investment problem with the best strategy for solving the problem.

Investment problem

Best strategy for solving the problem

1. Large lump sum settlements at retirement (other than pension) will trigger higher taxes.

A. Choose a different investment, particularly if the investment is starting to decrease the dividend amount, or interest rates are less attractive than when you started.

2. Investor has a 401k and a mutual fund set up for systematic withdrawals, but still needs other income.

B. Try to live off the interest for the first 10 to 15 years of retirement.

3. Investment has lost the potential to meet your financial expectations.

C. Try to increase your 401k contribution and ask your employer to break up the payment into two tax years.

4. You're fearful of tapping into the investment principal too soon.

D. Check out variable-rate annuities for their higher-than-average rates of return and tax-deferred growth.

Fill in the correct answers (worth $25,000 each)

58. What is the best way to insure that your investments give you a "pay raise" every year? _____
_____
_____

59. Ideally, how much money should you have set aside to cover emergencies? _____
_____

60. If you retire and maintain residences in two different states, can you declare that your principal residence is the one that imposes less or no state income tax? _____
_____

Making real estate decisions *real* easy
(Chapter 7)

True or false (worth $2,500 each)

61. _____ Home equity is the difference between the balance of your mortgage and the house's current appraised value.

62. _____ Trading down is when you sell home for well under market value.

Multiple Choice (worth $7,500 each)

63. In order to take advantage of the $125,000 capital gains exclusion:

    A. You or your spouse must be at least 55 years old

    B. You or your spouse must never have claimed this exemption at any other time

    C. Your property must have been owned and occupied by you and/or your spouse as your principal residence for three out of the past five years preceding the sale

    D. All of the above

64. The reason that the capital gains exclusion can be so advantageous is because it:

    A. Allows you to sell your house and avoid paying taxes on the first $125,000 of profits

    B. Allows you to defer the taxes on any excess profits by rolling them over to purchase a different, less-expensive home

    C. Gives you $125,000 tax-free dollars to invest in your retirement nest egg

    D. All of the above

Matching (worth $10,000 each)

65. Match the real estate problem with the best strategy for solving the problem.

Real estate problem

1. You're thinking of moving to Florida, but don't want to sell the house in case you come back. Without selling, you can't afford to move.

2. The market is soft and it's very hard to sell a home, but you've already purchased another house in another state.

Retirement Ready or Not

3. You want to buy a smaller home for retirement, but can't decide between paying cash or taking a mortgage.

4. You're confused by all the mortgage options and don't know which is best.

Best strategy for solving the problem
A. Price the home fairly, choose an aggressive broker and, if possible, be willing to provide seller financing.
B. Determine whether you are still in a high tax bracket and need the deductions, if you will have a predictable cash flow after you retire and could afford payments, and are willing to carry a long-term obligation. If this is the case, it's probably OK to apply for the loan.
C. Don't sell the house, rent it out for a year or two. If the move works, then sell. In the meantime, if you discover you like the new area, take some of the equity of the house to use as a down payment on another home.
D. Avoid variable-rate mortgages because of their unpredictable fluctuations, but consider fixed-rates or adjustables.

66. Match the following terms with the correct definition.

Adjustable-rate mortgage

A. Retired homeowner transfers ownership of house to a family member but continues living in the house paying rent, while the family member pays the retiree a down payment and all taxes, mortgage payments, insurance, etc.

Reverse mortgage

B. Conventional 15- or 30-year loan that results in the same payment of principal and interest every month for the life of the loan

Sale leaseback

C. Mortgage interest can be adjusted at regular intervals based on a fluctuating index

Fixed-rate mortgage

D. A home equity conversion that enables retirees to sell off the equity in their home to the bank in exchange for being able to live there until they die and receive monthly income from the bank

67. Match the following terms with the correct definition.

Negative amortization

A. The pre-payment of interest a buyer pays at the closing on the house

Points

B. Some adjustable-rate mortgages have a clause in the contract that if, due to the cap on interest, the bank had to pay more interest on the money than they charged you, they can tag that expense on to your last mortgage payment

Annual percentage rate (APR)

C. The profits for administrative expenses the bank adds to your adjustable rate mortgage over and above the financial index

Margins

D. The advertised interest rates on a mortgage, plus points, service charges, origination fees, mortgage insurance, etc.

Fill in the correct answers (worth $25,000 each)

68. If you have an adjustable-rate mortgage and the index it is tied to goes up by 5 percent what will happen to your next mortgage payments? _____
_____
_____

69. Is it better to go with a mortgage that offers lower interest and higher points, or higher interest and lower points? _____
_____

70. Can you still deduct interest on a home equity loan? _____
_____

Early retirement: Ready or not
(Chapter 8)

True or false (worth $2,500 each)

71. ____ An estimated 90 percent of all Americans will not be financially prepared to retire at age 65.

72. ____ If you are forced to retire by your employer, you may still be entitled to unemployment benefits, even though you are receiving termination pay.

Multiple Choice (worth $7,500 each)

73. ____ The reason that older workers who are forced to retire are most at risk for not finding other jobs is because:

A. Companies that follow Equal Employment Opportunity guidelines have age quotas
B. Most companies have younger executives today who are uncomfortable bossing employees who are their parents' ages
C. The salaries and benefits of older workers are much costlier than the average younger workers and, besides, there is no shortage of younger workers
D. None of the above

74. ____ People who are most likely to be in a position to retire early by choice are those who:

A. Consistently put away 20 percent of their earnings every year and who live within their means
B. Accumulated significant wealth throughout their careers
C. Received sizeable inheritances or major lottery winnings
D. Invested in real estate and/or the market and made a killing
E. All of the above

Matching (worth $10,000 each)

75. Match a person's total investment amount with the correct amount of his or her return if at age 35 vs. age 45 (based on annual 10-percent return).

Investment amount	Total return
$157,500 (age 45)	$728,962
$50,000 (age 35)	$561,417

76. Match the following terms with the correct definitions.

Retirement window   A. The tough decision faced by a two-income household as to when and if one or both should retire

Sweeteners   B. The special retirement offer made by a company to encourage workers to retire early

Dual retirement dilemma   C. The specific incentives or bonuses an employer offers to convince the employee it is worthwhile to retire early

Employee burnout   D. The amount of time the employer allows for the employee to accept or decline the early retirement offer

77. Match the best strategy with the proper circumstances.

Circumstances	Strategy
Plan to retire early	A. Network, ask friends/colleagues for contacts, bury your losses and move on.
Weighing an early retirement	B. Save 20 percent of your annual earnings, be an aggressive investor, live within your means.
Forced to retire due to health	C. Determine the after-tax value of the sweeteners, the overall impact on your benefits and figure out the extent of your personal financial obligations.
Laid off/forced to retire because of lack of job opportunities	D. Check with Social Security, your pension department, your insurance agent to determine if you are eligible for early benefits, can suspend premium payments or can withdraw funds without penalties.

Fill in the correct answers (worth $25,000 each)

78. Which is better? To retire before or after your company's fiscal year begins?_____

79. If you want to retire early, what is the single most important step you can take to build a retirement nest egg?_____

_____

80. When is the best time to present your employer with your own early retirement offer, an offer to become an independent contract or an offer to retire but fill in during the busy season, etc?_____

_____

Answers

1. True

2. False. Retirees may be in a lower tax bracket, but the effective tax rate may only be minimally lower because of the loss of possible deductions and exemptions.

3. C

4. D

5.
5	$3,402
10	$1,367
20	$424
30	$168

The idea is, the longer you have to save for retirement, the less money you will need to put away each month.

6.
Cash reserve assets	C
Equity assets	D
Retirement assets	A
Personal property	B

7.
$19,827	55
$12,982	60
$30,283	50
$70,638	40

8. To save money, the best thing to do with your paycheck is arrange to have a certain amount taken out before you receive it so that you get into the habit of living on a smaller sum while you are guaranteeing that you are saving money every month. (Any answer that is close in concept is acceptable.)

9. What percentage of your current income will you need to live on when you retire? If you answered 75 percent or more, you are correct.

10. According to the inflation table on page 30, if you lived on $3,000 today and the inflation rate continued at 4 percent a year, you would need $5,400 a month to live on to have the same purchasing power. (Per $1,000 in 15 years would need $1,800 X 3 = $5,400).

11. True

12. False. In order to apply for your own benefits, you must have earned 40 work credits. If you have less than that, or none at all, the only way to receive any benefits is to be married to a fully insured worker.

13. D

14. A

15.
Fully insured worker	B
Delayed retirement credit	D
Normal retirement age	A
Personal Earnings and Benefits Statement	C

16.
100%	65
80%	62
93%	64
87%	63

17.
50%	65
45%	64
41.7%	63
37.5%	62

What is important in both questions 16 and 17 is the understanding that the earlier the worker retires, the less benefits the worker and spouse will be entitled to for the rest of their lives.

18. 66

19. Half of your annual Social Security benefits.

20. $7,440

21. True

22. True

23. B

24. C

25. Long-term care   C
    Medicare   A
    Medigap   D
    Medicaid   B

26. Catastrophic policy   B
    Hospital/medical/surgical policy   C
    Major medical policy   D
    Mailorder health care policy   A

27. Under Medicare Part A   C and D
    Under Medicare Part B   A and B

28. One of the most important advantages of a long-term care policy is that it prevents the reliance on Medicaid, which means the spouse will not have to spend down or divest assets.

29. Thanks to the COBRA laws, no company that employs 20 or more people can discriminate against an employee because of age.

30. Only those individuals who are age-eligible can apply. If your younger spouse is not covered under a medical plan, your former employer must allow your spouse to continue medical coverage under the company's group rates for 36 months.

31. True

32. False. Profit-sharing is not like a Christmas bonus. It is a payout you receive at retirement from money that was put aside for you by your employer during your tenure with the company.

33. A

34. B

35. IRA   A
    ESOP   C
    401k   D
    SEP   B

36. Joint and survivor options   D
    Maximum pension benefit   A
    10-year certain   B
    Pop-up feature   C

37. IRA rollover   D
    Portability   A
    Withholding tax   B
    Partial distribution   C

38. One of the key advantages of an IRA rollover is the ability to defer taxes on the lump sum distribution.

39. To further reduce your IRA withdrawal amount at age 70½, name your child or grandchild as your beneficiary, since the IRS bases the amount you must withdraw on the combined life expectancy of you and your beneficiary.

40. If you tap into your IRA before age 59-and-a-half, you must agree to take

the same payment amount for no less than 60 months.

41. True

42. False. CDs have proven to be one of the worst investments for beating inflation.

43. C

44. D

45. Annuities — A
    Municipal bonds — B
    REITs — D
    Income mutual fund — C

46. Preferred stocks — D
    Government mutual funds — C
    High yield bonds — B
    Mutual funds — A

47. Growth and income — D
    Tax-free income — A
    Safety — B
    Growth — C

48. Over the past 66 years, stocks have outperformed CDs, T-bills and Treasury bonds. The annual rate of return of the S&P 500 Index was 10.38 percent.

49. A retirement annuity can either pay you for a *period certain* or provide income for life.

50. Money market, money market funds and savings accounts should support your investment pyramid. These short-term, interest-bearing, liquid investments give you stability of principal and are needed for cash emergencies.

51. False (although it would be a great device if you could buy it). A funnel force is your investment pyramid turned upside-down, positioning your riskiest investments at the bottom so they are the first to be liquidated. Your safest investments are at the top and the ones that will be preserved the longest.

52. True

53. D

54. A (If you picked C, it's a nice try, but states only impose state income tax.)

55. Adjusted gross income (AGI) — B
    Dollar cost averaging — D
    Annualized rate of return — A
    Multiple support agreement — C

56. Investments in the funnel force should be positioned in this order, starting from the top:

Safety and emergency investments
Income and tax-free investments
Growth and income investments
Growth, international funds, specialty markets
Speculative investments, collectibles, tangible assets

57. 1 — C
    2 — D
    3 — A
    4 — B

58. To insure an annual pay raise, make sure that around 10 percent to 25 percent of your portfolio is invested in growth funds that are projected to outpace annual inflation rates.

59. It is important to have enough money to cover three to six months of expenses sitting in a liquid investment.

60. In order to claim a state as a principal residence, you must actually live in that state for six months of the year. There are other stipulations, so check with your accountant or financial planner before filing.

61. True

62. False. Trading down is when you sell a larger, more expensive home and, subsequently purchase a smaller, less-expensive home so that you can help reduce your overall living expenses at retirement.

63. D

64. D

65. 1   C
    2   A
    3   B
    4   D

66. Adjustable-rate mortgage   C
Reverse mortgage   D
Sale leaseback   A
Fixed-rate mortgage   B

67. Negative amortization   B
Points   A
Annual percentage rate (APR)   D
Margins   C

68. When an index jumps by a large percentage, homeowners with adjustable mortgages are protected by two caps in their contract. The first cap only permits interest to go up by around 2 percent annually (on average). A second cap prevents the interest from going up or down by around 6 percent (on average) over the life of the loan.

69. If you plan to live in a house for five or more years, go for the deal that offers lower interest but higher points. If you plan to live there between one and five years, go for lower points and higher interest. Why pay a steep fee for the short-term use of the money?

70. Home equity loans up to $100,000 are fully deductible.

71. True

72. True

73. C

74. E

75. $50,000 (age 35) $728,962
$157,500 (age 45) $561,417

76. Retirement window   D
Sweeteners   C
Dual retirement dilemma   A
Employee buyout   B

Don't ever forget, the earlier you start saving for retirement, the greater amount you will accumulate—even if you invest three times as much starting as little as 10 years later.

77. Plan to retire early   B
Weighing an early retirement offer   C
Forced to retire due to health   D
Laid off/forced to retire   A

78. It is generally better to retire after the start of your company's fiscal year. In many cases, it may be possible to chalk up another year of service insofar as calculating pension benefits are

concerned. Check with your benefits department for specific guidelines.

79. The single most important step you can take to build a retirement nest egg so you can retire early is to take maximum advantage of an employer's retirement savings programs so that you enjoy investment growth, potential matching dollars from the employer and tax-deferred growth on the money over a period of years.

80. The best time to make deals with your employer is before the you-know-what hits the fan—before they start issuing their own early retirement offers. Once their offers are on the table, they will be less willing or able to negotiate terms that are more favorable to you.

Retirement Jeopardy Score Card

INSTRUCTIONS: Place a check mark by each question you answered correctly and write down the dollar value for that answer. Then, add up all the money you earned from being such a good student, and you'll have your final score. (The value of the correct answer for each question is shown at the right in parentheses.)

Question	Money earned	Question	Money earned
1._____	$_____($2,500)	31._____	$_____($2,500)
2._____	$_____($2,500)	32._____	$_____($2,500)
3._____	$_____($7,500)	33._____	$_____($7,500)
4._____	$_____($7,500)	34._____	$_____($7,500)
5._____	$_____($10,000)	35._____	$_____($10,000)
6._____	$_____($10,000)	36._____	$_____($10,000)
7._____	$_____($10,000)	37._____	$_____($10,000)
8._____	$_____($25,000)	38._____	$_____($25,000)
9._____	$_____($25,000)	39._____	$_____($25,000)
10._____	$_____($25,000)	40._____	$_____($25,000)
Subtotal $_____		**Subtotal** $_____	
11._____	$_____($2,500)	41._____	$_____($2,500)
12._____	$_____($2,500)	42._____	$_____($2,500)
13._____	$_____($7,500)	43._____	$_____($7,500)
14._____	$_____($7,500)	44._____	$_____($7,500)
15._____	$_____($10,000)	45._____	$_____($10,000)
16._____	$_____($10,000)	46._____	$_____($10,000)
17._____	$_____($10,000)	47._____	$_____($10,000)
18._____	$_____($25,000)	48._____	$_____($25,000)
19._____	$_____($25,000)	49._____	$_____($25,000)
20._____	$_____($25,000)	50._____	$_____($25,000)
Subtotal $_____		**Subtotal** $_____	
21._____	$_____($2,500)	51._____	$_____($2,500)
22._____	$_____($2,500)	52._____	$_____($2,500)
23._____	$_____($7,500)	53._____	$_____($7,500)
24._____	$_____($7,500)	54._____	$_____($7,500)
25._____	$_____($10,000)	55._____	$_____($10,000)
26._____	$_____($10,000)	56._____	$_____($10,000)
27._____	$_____($10,000)	57._____	$_____($10,000)
28._____	$_____($25,000)	58._____	$_____($25,000)
29._____	$_____($25,000)	59._____	$_____($25,000)
30._____	$_____($25,000)	60._____	$_____($25,000)
Subtotal $_____		**Subtotal** $_____	

Retirement Ready or Not

Question	Money earned	Question	Money earned
61._____	$_____($2,500)	71._____	$_____($2,500)
62._____	$_____($2,500)	72._____	$_____($2,500)
63._____	$_____($7,500)	73._____	$_____($7,500)
64._____	$_____($7,500)	74._____	$_____($7,500)
65._____	$_____($10,000)	75._____	$_____($10,000)
66._____	$_____($10,000)	76._____	$_____($10,000)
67._____	$_____($10,000)	77._____	$_____($10,000)
68._____	$_____($25,000)	78._____	$_____($25,000)
69._____	$_____($25,000)	79._____	$_____($25,000)
70._____	$_____($25,000)	80._____	$_____($25,000)
Subtotal $_____		**Subtotal** $_____	
		TOTAL $_____	

Epilogue

As the publisher was going to press, a very important new study* about retirement planning was released. The good news is that it corroborates everything I've talked about in the book insofar as the vast number of Americans who are not adequately preparing for their golden years. In other words, the study didn't make a liar out of me. The bad news is that it revealed that, financially speaking, people are less prepared than ever and are still failing to take advantage of the variety of investment opportunities and retirement plans that are now widely available. Here is some of what the study revealed:

- An estimated 76 million U.S. households (nearly 8 of every 10) will have less than one-half the annual income they will need to retire comfortably.
- If individuals in these households did not participate in an employer-sponsored retirement savings plan, they will likely have one-quarter the income they will need to retire. An estimated 47 percent of all Americans are currently not participating in such plans.
- Of those who are eligible to participate in an employer-sponsored retirement plan, 25 percent of employees make no contributions. But even those who do frequently dip into their retirement savings or liquidate the account when they switch jobs.

I thought it would be very helpful to share the highlights of this timely study. Now, before you close this book and move on to your day-to-day life, you will come away with some of the most compelling evidence yet that saving for retirement has to be your number-one financial priority in the years to come.

* **Source:** A study conducted jointly by the consulting firms of Arthur D. Little, Inc., and the WEFA Group (Wharton Econometric Forecasting Associates), commissioned by Oppenheimer Funds (July 1993).

About the author

As the co-founder of ARS Financial Services, Inc., Lee Rosenberg, CFP, brings more than 18 years of solid financial management experience to his company. Mr. Rosenberg is a Registered Representative of Cadaret Grant, Inc. (member firm of the National Association of Securities Dealers).

With his expertise in the areas of investments, estate and retirement planning, Mr. Rosenberg has been interviewed frequently by the national media, including Oprah Winfrey, CNN, CNBC, *The Wall Street Journal* and *Money* magazine. He has also been a guest on hundreds of local television and radio talk shows throughout the country.

Locally, Mr. Rosenberg has been a frequent guest of the New York media. He has appeared on Fox 5's "Good Day New York," WABC TV's "Eyewitness News," WABC, WOR, WMCA, WEVD Radio and the ABC Radio Network. He has also been quoted in *New York Newsday* and *The Daily News* on numerous occasions.

He recently served as the chairman of the Long Island Society of the Institute of Certified Financial Planners and is listed in *Who's Who of Financial Planning* (1989-1993). He is also a recognized member of the International Association of Financial Planners and the International Association of Registered Financial Planners.

Mr. Rosenberg is a well-known public speaker and guest lecturer, conducting financial planning seminars at local colleges, libraries, banks and Fortune 500 companies throughout the tri-state area. He is a graduate of Brooklyn College and the College for Financial Planning.

In addition, he is also the co-author of *Destination Florida: The Guide to a Successful Relocation, 50 Fabulous Places to Retire in America* and *50 Fabulous Places to Raise Your Family*.

He lives on Long Island, N.Y., with his wife, Saralee, and their three children.

Index

A

A.M. Best, insurance ratings, 77, 81
AARP, 64, 84
Adjustable rate mortgage,
    183-184, 188-189
Adjusted gross income, 93, 162
    chart, 93
Age of retirement, chart, 48
All-weather fund approach,
    investments, 139
Alzheimer's disease, long-term care
    policies, 81
American Guidance for Seniors, 77
Annual Percentages Rate, 182ff
Annuities, equity assets, 24, 128
Annuitization, 94-95
    disadvantages, 95
    joint and survivor options, 94
    lifetime payments to beneficiary, 94
    maximum benefits, 94
Arthur Andersen & Company, 83
Assets, 24

B

Back-load mutual funds, 142
Bankcard Holders of America, 38, 41
Bankruptcy, 40

Base amounts, Social Security, 53
Blue-chip stocks, 124
Bond calls, 139
Bond funds, 125-126
Bond trusts, 125-126
Bonds,
    equity assets, 24
    high-grade, 126
    high yield, 126
    junk bonds, 126
    municipal, 126
    rate of return, 139
Budgeting, 33-36
    bank account, 36
    credit cards, 36
    envelope system, 33
    monthly reviews, 33
    reward systems, 36
    spreadsheets, 33
    systems, 33-36
    tips, 36
Burns, George, 16
Business retirement plans,
    11, 24, 92-93
Buying a home, 181-185
    paying cash, 181-182
    taking a mortgage, 181-185

R

Refinancing, home ownership, 178
Registered Investment Advisors, 136
REITs, 140
  investments, 129
Relocating, 180-181
  advantages of renting, 180-181
RELPs, 140
  investments, 128-129
Request for Personal Earnings and
  Benefits Estimated Statement, 58
Retirement funds, 87-111
  disbursement, 94-104
  investing in market, 106
  liquidity, 104
  types of, 89-93
Retirement income sources, chart, 114
Retirement planning, 15-43
  diversification, 20
  late start, 41-42
  lower cost of living, 20
  myths, 19-21
  single, 43
  tax breaks, 20
  worksheets, 22-23
Retirement window, forced
  retirement, 204
Reverse mortgages, 184-185
Risk tolerance level, investing, 116

S

Safety, investments, 117
Sale leasebacks, 185
SARSEPs, 92, 108
Saving for retirement, 32-39
  pay yourself first, 42
Scott, Willard, 79
Security and Exchange
  Commission, 136
Seller-financing, 180

Selling, home, 172-175, 179-180
Semi-retirement, 206
  Social Security implications, 54-55
SEPs, 92, 107
Short-term bond mutual funds, 127
Short-term government bond mutual
  funds, 127
Social Security, 45-59, 70f, 113, 160
  age of retirement, 48
  arrival of monthly check, 56, 152
  benefits chart, 26
  contacting, 57-58
  countable income, 53
  death of a spouse, 55
  disability, 47
  divorce, 55
  early retirement, 51-52
  eligibility, 46, 55
  exemptions from state taxes, 163
  forced retirement, 56
  increase of benefits, 11
  Independent Entitlement clause, 57
  inflation, 54
  later retirement, 55
  maximum benefits, 45, 56
  mid-year retirees, 56
  overpayment, 58
  paying taxes, 53
  quarters of coverage, 46
  retiring early, 48-49
  semi-retiring, 54-55
  spouse's benefits, 46, 55
  stability of system, 45
  taxes, 57
  two-worker households, 51
  upon death, 47
  upon retirement, 47
  work credits, 46
Source tax, 166
Stair-step, CDs, 137
"Standard & Poor's Stock Guide," 122
Standard and Poor's Corp., 81

LFE